The Osborne/McGraw-Hill CP/M® User Guide

Third Edition

by Thom Hogan

Osborne/McGraw-Hill
Berkeley, California

Published by
Osborne/ McGraw-Hill
2600 Tenth Street
Berkeley, California 94710
U.S.A.

For information on translations and book distributors outside of the U.S.A., please write to Osborne/ McGraw-Hill at the above address.

THE OSBORNE/McGRAW-HILL CP/M® USER GUIDE

1234567890 DODO 8987654

ISBN 0-88134-128-2

Karen Hanson, Acquisitions Editor
Ralph Baumgartner, Technical Editor
Ellen Guethlein Silge, Copy Editor
KLT van Genderen, Text Design
Yashi Okita, Cover Design
Photography by Richard Cash and Harvey Schwartz

An earlier version of this book was reviewed for technical content by William Fairman of Faircom and Doug Huskey of Digital Research. Technical editors were Curtis A. Ingraham and Martin McNiff. Compositional editor was Denise E.M. Penrose.

Hogan, Thom, 1952-

The CP/M User Guide: For all CP/M-80 and CP/M-PLUS Users
Bibliography: p 267
Includes index.
1. CP/M (Computer program) 2. Operating Systems (Computers)
I. Title. II. Title: CP/M user guide

This book is dedicated to Lore Harp, Carole Ely, Steve Jobs, Steven Wozniak, Gary Kildall, and Seymour Rubenstein, who gave me the tools to write it.

Contents

Introduction

Your computer is not a single unit but an interrelated system of devices and programs. You must direct these components to carry out any program you wish to run. CP/M-80 and CP/M-PLUS are operating systems that do much of this job for you. They direct the activities of your computer's components and manage files that contain computer instructions or data.

Although CP/M-80 and CP/M-PLUS are complex computer programs, you can learn to use them even if you do not have any prior computer experience. This book introduces the novice computer user to the microcomputer system and examines CP/M's function within that system.

Chapters 1 and 2 provide the basic, practical information you need to get started, and they present a history of CP/M's development. Chapter 3 rounds out the fundamentals you need to know to use CP/M. Chapters 4 through 6 detail the CP/M-80 and CP/M-PLUS commands. Chapter 7 describes how other programs you purchase (or create) relate to CP/M; you'll be introduced to the concept of computer languages and application programs in this section. This is information you will use every day, so we recommend that you study the examples carefully. The beginning seven chapters of this book provide a solid foundation for understanding what CP/M is and how to use it.

Beginning with Chapter 8, the book goes beyond the functions normally needed by business or casual computer users and starts a discussion of emphasis on how these relate to assembly language programming. Chapter 11 combines the information presented in the previous three chapters to provide a step-by-step example of how to program in assembly language using CP/M.

The last chapter, Chapter 12, discusses CP/M's relatives: how they differ, what they do, and why you might be interested in them. An annotated bibliography provides directions for additional reading, and several other appendixes offer practical consumer information about CP/M-compatible programs, languages, and products.

Some special introductory comments regarding this revised edition of the *Osborne/McGraw-Hill CP/M® User Guide* are in order.

The primary concerns in rewriting, restructuring, and adding to the text for this third edition were to make the book more up-to-date and to include CP/M's latest generation, CP/M-PLUS. As happens with many works, the author had second (and third) thoughts about how to make some sections clearer. The CP/M-PLUS commands and information have been integrated into the text in a manner that allows owners of either CP/M-80 or CP/M-PLUS to make equal use of this book. For readers interested in learning about 16-bit versions of CP/M, Osborne/McGraw-Hill publishes a user's guide specifically for those operating systems.

Much effort has been expended to make this revision the most complete and accurate manual for 8-bit CP/M users. If you have a working computer system, read this book while seated in front of your computer. Try the commands and examples presented here; do not just read about them. You will be comfortable with CP/M much sooner than you expected.

One last comment: The terms CP/M, CP/M-80, and CP/M-PLUS are used in this book with specific meanings. Whenever we refer to CP/M, we are writing about *all* versions of CP/M. However, whenever we refer to CP/M-80 or CP/M-PLUS, we are referring to specific (and different) versions of the operating system.

Books, like computer programs, are never completely error-free. The author and publisher invite your comments and criticisms.

This book is the work of the author and the publisher; it has not been reviewed, authorized, or endorsed by Digital Research.

th
Palo Alto
1984

CHAPTER

1 Computers, CP/M, and Operating Systems

This chapter presents the basic information that allows you to understand what an operating system like CP/M is, why it is necessary, and how it relates to the specific parts of the computer. You'll also learn a few computer terms and information about the diskettes used by CP/M.

CP/M is a disk operating system for microcomputers produced by a company named Digital Research. When CP/M was first introduced, its creator indicated that the initials stood for "Control Program/Monitor." Since then, however, it has become more popular to refer to it as "Control Program for Microcomputers."

Versions of CP/M are available for a wide variety of microcomputers from a number of different sources, and the introduction of new versions of CP/M can be expected when new central processors are invented. CP/M-80 and CP/M-PLUS can be used on almost any microcomputer that uses the 8080, 8085, or Z80 central processor unit and has 8-inch or 5 1/4-inch floppy disk drives. If the numbers confuse you or the term *central processor* has no meaning to you, read on; the concepts should be clear to you by the time you finish this chapter.

THE FUNCTION OF CP/M WITHIN A MICROCOMPUTER SYSTEM

Before starting to use CP/M, it is important to understand the functions served by CP/M within a microcomputer system. If you know what is going on and why CP/M is necessary, you are less likely to make mistakes.

In this section, we describe the function of CP/M (or for that matter, any operating system) within a computer system. This description assumes an elementary understanding of microcomputers and how they function. If you need more information about microcomputer systems, see *An Introduction to Microcomputers, Volume 0, The Beginner's Book* by Adam Osborne (Osborne/McGraw-Hill, Berkeley, California, 1978).

A microcomputer system is illustrated in Figure 1-1. The system shown is typical of configurations that you may encounter. It includes the microcomputer itself, a keyboard, a video display, a pair of disk drives, and a printer.

Numerous permutations abound. You might have a single integrated terminal (keyboard and display) or a display separate from the keyboard. The keyboard could be part of the microcomputer while the display is separate, or the keyboard, display, and microcomputer may be packaged together. For the purposes of this book it does not matter how many "boxes" the basic components come in, just as long as you have the basics.

Figure 1-2 is a functional diagram of the components of a typical microcomputer.

Microcomputers spend much time transferring information between the microcomputer and various other components of the system. This process of transferring information is called "I/O" (short for Input/Output) and is done through "ports" (the channels through which the input and output must be routed). A disk controller is simply a specialized I/O port, but we show it as a separate functional block in Figure 1-2 because it is a unique type of I/O device.

FIGURE 1-1. Typical microcomputer system

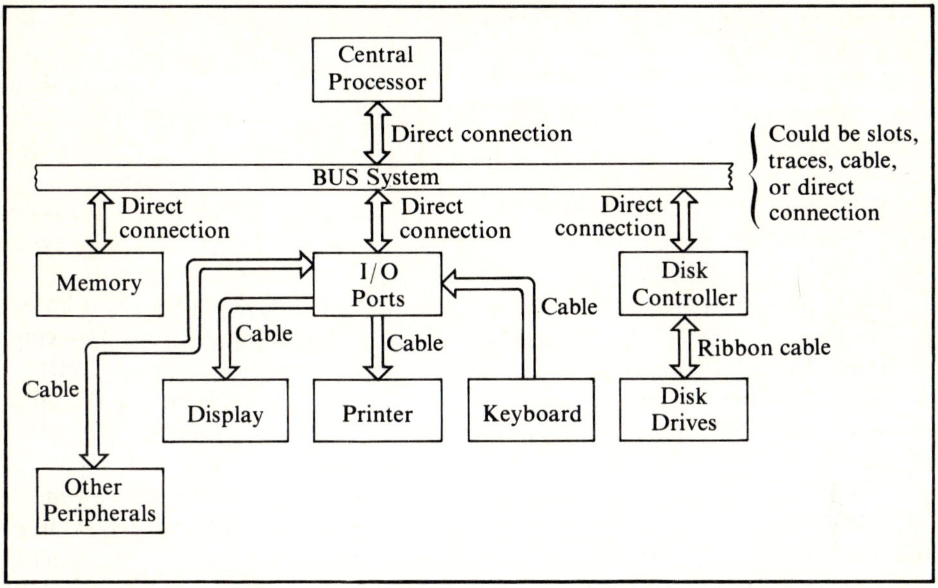

FIGURE 1-2. Functional diagram of a typical microcomputer

How does a microcomputer know what components are present and how to control them? The answer is that a set of instructions, called an *operating system,* is necessary for the microcomputer to function.

CP/M is such an operating system. By using appropriate CP/M commands, you can transfer data from a diskette to the microcomputer, print data from memory on a printer, or perform any operation that the microcomputer system is physically capable of handling.

In order to perform these microcomputer system functions for a wide variety of different configurations, CP/M (like most other operating systems) ignores the physical components that make up the microcomputer system, dealing instead with logical components. In other words, rather than addressing a printer, the operating system assumes that a "listing device" is present. Likewise, rather than reading information directly from a modem, the operating system assumes that the input comes from an "auxiliary device."

The manufacturer of your microcomputer system usually ensures that the system's actual physical units connect properly to the logical units CP/M uses. If you put together a system by "mixing and matching" components from several manufacturers, you may have to make some changes to CP/M yourself. These program modifications are invisible if made correctly, but if the proper changes are not made, CP/M may work inaccurately, if at all.

As an operator of a microcomputer system, you may occasionally be concerned with physical as well as logical units. For example, you may have the option of sending program output to a specific printer or display. Likewise, you may have the option of typing input at the keyboard or of telling the computer to receive input over a telephone line from a remote terminal. You can make such physical unit choices easily using the appropriate CP/M commands described later in this book. For the moment, you need only understand the general function of CP/M or of any operating system. You do not need to understand CP/M's specific activities in order to use it.

An operating system like CP/M is itself a computer program that must be executed by a microcomputer. Being a program, CP/M must be written in a programming language. The programming language that a microcomputer understands is determined by the microprocessor (sometimes called *central processing unit*, or *CPU* for short) that the microcomputer contains.

A microprocessor is a very small and unassuming device; Figure 1-3 shows a typical microprocessor. The microprocessor is a microcomputer's most important component—it actually translates the instructions that constitute a program and causes the action associated with each instruction. Some microprocessors can execute CP/M, but others cannot.

CP/M was initially written for the 8080 microprocessor designed by Intel. Since the later 8085 and Z80 microprocessors also execute 8080 instructions, CP/M-80 and

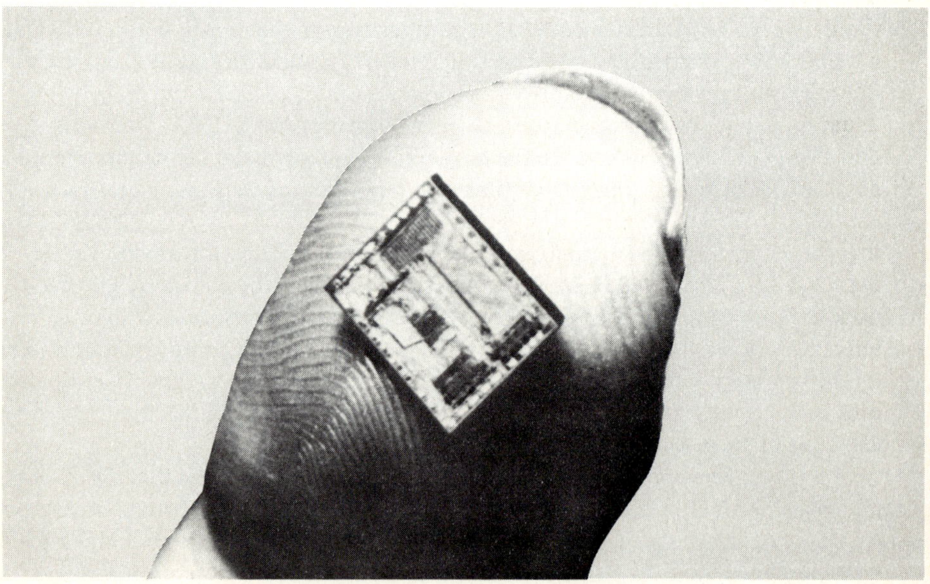

PHOTO COURTESY OF INTEL CORPORATION

FIGURE 1-3. Typical microprocessor

CP/M-PLUS run on microcomputers containing either of these two microprocessors. In addition, in early 1981 Digital Research introduced CP/M-86 for the 8086 and 8088 microprocessors. A fuller discussion of the different types of CP/Ms appears in the next chapter.

SOME USEFUL TERMS

Like most disciplines, computing has a vocabulary of its own. So that we can be as precise and clear as possible throughout the rest of this book, we will present a short glossary of the more common terminology we will be using. Specifically, we want to make sure that you understand the "units" of information we discuss. When one talks about language, one uses the terms *words, sentences, phrases,* and *paragraphs.* Similarly, when one talks about computers, one talks about *bits, bytes, sectors,* and *tracks.* If you are familiar with computers and the difference between bytes and bits, and so on, you might wish to skip ahead to the next section. Newcomers to computing should study the following information carefully.

BIT

A bit is the smallest piece of information a computer can maintain. All of a computer's data is stored internally as a series of 1's and 0's. A single bit is a single 1 or 0. You will encounter this term later in this book when the technical details of CP/M are discussed.

BYTE

The storage capacity of a microcomputer's memory, or its disks, is always described as some number of bytes. A byte is a memory unit capable of storing a single character. For example, the letter A or the digit 1 could be stored in one byte of memory. Numbers without decimal points (termed *integers*) are usually stored in two consecutive bytes of memory, while numbers with decimal points (termed *floating point numbers*) are stored in four or more consecutive bytes of memory per number.

Memory size is usually expressed not as thousands of bytes but as some number of *K* bytes. 1K equals 1024. All computers are binary machines; in other words, they count in twos. For example, you get the number 1024 if you double 2 to give 4, then double 4 to give 8, and keep on doubling in this fashion ten times.

A byte, by the way, consists of eight consecutive bits. Since a bit can contain only a 1 or a 0 value, a little binary arithmetic soon shows you that a byte has 256 possible values. In most microcomputers each possible byte value is assigned to one symbol, letter, or digit. A "1," for instance, is stored by the computer as a byte value of 49, while an "A" is stored by the computer as a byte value of 65. The "code" that determines what value is assigned to what letter, digit, or symbol is called the *ASCII* code (which stands for American Standard Code for Information Interchange—see Appendix A).

TRACK

When information is stored on a cassette tape, it is stored as a single track of data down the length of the tape. When information is stored on a disk, the surface of the disk is a series of concentric circles called *tracks*. The outermost circle is referred to as track 0; while on standard 8-inch CP/M disk systems, the innermost concentric track is called track 76.

SECTOR

Each concentric track of information on a diskette is further subdivided into units called *sectors*. On standard 8-inch CP/M disk systems each sector stores 128 bytes (characters) of information, and there are 26 sectors on each track. The smallest unit of information that CP/M manipulates on a diskette's surface is one sector. Manipulations of a single byte at a time are done in the computer's memory and not directly on the diskette.

Figure 1-4 illustrates the concept of sectors and tracks.

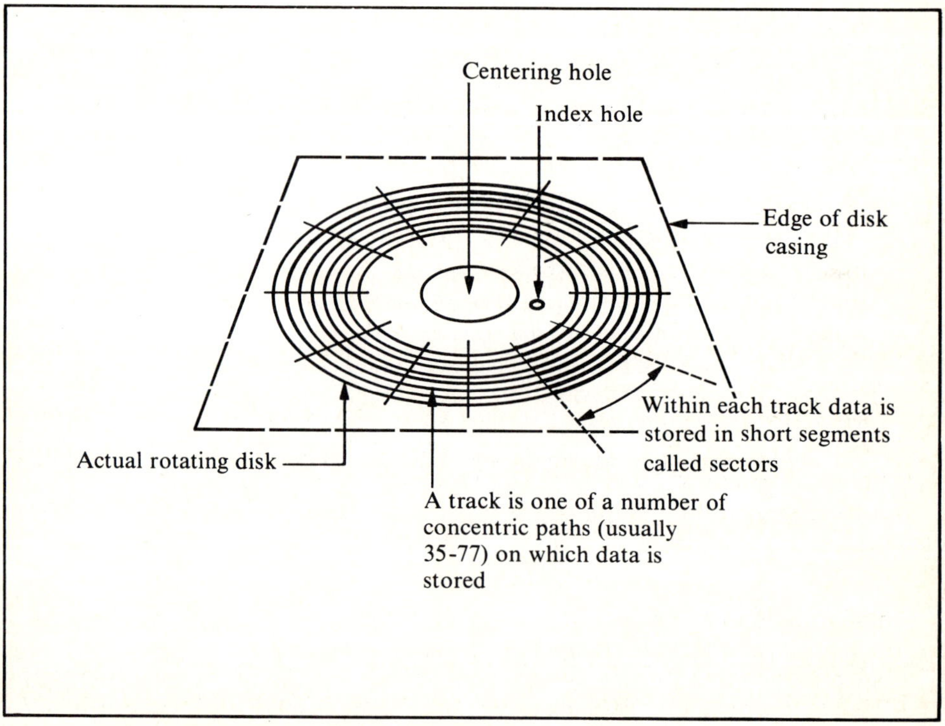

FIGURE 1-4. Sectors and tracks

DISKETTES

There is more to diskettes than just tracks and sectors, however, and it is important that you understand as much about diskettes as possible, since so much of CP/M's use revolves around them. Let us take a closer look at the terminology of diskettes.

A floppy diskette is the flimsy removable medium used by a disk drive, which is a mechanical device used to write information to and read information from diskettes. Disk drives that utilize polished metal "platters" instead of removable floppy diskettes are *hard disk drives* (because the medium is hard). For the sake of conciseness, we will normally abbreviate floppy diskette to "disk," disk drives to "drives," and hard disk drives to "hard disks."

The backbone of any disk operating system is, of course, the disk itself. It may be difficult to comprehend that 150 single-spaced typed pages (the equivalent of 30 hours of typing) can be stored on one flimsy magnetic disk. Unfortunately, one can easily forget to take the proper steps to protect the information stored on the disk. Before discussing detailed information about CP/M, we will pause for a quick course on disk types, care, and usage.

Comparing Disks

Walk into a computer store and ask for a disk, and the salesperson will ask you what kind you need. For an idea of the possibilities, here are some features to consider:

- 8-inch versus 5 1/4-inch disks
- Single-sided versus double-sided disks
- Single-density versus double-density disks
- Soft-sectored versus hard-sectored disks
- 10-sector versus 16-sector hard-sectored disks
- Write-protect notch versus no write-protect notch.

This is a confusing array of choices, and there are as many brands as there are types. We could not possibly list all of the combinations. Diskette manufacturers publish long lists of compatible diskettes, computers, and disk drives. Check with any reputable computer store to learn which diskettes to use with your microcomputer. Better yet, check with the vendor who sold you your computer.

A brief summary of the more popular types of diskettes and microcomputers is provided in Appendix B.

Describing Disks

Disks, as mentioned previously, are flimsy. That is why they are sometimes called "floppies." If you have an extra disk around, you may want to get it, as we are about to take a "disk tour."

You notice first that the disk is accompanied by a paper envelope. This envelope protects about two-thirds of the disk from such data killers as dirt, liquids, and thumbprints. Since it is a thin envelope, it provides limited protection, so be careful. Many disk manufacturers print handling tips on the back of the envelope. Read any such information; someday it may mean the difference between retyping for five hours and spending a relaxing evening at home.

Carefully pull the disk out of the envelope. (**Note:** It slides right out. If it looks as if you must cut something open to get inside, you are mistaking the disk "sleeve" for the envelope.) The disk has a square vinyl sleeve that protects a thin circular disk. The sleeve has a circular hole in the center (as does the disk surface inside), and there is an oblong cutout at one edge of the sleeve (see Figure 1-5).

5 1/4-inch disk

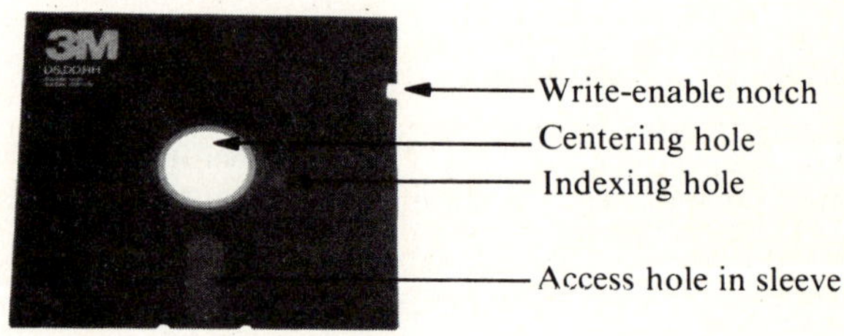

8-inch disk

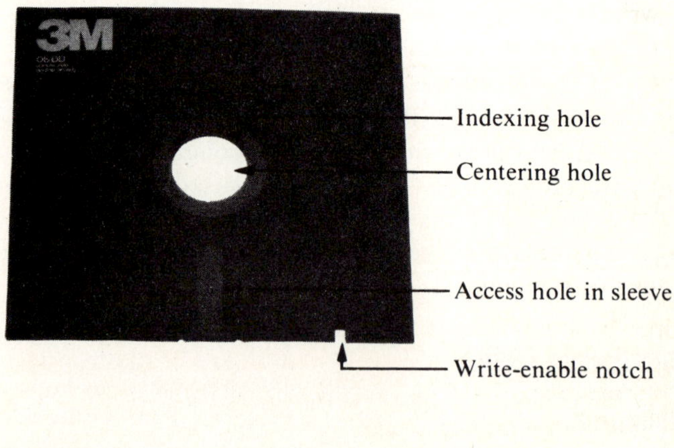

FIGURE 1-5. 5 1/4-inch and 8-inch disks

Also, there is a smaller hole just to one side of the central hole.

Identify these parts:

CENTERING HOLE

The disk drive mechanism locks onto this hole to spin the disk inside the sleeve.

INDEXING HOLE

The disk drive looks here to find the starting sector (and, in the case of hard-sectored disks, each individual sector) for each track on the disk. Imagine a line drawn across the disk surface at this point; the drive waits for this starting line and then counts characters of information from there.

ACCESS HOLE

The head of the disk drive comes in contact with the magnetic surface through this cutout. The head moves back and forth in this opening, from track to track. Note that there are access holes on each side of the disk.

NOTCH

This is a write-protect notch. Writing on the disk means adding information to the disk.

A point of confusion arises here: On 8-inch disks, if the write-protect notch is covered up, you can write on the disk; if the notch is left uncovered, you cannot write on it. On 5 1/4-inch disks, if the notch is uncovered, you can write on the disk; if the notch is covered, the disk is protected against writing. (You may want to circle the appropriate section of this paragraph for future reference.)

To compound the problem further, the write-protect notch on 8-inch disks is located at the bottom of the disk, while that on the 5 1/4-inch disks is located on the side of the disk (see Figure 1-5).

As if this were not enough, some manufacturers buy disks that have no write-protect notch at all. Software vendors who sell programs on 5 1/4-inch media usually buy such disks so that you can never make any changes to the original disk you receive.

Handling Disks

Now that you are familiar with the parts of the disk, it is time to learn how to handle it.

First the don'ts:

Never touch the disk surface. You may handle the vinyl sleeve when necessary, but do not touch the actual magnetic surface of the disk. No matter how clean your hands appear, even a slight residue may prohibit your computer from reading some data.

Keep disks away from magnets. Silly instruction, you say? You think you have no magnets where you work? Think again. If your computer has a video terminal (one with a television-like display tube), you have a magnet. Strong electrical fields can also act as magnets. The speakers in any sound system almost certainly contain magnets. Actually, the magnetic field most appliances generate is not enough to erase the information on your disks except through direct contact. Even so, it is a good idea to keep your disks at least a foot away from anything magnetic. Also, contrary to popular belief, it is best to store magnetic media in a metal box, not a plastic one. Plastic does not intercept stray magnetic fields; metal does.

Do not bend your disks. The information on a disk is packed into a very small area. Think about it for a moment: 2 million characters (on some disks) in an area of two surfaces 8 inches in diameter. Any crease in the disk can make the head of the disk drive lose contact with the disk surface, and a lot of information could be lost in that crease.

Do not keep disks in a dirty environment. If you eat, drink, or smoke while using the computer, you are asking for trouble. Filmmakers routinely use cola to erase extraneous noises from magnetic sound tracks; if you should accidentally spill a cola drink on your disk, you would probably destroy all its information.

Never leave a disk in the computer when you power down. Remove the disks before you turn off the computer or the disk drives. Likewise, turn the power on before inserting the disks. Most of the time, if you do not follow this advice, nothing happens. However, a "spike" of power could reach the magnetic head of the disk drive and write spurious information. This can prove disastrous.

Do not let your disks get too full. Many programs use a disk to store data temporarily or to generate data. If this temporary or new data does not fit, you could lose it.

Two factors limit disk capacity: the number of files and the number of characters. Some implementations of CP/M allow as few as 32 files, while some versions of CP/M allow as many as 8192 files (on a hard disk). Most versions of CP/M allow 64 or 128 files to be stored on a floppy disk and 256, 512, or 1024 files to be stored on a hard disk.

The number of characters on a disk is determined by the drive and ranges between about 80,000 and 1.2 million characters for floppy disks. Hard disk drives can generally store a minimum of 5 million characters and range in size up to 30 or more megabytes of storage.

Now for some do's:

Always insert disks slowly and carefully. Many of the 5 1/4-inch disk drives have a very small tolerance for alignment between the disk and the magnetic head that reads and writes information. In particular, Micropolis drives can be made to miscenter a hastily entered disk. This is because the drives actually move the disk before it is positioned for reading. Disks are fragile; they should be handled slowly and deliberately. Saving one second by rushing to get the disk into the drive may waste hours when you must reenter the lost information.

Label all your disks. Nothing is more frustrating than having 50 identical disks and not knowing their contents. Disks, especially if you follow the backup recommendations given later in this guide, have a tendency to multiply like rabbits. Consider this book. The text barely fits onto one high-capacity disk. Copies of the last three revisions, plus backups, are also stored on disks. In addition, the text editor program occupies most of another disk. Add the programming disks, another set of disks to keep important records and data, plus a few for games and recreational purposes, and you can imagine the stack of paper envelopes you might accumulate.

So take heed. Label your disks. Develop procedures to distinguish older versions or copies of your data from the current (or "use") ones. The label should contain your name and the date, the name and version number of the operating system, and some description of the disk's contents.

Keep backup and rarely used disks away from the computer. Limit those disks you keep at the computer to those you constantly use. Since you will generate a number of disks, why complicate the task of locating the one you need?

Make sure your disks are stored correctly. Just like phonograph records, disks are damaged if they are stored for long periods of time in other than a horizontal or perfectly vertical position. If disks are allowed to slant diagonally, gravity will subtly bend them in time. While disks do not warp like records, when that bend gets to a certain point it creases the disk. If you store disks horizontally, do not pile large numbers of disks on top of one another. Disk manufacturers recommend that you stack disks no more than ten deep.

Maintain your equipment. Disk drives are not as difficult to maintain as cars; they do not require oil changes every 10,000 reads. Actually, disk equipment can be overmaintained. Constant adjustment of the mechanism may erode the tolerances built into the drives. Too frequent cleaning of the magnetic heads may be more abusive to the heads than is normal wear. Use a cleaning disk (available from disk suppliers) once every three months or whenever you suspect disk drive errors. The latest disk drives need maintenance only once a year, and in the case of the newer Winchester-technology hard disk drives, there is nothing to adjust—the unit is a sealed mechanism.

Buy quality disks. Mail-order bargains for disks are priced below what most dealers pay. At that price the disks have not been verified or checked for their ability to store and retrieve data. You can hear the difference in quality between disks; a poor-quality disk makes raspy rubbing noises. You don't keep your personal and business records on napkins and paper towels, so don't entrust your valuable information to their computer equivalents.

Inserting and Removing Disks

Consult the manual for your microcomputer to learn how the disk goes into the drive. For horizontally mounted drives hold the disk (remember not to touch the magnetic surface) so it is also in a horizontal plane. The label side should be up. Insert the end with the head access hole (the oblong one) into the drive first (see Figure 1-6).

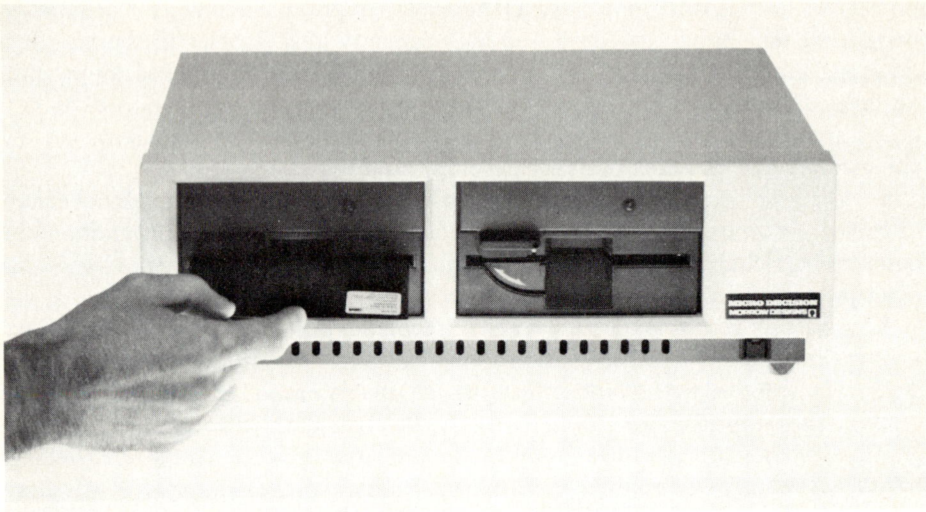

FIGURE 1-6. Inserting a disk

The writing on the label usually faces away from you as you insert the disk. Examples of computers for which the above process is correct are the Apple, IBM, and Osborne computers.

There are exceptions even to this simple process. Altos, for instance, mounts its disk drives upside down in the chassis for ease of maintenance. The label side of the disk therefore faces down when you insert a disk into an Altos system.

Vertically mounted drives are a bit more difficult to describe, as they may be mounted so that the label goes in either on the left- or right-hand side as you insert a disk. If you do insert a disk upside down, there is a possibility that you may damage it. When you are in doubt about the process of inserting a disk, be sure to consult the manual for your microcomputer.

Almost all disk drives tell the user when the drive is using (or "accessing") a disk. A small red light, the disk activity light, comes on each time a disk is accessed. Do not put a disk into or take a disk from a drive when the disk activity light is on unless the manual for your computer says you can do so. On many systems taking a disk out while the activity light is on may cause information to be written randomly across the disk surface. You stand more of a chance of damaging the integrity of the data on a disk if you remove it from the drive with the disk activity light on when the computer is trying to write information onto the disk (as opposed to merely reading from it).

Rational handling of disks is applied common sense. Though disks are new to the computer novice, there is no excuse for ignoring the implications of misuse. CP/M can only be as good as the environment you create for it. Properly maintain the equipment and carefully handle your data on the disks.

SUMMARY

This chapter, of course, is not a complete introduction to the meanings of computer terminology or to disk use. We have selected the main aspects that are appropriate for users of CP/M and have defined the most important terms we will be using in this book. If you find yourself confused by an unfamiliar term, try looking it up in the glossary at the end of the book.

CHAPTER

2 The Development Of CP/M

This chapter provides a history of how CP/M developed and a detailed guide to how different types of CP/M relate to one another.

HISTORY OF CP/M

CP/M has its roots in the very genesis of microcomputing. In the early 1970s CP/M's designer, Gary Kildall, was a software consultant for Intel, one of the first manufacturers of integrated circuits and the inventor of the first "microcomputer on a chip," the 8008. Kildall's everyday job was as a computer-science professor at the Naval Postgraduate School in Monterey, California. His two jobs gave him a unique position to observe and tinker with the fledgling microcomputer industry.

Kildall began collecting the pieces that by 1973 formed a home-grown microcomputer system. The main processor (the "brains" of the computer) and its memory were integrated circuits from Intel, the disk drive was a recycled test drive from Shugart, and the console consisted of a teletype device he had access to.

Needing something to tie all these components together into a usable whole, Kildall wrote a simple "operating system" in his then-favorite language, PL/M. The result he called "Control Program/Monitor," or CP/M for short. CP/M is a set of software that controls the basic components of the computer — an operating system.

Kildall showed his earliest versions of CP/M to Intel, but that company declined to market or develop the project further. This is not surprising, because in 1973 and 1974 microcomputers were a rarity, and users had not completely realized their potential.

By 1975 a number of small companies were marketing microcomputers to curious hobbyists. When most of these companies developed computers that incorporated disk drives, they usually generated their own operating system. Had these pioneers—Altair, IMSAI, Polymorphic, and Processor Technology, for example—been able to get their products to consumers quickly, CP/M might not have become the quasi-standard operating system it is today.

The insatiable microcomputer owners, however, were not about to wait for the industry leaders to come out with new products, so they bought whatever they could find. NorthStar, Vector Graphic, Cromemco, and a number of other companies got their start selling pieces that could be added to an IMSAI or Altair computer.

Several of these small microcomputer manufacturers decided to eliminate a costly research and development stage and adopted Kildall's CP/M operating system for their products. Most notable among these smaller companies were Tarbell Electronics and Digital Microsystems. These two firms were among the first to ship working disk systems. Because these firms manufactured "add-on" components—that is, peripherals that could be used on virtually any system—owners of Altairs, Vectors, Polys, and others did not have to wait for their computer's manufacturer to get around to producing drives. In addition, IMSAI, another microcomputer pioneer, had been shipping disk systems without any software to run them, promising to ship an operating system as soon as it was ready. This operating system turned out to be IMDOS, which was really a disguised version of CP/M.

Another important element in CP/M history is the enthusiasm of its first users. These true hobbyists tackled seemingly insurmountable problems in their pursuit of new knowledge and experience. Theoretically, CP/M-80 could link any 8080- or Z80-based microcomputer with any disk system, and a group of hobbyists with "mix and match" systems emerged to test Kildall's product. These hobbyists developed a number of refinements and, more important, a strong and visible users' group.

The support of a strong users' group cannot be underestimated. During the infant years of the microcomputer industry, accurate product information was not readily available. Manufacturers often released products with incomplete documentation; computer stores were still relatively unknown; and in some cases, users' groups were more stable than the companies that developed the product the group was formed to support.

After manufacturers delivered reliable disk drives, software developers launched the next vital phase of CP/M's evolution. The key to making software development financially feasible was to write programs that run on as many different microcomputers as possible. CP/M-80 was one of the few operating systems that could run on just about any 8080- or Z80-based microcomputer and was not restricted to only one type of disk drive.

Fortunately for CP/M's development, the first programs that became available were development tools—programs that help programmers generate other programs. Among the development tools that helped establish CP/M as the leading operating system for microcomputers were CBASIC (and its predecessor, EBASIC),

Microsoft BASIC, and several special assembly language programs. These tools, in turn, were used to write application programs, such as general ledgers, database and inventory programs, and word-processing programs.

The popularity of the CP/M operating system thus became part of an escalating pattern: CP/M spawned programming languages and development tools, which in turn gave birth to application programs. These CP/M-dependent application programs increased CP/M sales, which again increased the number of development tools being introduced. This pattern—an upward spiraling of sales leading to more tools leading to more application programs leading to more sales—has continued unabated for several years and shows no signs of stopping.

But during this rapid growth of popularity, CP/M did not remain the same. The original CP/M Kildall wrote (and his wife, Dorothy McEwen, marketed for him) was called CP/M version 1.3. CP/M 1.3 had a number of minor problems—after all, it was put together quickly and for Kildall's own use. So Kildall rewrote it, tightened up some of the code, and recreated some of the utility programs that came with it. This became CP/M 1.4. At about the same time, Kildall and McEwen's company, Digital Research, sold the rights to CP/M 1.3 to Cromemco, which made some modifications of its own, creating CDOS (Cromemco Disk Operating System).

A few comments are in order about CP/M 1.4 and the equipment it was designed to work with. CP/M 1.4 was designed at a time when memory was expensive and disk drives came in only one flavor: single density. Add to this the fact that paper tape systems and teletype consoles (keyboards and printer) were still extremely popular. The result is that CP/M 1.4 was designed with the limitations of these devices in mind. CP/M 1.4 takes up little memory (and therefore is limited in what it can do), assumes no intelligence on the part of the accessories attached to the system (and is thus simplistic), and was designed to allow a mixture of then-available peripherals to be attached. In some respects these are characteristics that made CP/M popular and established its identity as a quasi-standard—it was not specific to a single computer and could work on a minimally equipped one.

Computers changed in 1979 and 1980. With the introduction of programs like VisiCalc and WordStar and with new hardware, such as higher-capacity disk drives and low-cost memory, computers took on a more serious tone. CP/M 2.2 was introduced to update the original operating system to make it more compatible with the changing microcomputer. Whereas CP/M 1.4 was severely limited in the amount of disk storage it could address, CP/M 2.2 was expanded to allow for up to 16 drives, each with megabytes of storage space.

Other changes also occurred. Most of these were minor enhancements or modifications that made CP/M more flexible than before. The ability to address more than one type of disk drive at a time (like mixed 8-inch and 5 1/4-inch systems) was added.

But CP/M's original features were still evident: it remained compact and flexible. Digital Research emphasized sales primarily to manufacturers and distributors. Thus modest sales efforts on the part of Digital Research often meant large numbers of new users. Probably the best example of this was when Microsoft introduced the Z80

SoftCard with CP/M 2.2 for the Apple II computer. Within months, tens of thousands of CP/M users were added.

(**Note:** When we refer to CP/M-80 in this text, we mean CP/M version 2.2; very few version 1.4s are still in use. All commands and descriptions in this book referring to CP/M-80 refer directly to CP/M version 2.2.)

During the years 1979 and 1980, CP/M became self-perpetuating. Its popularity attracted software companies, whose software in turn attracted more users, who then attracted more manufacturers. This circular growth pattern accelerated very rapidly, with CP/M-80 going from about 300,000 users in 1979 to almost 1.5 million in early 1983.

The watershed year for CP/M was 1981. With the introduction of new microcomputers by computer giants like IBM, Hewlett-Packard, and Xerox, all of which were offered with CP/M as a standard or optional operating system, the number of users of CP/M increased at an accelerated pace. During this same year, however, the rapidly changing technology of computers again caught up with CP/M, so Kildall and Digital Research once more refined the original operating system.

CP/M was originally designed to work on an 8080-based microcomputer. Not to disparage the poor 8080, but it just was not a state-of-the-art central processor when 1981 rolled around. After the 8080 came the Z80. Not only was the Z80 faster than the 8080, but its expanded instruction set allowed for better and faster software. Fortunately, a Z80 can perform any computer instruction that an 8080 can, with the result that the original CP/M can run on a Z80- or 8080-based microcomputer.

The Z80's speed inspired computer designers to make microcomputers that could support more than one user at a time. In addition, the rapidly dropping cost of microprocessors meant that a designer could simply add a processor for each user envisioned. Multiuser microcomputers began to be popular. CP/M works only for a single-user computer, however. Digital Research therefore started a second branch of CP/M by creating a product called MP/M (an acronym for Multi-Programming Monitor control program).

MP/M works in a way similar to CP/M (therefore, someone who has used CP/M can generally learn to use MP/M in an hour or two), but is not exactly the same; software that works with CP/M does not always work under MP/M. One feature Digital Research retained from CP/M while creating MP/M was the disk format. That means a disk created on an MP/M system is directly compatible with a CP/M system (assuming the same format and size) and also means that data and some programs can be used on either a CP/M or MP/M system. This is an important attribute of the CP/M family of operating systems. We will briefly describe the other features and utility programs that make up MP/M in the last chapter of this book.

Another branch of CP/M came with the introduction of 16-bit central processors. The first 16-bit processor to become available in systems was the 8086 (and its slightly different cousin, the 8088). Digital Research had always planned to produce CP/M-86 but was beaten to the punch by Seattle Computer Products, which offered a CP/M-like operating system it called QDOS, later renamed 86-DOS.

86-DOS was patterned after CP/M 1.4 with one very important difference: the disk format was changed, and the resulting structure of information stored on the disk was entirely different. 86-DOS went on to become Microsoft DOS, then IBM PCDOS, and is now generally referred to as MSDOS. While it is similar to CP/M and originated from CP/M-like beginnings, it is important not to confuse MSDOS with versions of CP/M.

Digital Research went on to introduce CP/M-86, a version of CP/M that worked on 8088 and 8086 central processors. While it, too, is similar to earlier versions of CP/M, it does have some differences in operation. Later versions of CP/M-86 are Concurrent CP/M-86, a version that allows one user to run multiple programs simultaneously, and MP/M-86, which allows multiple users to work from a single computer.

CP/M has continued to change and develop. In early 1983, Digital Research introduced improvements in the original version and expanded CP/M to other central processors. Versions of CP/M for 68000 CPUs and Z8000 CPUs are now available (called CP/M-68K and CP/M-Z8K, respectively).

At the same time Digital Research was expanding CP/M to new central processors, the company took what was learned in these new versions and applied it backward to the original version of CP/M. The result is a product called CP/M-PLUS. CP/M-PLUS is ostensibly CP/M-80 version 2.2 with additions similar to those found in CP/Ms for other processors. At one time Digital Research was going to call this CP/M-80 version 3.0—indeed, its documentation makes reference to CP/M 3.0—but the name was changed to CP/M-PLUS at the last minute to indicate that this was a significantly different version of CP/M-80.

This book specifically deals with only the CP/M-80 version 2.2 and CP/M-PLUS branches of the CP/M family (although Appendix C, listing differences between CP/M 1.3, 1.4, and 2.2, should allow all CP/M-80 users to benefit from this book.) CP/M-PLUS users should note that it is available in two versions, banked and nonbanked. Some commands, most notably the control characters used in line editing, are not available to users of the nonbanked CP/M-PLUS. The differences between banked and nonbanked versions of CP/M-PLUS are dealt with in Chapter 10. In addition, MP/M-80 version II overlaps CP/M-80 and is covered by this book.

It is important that you understand the development of CP/M over the last ten years. Most of CP/M's advantages come from its ability to be used on a wide variety of computer hardware. Figure 2-1 shows the "family tree" for the development of the various CP/M operating systems.

It is estimated that over 500 computer manufacturers now offer CP/M with their equipment. Even owners of microcomputers that normally do not use CP/M as an operating system are now able to make use of CP/M with the recent introductions of add-on processing boards. These include 8-bit computers, such as the Apple, Atari, and Commodore computers, as well as 16-bit computers such as the IBM and Hewlett-Packard computers. This book is relevant for any computer that uses the 8-bit version of CP/M, no matter whether CP/M is the primary or secondary operating system.

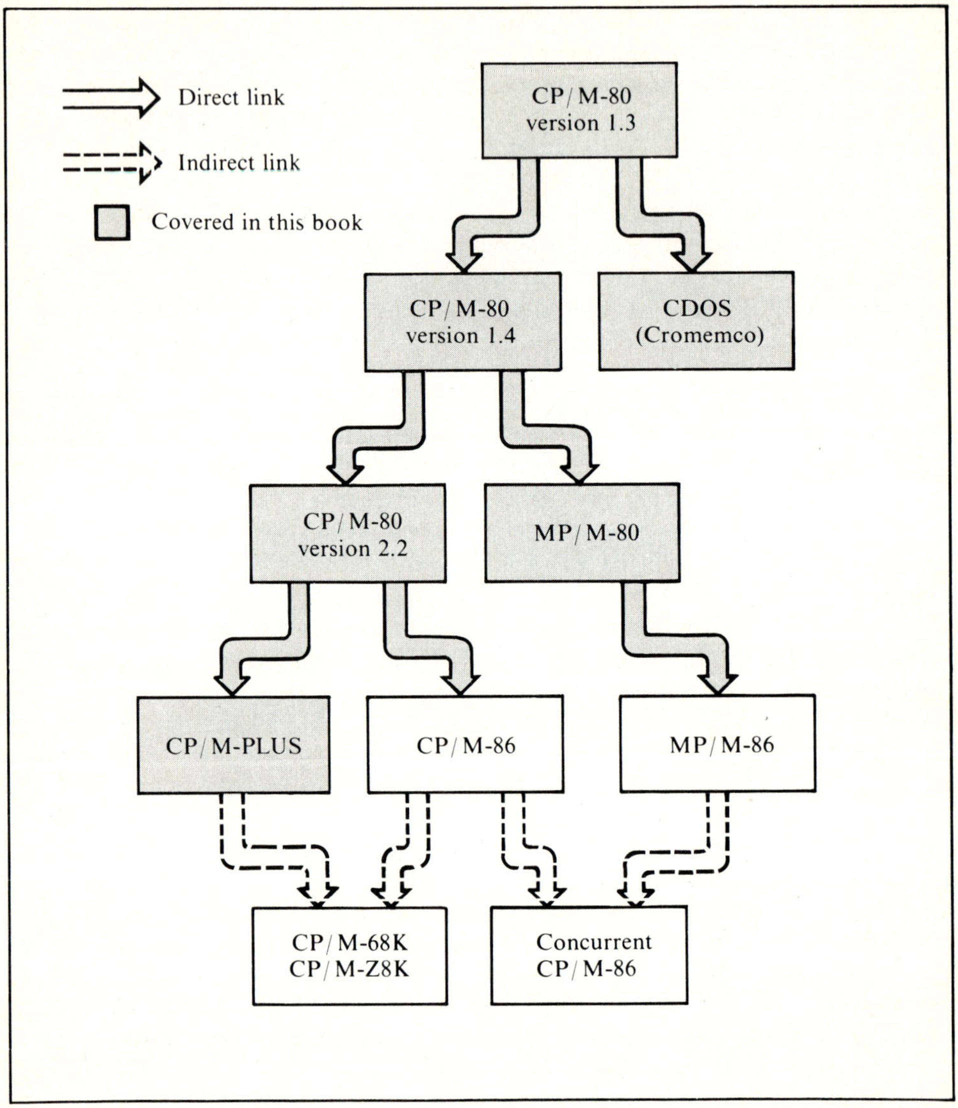

FIGURE 2-1. CP/M "family tree"

From CP/M's modest beginnings, it has become the most widely used operating system for microcomputers (and possibly for all computers, if number of installations is counted instead of number of users). Many changes have been made to Kildall's original operating system, and, despite its simplicity, there is much to learn about CP/M.

TYPES OF CP/M

CP/M may be a quasi-standard operating system in the microcomputing field at present, but as you saw earlier, all CP/Ms are not equal. CP/M varies with the input and output (I/O) instructions for each machine and varies in other ways as well.

Since CP/M was originally designed for floppy disk systems, it required changes for use in hard disk units. This is the primary difference between versions 1.4 and 2.2 of CP/M-80 (see Appendix C for a complete list of the differences between versions).

The different types of CP/M also reflect the large number of manufacturers using CP/M. Each may add utility programs or refinements to CP/M to improve performance on a particular machine. Let us examine the differences between types of CP/M in more detail.

CP/M Compatibility

Unfortunately, not all CP/Ms are compatible, and even the degree of compatibility can vary. The primary ways CP/M varies are:

- Version number (for example, 1.3, 1.4, 2.0, 2.2, PLUS).
- Location of CP/M within memory (for example, 48K CP/M, 60K CP/M).
- Type of disks used (single density, double density, 5 1/4-inch, 8-inch, etc.).
- Logical layout on the disk (usually, differences in the number of sectors or tracks used).
- Vendor (normally a combination of the first four variations).
- Processor type (8-bit versus 16-bit).

To list every different type of CP/M would be futile: The list would be out-of-date by the time you read this book. But despite the possibilities for variation, CP/M still remains more machine independent than most operating systems. By linking computers using two disparate versions of CP/M, program interchanges or data transfers can usually be accomplished.

CP/M Version Numbers

As stated earlier, there are several versions of CP/M. In general this book is applicable to CP/M-80 version 2.2 and to CP/M-PLUS, but owners of earlier or subsequent versions also will find this book useful.

CP/M-80 versions are identified by one number to the left of the decimal point, which refers to the overall version number, and one number to the right of the decimal point, which refers to a revision within a version. A second number to the right of the decimal point, as in 1.42, identifies subtle or machine-dependent modifications. Versions of CP/M include:

- 1.3 The original version of CP/M-80.
- 1.4 An improved version of CP/M-80 release 1.
- 2.0 The original release version of CP/M-80 release 2.
- 2.1 A field update of version 2.0.
- 2.2 The current revision of CP/M-80 version 2.
- PLUS Developed at Digital Research as version 3.0, but name changed to distinguish it from other versions.

If you are using a version of CP/M earlier than 2.2, you should immediately have your version updated, as significant problems may result from your using it.

Version numbers can vary from vendor to vendor. Some CP/M-80 vendors released several different CP/M-80 revisions as version 1.4, while others indicated their own updates by numbers 1.41 and 1.42. In general, only the first two numbers in a version number indicate changes to CP/M-80 by Digital Research.

DIGITAL RESEARCH CP/M PRODUCTS

Since Digital Research wrote CP/M and supports it, we will compare other products with theirs. Currently, Digital Research supports the following 8-bit CP/M products:

CP/M
: Uses a predefined (IBM 3740) format for storing information on the disk. CP/M-80 was originally designed for this format. Versions for 2.2 and CP/M-PLUS are available. As supplied by Digital Research, CP/M-80 and CP/M-PLUS come ready to use only on an Intel MDS development-system microcomputer; if you own any other microcomputer you will have to make modifications to portions of CP/M-80 in order for it to work properly.

MP/M
: A multiuser form of CP/M. Instead of supporting just one terminal, MP/M supports several. See Chapter 12 for more information about MP/M.

CP/NET
: A multicomputer form of CP/M that allows one computer to use the resources of another computer (printers, disk drives, and so on). In order to use CP/NET, at least one of the computers must be equipped with MP/M, and all others must use CP/M. Again, see Chapter 12 for more details on this operating system.

Note that Digital Research provides a ready-to-run CP/M implementation for specific equipment only. For microcomputer systems that Digital Research does not support, special instructions for the terminal, modem, printer, and disk drives are necessary. Only a skilled assembly language programmer should buy CP/M directly from Digital Research. Consultants can be hired to install CP/M if an off-the-shelf implementation is not available for your hardware.

OTHER MANUFACTURERS AND LOOK-ALIKES

Many microcomputer manufacturers and distributors provide CP/M as a standard or optional operating system on the computers they sell. Such manufacturers include Altos, CompuPro, DEC, Digital Microsystems, Dynabyte, Exidy, Hewlett-Packard, IBM, IMS International, Micromation, Morrow Designs, NorthStar, Onyx, Osborne, Texas Instruments, and Vector Graphic.

These CP/M products may differ slightly from Digital Research's CP/M products; all manufacturers reconfigure portions of CP/M for their own equipment. Some manufacturers add subtle traps for the unwary, however. These traps are often labeled as "features." For example, Vector Graphic's CP/M-80 version 2.2 includes some complicated checking for the computer model in use. It also includes a routine to check for the depression of certain keys. These additional routines make some otherwise standard CP/M-80-compatible programs incompatible with Vector Graphic's implementation of CP/M-80.

At least one manufacturer has also made modifications to the internal structure of CP/M-80 to make it work faster. While speed is certainly a benefit, it comes at the cost of compatibility with systems that use a standard version of CP/M-80.

Yet other manufacturers, like Cromemco and Epson, have produced operating systems for their equipment that are similar to, but not exactly like, CP/M. Again, there may be significant advantages to using such operating systems, but they are simply not CP/M, and users of these "look-alikes" should be aware of this.

Manufacturers of add-on products for the Apple, Atari, and Commodore computers also provide their own customized versions of CP/M, usually because the additional hardware dictates that the internal operation of CP/M needs to be different. On Microsoft's Apple Z80 Softcard, which comes with CP/M-80, the additional hardware "changes" the locations of the normal Apple memory to something the Z80 and CP/M can use. The user of the Softcard never has to know that this is happening, but if you decide to do assembly language programming under CP/M on an Apple computer, you should be aware of this "trick."

While data on CP/M-86 storage disks may be compatible, program files are not compatible between the two versions, at least not without some conversion.

Besides computer manufacturers, a number of software firms have produced CP/M look-alikes. Like CP/M, most of these look-alike products can be used on a wide range of microcomputers. Some, however, are more restrictive than CP/M-80 and require that the microprocessor be a Z80. TP/M from Computer Design Labs is one such product.

Other popular CP/M-80 look-alikes are SDOS from SD Systems, developed originally for the SD computer, then marketed separately; I/OS (also offered under the name TSA/OS) from InfoSoft; and TurboDos, a special look-alike that emphasizes speed of memory-to-disk transfers. In addition, CDOS, the Cromemco Disk Operating System, claims compatibility with CP/M-80 version 1.3.

For the most part, these look-alikes will run standard CP/M-80 software. CP/M look-alikes will be covered in more detail in Chapter 12.

SUMMARY

You should now realize that when we use the term *CP/M* we are actually referring to a family of similar operating systems. If you have already purchased a computer that uses a version of CP/M, the information in this chapter should have been sufficient for you to understand the history behind your version's development and how it might differ from other CP/M versions.

CHAPTER

3 Using CP/M

In this chapter we will present the information you will need to start using CP/M. You will be introduced to the special characters CP/M understands, the concept of files, and the messages CP/M presents to you. By the end of the chapter you will know how to start CP/M and how to turn off your computer when you are finished using it.

STARTING AND USING CP/M

The first thing you need to know is how to get CP/M started on your computer and how the computer will respond. Some manufacturers' versions of CP/M may behave slightly differently, however. Check your system's manuals if you have difficulties matching our description with what happens on your computer.

When any version of CP/M is loaded into your computer, several things happen. First a *cold start loader* moves into your computer's memory from the disk. This loader varies from machine to machine and may differ between CP/M versions, but its function is always to load CP/M. The cold start loader is a distinct program stored with CP/M on the disk.

Why load something into your computer in order to load something else? The reasons are complex (and are discussed later in this book when we describe the technical layout of CP/M), but primarily the loader facilitates machine independence, which means, in effect, that completely different computers can use the same disk drives and the same copy of CP/M.

After the cold start loader brings in CP/M, the following things occur:

1. CP/M is loaded into your computer's memory
2. Control of the computer is passed to CP/M
3. CP/M performs various initialization operations

4. CP/M places a "sign-on" message on your screen
5. The prompt A> appears on your screen
6. Finally, CP/M waits for you to type a command.

This is true of both CP/M-80 and CP/M-PLUS, although the details of each step vary between these versions.

At this point, your display looks something like this:

```
56K CP/M-80 Version 2.2
                     |
A> ■                 |________ Sign-on message
|  |
|  |______________ Cursor position
|_________________ Command prompt
```

As you can see, CP/M does nothing particularly mysterious when you start your computer. The whirring and clacking you hear from the computer's disk drives indicate that everything is working properly and that the information needed to get CP/M running is being transferred from disk into memory.

Next consider the physical process *you* undertake to initialize CP/M. Since every computer system is different, we will speak in general terms. If you are not sure of the correct procedure, read the manuals that accompanied your computer.

Some peripheral devices must be turned on first. If you have a hard disk drive, turn it on first, as some hard disk drives take several minutes to "get up to speed" before they can be used.

If you have floppy disk drives, do not insert any disks at this time unless your computer manual tells you to do so (the IBM and Apple computers are examples of this). If you insert a disk and then turn the computer on or off, a small transient voltage may be applied to the disk drive head, accidentally erasing or changing information on the disk.

Turn the computer on. In some cases the computer immediately attempts to load programs from the disk when you turn the power on. Do not insert a disk into a drive while the drive is attempting to access a disk.

Most manufacturers use a special routine to get things started. When you "power on" such machines, they display a message on the screen and wait for your instructions. Some wait for you to press the CARRIAGE RETURN key several times (to determine the speed the keyboard sends characters). On some systems you need to press a single key (like B, which stands for "boot," or the RETURN key). On these systems you turn on the power, place your disk in the first drive, and press the key your system requires.

Here is a summary of the startup steps we have discussed:

1. Switch on peripherals' power
2. Insert disk (some systems)
3. Power on computer
4. Insert disk (remaining systems)
5. Press the CARRIAGE RETURN key (some systems)

6. Type start instruction (some systems, usually B)
7. Wait for CP/M to "sign on."

See your computer manuals for more specific startup procedures.

RESET: PRESSING THE PANIC BUTTON

There are a number of "fatal errors" that can endanger the data on your disks. Fatal errors (errors from which there is no recovery) are guaranteed if you turn off the power or press the RESET button while the disk drives are writing information on the disk. Unfortunately, there is no steadfast rule on this. You may resort to pressing the RESET button to stop an "endless loop" of continuously executed instructions. Thoroughly tested programs rarely become stuck in such a loop, but newly developed programs can and often do. If one of these endless loops includes an instruction to write information onto the disk, the disk activity light could come on and stay on. After a few minutes of waiting for something to happen, you may panic. Be certain the computer is in an endless loop before proceeding. Good computer programs give periodic messages like I'M WORKING... or THIS MAY TAKE A WHILE.... While these messages are not exactly foolproof (how long is "a while"?), they are somewhat reassuring when the disk activity light comes on and stays on.

If you are entirely convinced that your computer is in an endless loop, press the RESET button on the computer. Almost all computers have one, but some of them are hidden on the back. Pressing the RESET button on most computers has the same effect as turning the power off and back on. However, the power to any component is not interrupted. Some computers even retain the program and/or data that was in memory at the time RESET was pressed, but this is not usually true.

If your manuals are not clear about what to do after pressing RESET, call your computer store before doing anything else. If important data still remains in the computer and you want to preserve it, reloading CP/M or another program will probably destroy it. You will, no doubt, be pleasantly surprised if you manage to recover information from memory after pressing RESET. The chance of doing so may be slim, but remember, it is the only chance you will get, so don't do anything else after pressing RESET until you are sure that the information in memory is either not recoverable or not important.

ENTERING COMMANDS

Before we can tell you what each command does, you need to know the conventions we use to denote commands and keystrokes:

Press means to press a single key.

Type means to press a sequence of keys.

<cr> means to press CARRIAGE RETURN (or ENTER on some machines).

^X means to enter the control character X. (CONTROL-X means the same thing.)

Underlines are used to distinguish user input from computer output (when necessary); anything *you* type is *underlined* in the examples we provide.

Note that the CARRIAGE RETURN key is represented by the symbol <cr>. A typical example we might use for a command entry would be

```
DIR<cr>
```

This means you type the letters D, I, and R and then press the CARRIAGE RETURN key. The CARRIAGE RETURN key may be labeled on your keyboard as RETURN, CARR RET, CR, ENTER, or some other abbreviation.

Control characters are subject to special interpretation by a computer. Just as you hold down the SHIFT key to type a capital letter on a typewriter, you hold down the CONTROL key to type a control letter (or control character, in computer jargon). This is illustrated in Figure 3-1. Therefore, ^C means press and hold down the CONTROL key, type and release the letter C, and then release the CONTROL key.

The CONTROL key is often abbreviated as CTRL or CTL or sometimes ALT; it is almost always found in the lower left-hand corner of the keyboard near the left-hand SHIFT key.

Your console displays both what you type and the computer's response. This book uses the following convention to differentiate between output from the computer and

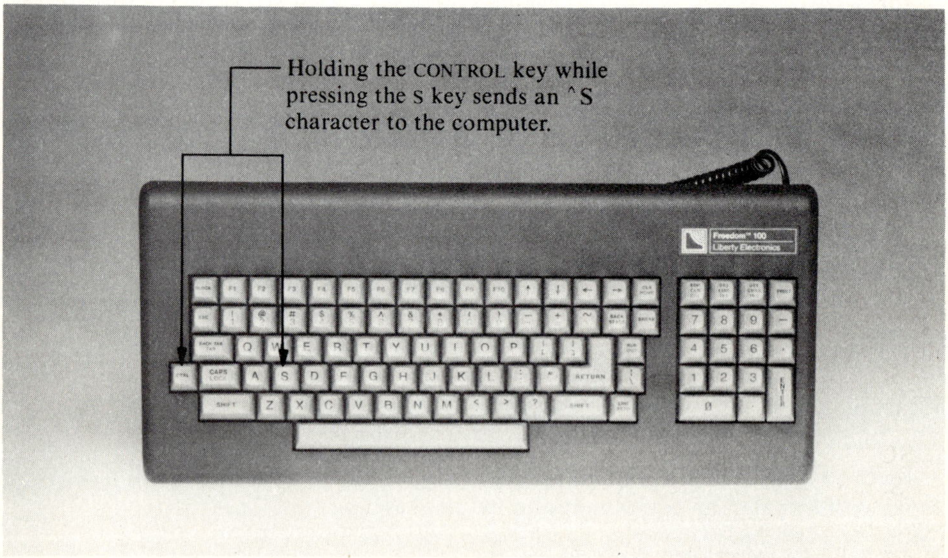

FIGURE 3-1. Typing a control character

data typed at the keyboard: operator input is underlined, while all computer-generated characters are not underlined. Here is an example:

```
A>DIR<cr>
A:STAT    COM : MBASIC4 COM : BACKUP  COM : MBASIC5   COM
A:CBAS2   COM : CRUN2   COM : XREF    COM : PIP       COM
A>MBASIC5<cr>
Microsoft BASIC version 5.3
copyright 1977, 1978, 1979, 1980
by Microsoft, Inc.
14,568 bytes free
OK
```

In this example the computer places the prompt, A>, on the screen (or printer). You type DIR<cr>. The computer replies with a listing of eight file names and another A>. Then you type MBASIC5<cr>. The five-line message typed by the computer indicates that Microsoft BASIC has been loaded and is ready to use.

The space character, which is typed by pressing the SPACE BAR, is frequently required in commands. Even though it appears to be "nothing" or a blank space when typed on a typewriter, within a computer system it is just as important as any other character. In fact, early versions of CP/M are quite finicky about spaces, although this is less true of version 2.2 and CP/M-PLUS. Generally, when the examples in this book show a space, you should press the SPACE BAR, and where no spaces are shown, do not press the SPACE BAR.

Uppercase and lowercase letters are used in command line and other user-input examples to differentiate the fixed variable from the portions of the input. You must type the uppercase portion exactly as it appears; this unvarying part of your input is usually the command name. In place of the lowercase portions you must substitute information of your choosing; this is the variable part of your input. For example, one form of the directory command is

DIR *.typ <cr>

You must type the DIR portion of the above command, but you must replace the typ portion with a file type of your choosing when you type the command. Here are some specific examples that would be acceptable forms of the above command:

```
A>DIR *.ASM<cr>
A>DIR *.BAS<cr>
A>DIR *.COM<cr>
```

Some computer keyboards have other special keys that may or may not have some function when you use CP/M. A list of these "other" keys includes

ESC
: Stands for escape; usually used to terminate an operation and go back to the function that called it.

DEL
: Deletes one character to the left and moves the cursor one space to the left.

BREAK
: Used in communications programs to inform the other computer (or terminal) that you wish to "break" from what it is currently doing.

CURSOR KEYS
: Cursor keys (keys with arrows on them) are used to move the cursor in the direction of the arrow.

FUNCTION
: Special keys that perform an operation or function or sometimes type a sequence of characters. A function key is often labeled with the function it performs (if it is fixed), as in INSERT, DELETE, JOIN, HELP, and so on.

TAB
: Moves the cursor eight spaces to the right.

CP/M as supplied by Digital Research does not usually respond to these special keys (other than DEL, TAB, and the LEFT ARROW), although the computer manufacturer may have modified CP/M to take advantage of them. You will have to check your system's manuals to find out if any of the special keys are applicable to CP/M. In addition, some computers that run CP/M (most notably the Apple, Atari, and Commodore) may not appear to have some of the keys that are necessary to enter certain commands. Read the manuals that accompany these special CP/M versions carefully; they usually show you how to type those "nonexistent" keys.

Otherwise, your computer's keyboard works exactly the same as a typewriter. You hold down the SHIFT key when typing a capital letter (or press the CAPS LOCK or ALPHA LOCK to type all capital letters) or one of the symbols above the numbers on the keyboard, or you simply press the key that represents the character you wish to send to the computer.

FILES

CP/M accesses and manipulates information stored on disks in *files.* A file is any information stored as a single entity and given a unique name. The length of a file may vary from no characters to the maximum capacity of the disk. Here are some examples of this:

- A single program
- All of the data used by a program
- An entire mailing list
- A single list
- A large group of standard form letters
- A chapter of this book
- The entire contents of this book.

No rule determines the information you may store in a file. You define a file's contents when you create the file.

All files consist of *fields:* single words, numbers, or any other convenient, small unit of information. You can also divide files into *records,* a division of information that is larger than a field.

How files are divided into records and fields depends again on how you create the file. To see the difference between records and fields, consider a mailing list file. All the names and addresses may constitute a single file, but each name and address can be designated as a single record, while the name and each line of the address may each become a single field.

```
    FILE: [============NAME AND ADDRESS FILE============]
 RECORDS: [--name/address/city--] [--name/address/city--]
  FIELDS: [name] [address] [city] [name] [address] [city]
```

File Names

Each CP/M file has a unique name consisting of one to eight characters. Normally only uppercase letters are used for file names, although it is possible (using Microsoft BASIC, for instance) to create a file with a lowercase name, or even no name at all.

CP/M automatically converts characters you type in a command line (following the A>) from lowercase to uppercase and will not accept a blank file name in a command line. Several characters may not be used in a file name. These characters are

<> . , ; : = ? * [ ] ( ) / or <tab>

Since CP/M uses each of the above characters in special ways, they are invalid as file-name characters.

In addition, you may not use control characters (or any other characters that do not appear on the screen) in a file name. Here are some samples of valid CP/M file names:

FILENAME	
IS-FILE	
OH!	
87654321	
A+B+C	(Not recommended since the plus sign can be misinterpreted in some instances)

The following are all invalid CP/M file names:

ISFILENAME	Too many characters
IS,FILE	Contains illegal character
<FILE>	Contains illegal characters
IS)FILE	Contains illegal character
FILE^C	Contains control character
WORD*	Contains illegal character.

When you select a name for a file, it is best to pick a name that is meaningful and obvious. A file containing the instructions for your payroll program might be called PAYROLL, for instance. Naming your payroll program PR102 might make perfectly good sense to you, but it is more likely you will forget what is in such a file.

We suggest you avoid the common practice of shortening the file name to save keystrokes. Naming your payroll program P to save six letters may seem like a good idea at first, but imagine looking at the contents listing of a disk and seeing nothing but one-letter file names. If you have a lot of files, it may take you longer to figure out what files are on the disk than it does to type the extra six letters in PAYROLL.

File Types

It is also a good idea to identify files in a manner that lets you know what a file is going to be used for, since different types of information are handled in different ways. For example, certain program file operations could destroy the contents of a data file were it accessed by mistake.

To keep such disasters from happening, CP/M relies upon a file type to express the file function. The file type follows the file name and consists of up to three characters chosen from the list of valid file-name characters. The type is separated from the file name by a period; that is why a period cannot be embedded within a file name. When CP/M sees a period in the file identification, it assumes that what follows is the file type.

Table 3-1 is a listing of the most common file types you will encounter using CP/M (Appendix D contains a more comprehensive listing). In addition, if you use

TABLE 3-1. File Types Commonly Used by CP/M

Type	Description
.ASM	Assembly language source program file (CP/M-80)
.BAK	Backup file
.BAS	BASIC source program file
.CMD	Directly executable transient program (CP/M-86)
.COM	Directly executable transient program (CP/M-80)
.DAT	Data file
.DOC	Document file (text file)
.HEX	Intel HEX format object code file (CP/M-80)
.INT	BASIC intermediate code program file (CBASIC)
.LIB	Library file
.MAC	Macro assembly language source program file
.PRL	Page-relocatable file (MP/M)
.PRN	Assembly language print listing file
.SUB	Command file for SUBMIT program
.TXT	Document file (text file)
.$$$	Temporary file or improperly saved, unusable file.

business-oriented programs like SuperCalc, WordStar, or dBASE II, you may find files with types such as .CAL (SuperCalc data file) and .OVL or .OVR ("overlay" files).

While there are other file types in use, this list represents about 95% of those you will encounter. As you can see, some types help to identify particular programs. In addition, they aid in selecting files to use or to print.

You can also invent your own file types. For example, you might use the version number of a program during the development stages. If you were working on a BASIC program called THEBEST, your list of files on a disk might look like this:

THEBEST.001
THEBEST.002
THEBEST.003
THEBEST.004
THEBEST.BAS

THEBEST.BAS represents the finished product, and each of the other types represents the program at a different stage of development.

File types can be one, two, or three characters in length, or nonexistent. The file type may sometimes — but not always — be omitted when you name a file; it depends on the program you are using.

For the most part CP/M ignores the file type, but many programs demand specific file types. For example, the CBASIC compiler requires source program files to have the type of ".BAS", while a CBASIC compiled program needs the type of ".INT". But these types are meaningful to the CBASIC program only; CP/M-80 and CP/M-PLUS know nothing about the CBASIC program needs, nor do they take such needs into account in any way.

In early Digital Research documentation (and for that matter, the first edition of this book) you will often find file types described as file extensions. This nomenclature derives from the fact that the three-letter file type was originally considered an extension of the file name. The word *type,* in context, is more meaningful than *extension,* so we will use file type exclusively in this book. If you are reading other documentation that describes "CP/M extensions," simply substitute *types* for the word *extensions.*

Combining File Name and File Type

You can sometimes specify a file by typing just the file name (the eight-character label). Other times you must type both the file name and the file type. The file name and file type are always separated by a period, so valid examples of the combined file name and type are

WATNOWMY.LUV
ROBOT.1
MICRO.SFT

THX1138.PIK
KINGAND.EYE

Notice that eight characters are not required in the file name, nor are three characters required in the file type. A file name must have at least one character, though files need not have a type. In other words, you may have file names of one to eight characters in length and file types of zero to three characters. All CP/M versions ignore any characters after the eighth one in a file name and the third one in a file type. Thus, if you type

CPMUSERGUIDE.BOOK

when requested for a file name and type, CP/M interprets this as

CPMUSERG.BOO

In short, CP/M lops off any character after the eighth one in the name and the third one in the type.

Now for a caveat: Computer language is not standardized enough for universal definitions. For some programmers "file name" represents the entire combination of file name, period, and file type. Terms such as *file reference, file extension, primary name,* and *secondary name* are often used to refer to the various parts and combinations of the file identification. In this book, file name describes the label (one to eight characters in length) used to refer to the file, and file type refers to the function of the file. In examples where you are to fill in a specific file identification, we use the form

name filename.typ<cr>

which would mean you enter the command name, a space, the file name, a period, the file type, and then CARRIAGE RETURN. Remember, words in uppercase letters indicate information that must be typed exactly as shown, while lowercase letters indicate places where you must substitute your data of the type indicated.

Disk Drive Identifiers

CP/M refers to available disk drives with the letters A, B, C, D, and so on. The first, or *primary,* drive of your system is the A drive. Other drives follow in alphabetical order (for example, the second drive is the B drive, and so forth). The only exception occurs when hard disk and floppy disk drives are intermixed on a computer system. Some manufacturers use later letters (M, N, O, or P) to indicate the hard disk drives and early letters to indicate floppy drives (A, B, C, D, ...). Check your manuals if your system uses mixed drives.

Since file names also consist of letters, CP/M must distinguish between a letter referring to a drive and the same letter used as part of a command or a file name. To denote a disk drive, enter a colon (:) after the drive letter; for example,

A:

In this book and in all CP/M manuals, A:, B:, C:, and so on, always pertain to disk drives. When we provide examples in this book that require you to enter a disk drive identifier, we will do so as follows:

command d:filename.typ <cr>

which would indicate you are to enter the command, a space, a valid disk drive identifier, a colon, a file name, a period, a file type, and then a CARRIAGE RETURN. A disk drive identifier is not required if you want to use the current "default" d drive, the drive that CP/M assumes you want to use unless told otherwise. (More about default drives in a moment.)

If you have used other disk operating systems, you may have trouble with the disk drive identifiers; many operating systems use numbers instead of letters to identify drives. Since most manufacturers do not label the disk drives, it makes sense for you to place a label with the proper CP/M identifier on each drive in your system.

When you start CP/M, you will almost always use the A drive. Unless you specify another drive, the A drive is the default—or currently logged—drive for all commands and programs you invoke. This means that to use the A (default) drive, you need not type its identifier. If you make the B drive the default (by typing B:<cr>), then all activity takes place on the B drive unless you tell CP/M otherwise.

Wildcard References

Sometimes you may not know the name or type of a file you wish to use, or you may wish to specify more than one file at a time. Digital Research has provided for such occurrences with a set of wildcard references, sometimes called *ambiguous file references.* The asterisk (*), when used in a name or type, replaces the remainder of the file name or file type or both. The question mark (?), when used in a name or type, replaces a single character within the name or type.

In older Digital Research manuals, ambiguous file references are abbreviated *afn* (for ambiguous file name), while the complete file name is referred to as the *ufn* (or unambiguous file name). Newer Digital Research manuals refer to wildcard-filespec and filespec respectively.

Many CP/M commands require you to enter unambiguous file references (that is, the complete file name) in the command line. This means that you must precisely specify the complete file name and type to invoke the command properly.

The asterisk (*) can represent the entire set of characters on either side of the period in a complete file name. For instance, all of the following are valid, ambiguous file specifications in CP/M:

*.BAS	All files with type of BAS
THEBEST.*	All files with the name of THEBEST
.	All files.

Now wait a minute, you ask, what good is that? Consider the directory command. To learn the names of all the BASIC programs on drive A, type the following command line:

A>DIR *.BAS<cr>	DIR stands for directory

The computer displays all files with the type of BAS. To erase all BASIC source program files on the disk in drive A, type

A>ERA *.BAS<cr>	ERA stands for erase

The asterisk can be used as the last character in the file name or file type, in which case it serves to match any subsequent characters. An example of this use would be

```
A>DIR T*.BAS<cr>
```

which would display all files of type BAS whose names start with a "T."

You may have already guessed that we can use the question mark as we use the asterisk. For instance, if PROGRAM1.ASM is the only file with the type ASM, the following commands are treated identically by CP/M:

A>ERA *.ASM<cr>	Erase all files with type ASM.
A>ERA PROGRAM1.ASM<cr>	Erase specific file PROGRAM1.ASM.
A>ERA ???????1.ASM<cr>	Erase all files with type ASM and last letter of file name of 1.

Notice how seven question marks precede the 1 in the last example. This is because the question marks are considered to occupy one character position only, not several. Typing ?1.ASM and ???????1.ASM is not the same thing to CP/M.

Most CP/M systems have two or more drives. Remember that CP/M identifies a disk drive with a letter followed by a colon. The command

```
A>DIR B:*.*<cr>
```

displays *all* files on drive B. (The prompt A> indicates drive A is the default drive. If we did not type B: in front of the above command, all files on drive A would be displayed by default.)

MESSAGES FROM THE SYSTEM

CP/M presents messages or information on the screen at some points. It is important to know how to decipher these messages; otherwise you may find yourself lost or not understanding the result of a command you type.

Prompts

In CP/M a prompt is defined as being something that indicates where you are to type a command or response to the computer. The most common prompt in CP/M is the command prompt:

```
A>
```

This prompt provides information in addition to showing you that CP/M is waiting for a command. The A in the A> means that the default disk drive CP/M uses (unless you tell it otherwise) is drive A. If you see

```
B>
```

CP/M is telling you that the B drive is the default.

Under CP/M-PLUS, MP/M, and some other versions of CP/M, a number before the drive letter in a prompt indicates the "user area" you are currently in. For example:

`1A>`	Indicates user 1 on drive A
`5B>`	Indicates user 5 on drivc B.

No number in front of the drive letter in CP/M-PLUS indicates that the current user area is zero.

`B>`	Indicates user 0 on drive B.

You will read more about user areas later. The important factor to note here is that a number preceding a letter in the CP/M-PLUS command prompt tells you which user area has been selected.

Other prompts exist within CP/M. For instance, if you use a program called ED (short for editor), it presents a prompt that looks like this:

```
1:*
```

The number refers to the current line number, while the asterisk is the actual prompt (the earliest versions of CP/M only displayed the asterisk).

Other common prompts you will encounter using CP/M are

Prompt	Meaning
–	Used by the DDT program
#	Used by the SID program
*	Used by PIP, ED, and most Microsoft programs
1>	Used by SuperCalc
.	Used by dBASE II.

A more complete list of prompts is included in Appendix E.

Error and Advisory Messages

Sometimes CP/M needs to warn you about something or inform you of a problem. When this happens, CP/M displays an advisory or error message on your display.

Unfortunately, CP/M's messages are sometimes confusing for newcomers to computing. The problem is that CP/M's messages were designed to be brief and diagnosed by computer experts. A typical CP/M-80 message might look like this:

```
BDOS ERR ON A: R/O
```

This would be interpreted as "basic disk operating system error encountered on drive A; the disk was configured to be read from (not written to) only."

CP/M-PLUS's messages can be even more confusing:

```
CP/M Error on A: Disk I/O
BDOS Function = 21 File = YORE.FIL
```

or

```
BIOS error writing drive A: crc-error
(code = 01/01 - 0100800400070A01) Retry this operation
(Y or N)?
```

We will not attempt to explain everything these messages mean here. Suffice it to say that the information CP/M presents in its messages is often condensed or coded. Appendix F is a list of most of the error messages you will encounter and a description of what they mean and what to do about them.

Whatever else you do, do not press any key until you are sure that you understand the message CP/M is presenting to you. In some cases the message is presented to warn you that your action may have some severe consequence. The effect is obvious when the message is

```
Delete this file?
```

but it may not be so obvious with other messages CP/M presents.

SHUTTING OFF THE SYSTEM

Earlier you learned how to turn on your computer system. The procedure for shutting off the computer system is *not* the reverse of the power-on procedure.

First use a normal exit from any program you might be running. This step is extremely important because many programs do not correctly finish writing information to the disk until you tell the program that you are done.

Second, remove any disks from their drives. Then turn the power off on the disk drives, terminal(s), printer(s), and any other peripheral. Turn power off at the microcomputer last. If you have hard disk drives on your system, turn off the power to those drives before turning off the microcomputer's power. Failure to do so may result in loss of information on the hard disk. If your manual tells you to do the opposite, of course you should follow its instructions.

SUMMARY

You have learned in general how to start and stop your computer and some of the prompts, messages, and special characters that you will be using. In addition, you have learned about files and how they are named. At this point you are ready to learn some specific commands and programs for your version of CP/M.

CHAPTER

4 CP/M's Built-In Commands

We described how to start up CP/M in Chapter 3. Now it is time to make CP/M work for you. This chapter investigates the built-in commands in CP/M. You will find out what commands are and how to use them.

COMMANDS ARE INSTRUCTIONS

Commands are instructions to CP/M. When CP/M is ready to receive a command, it displays its prompt (usually A>). To get CP/M to perform a command, you type the command and then press the CARRIAGE RETURN key.

All versions of CP/M have two types of commands. They are called *built-in commands* and *transient commands*. The distinction is a subtle one. The short programs that carry out built-in commands are always present in memory with CP/M; indeed, they are a part of CP/M itself. The programs that carry out transient commands are not automatically loaded into memory when CP/M is started up. Instead, issuing a transient command causes CP/M to get a program from the disk, load it into computer memory, and then execute the program. The program, called a *transient program,* is not present in memory until moments after you type the command.

To make things clearer, we will distinguish between built-in commands and transient commands in this way:

- A built-in command is immediately executed by CP/M without consulting further instructions on disk.
- A transient command requires a set of instructions stored on disk to be brought into memory before each use.

It is important to note that CP/M controls the execution of all commands, whether they are present in memory or not. Both built-in and transient command programs are invoked by typing a command such as LOAD or DIR in response to the CP/M prompt.

We have to modify this distinction between types of commands in the case of CP/M-PLUS. Some CP/M-PLUS built-in commands are not complete; that is, parts of the command — normally the options portions — are stored on disk in order to save memory space within the computer. If you type DIR in CP/M-PLUS, the instructions executed are all memory-resident; if you type DIR [FULL], directions are brought in from disk. We will consider such hybrid commands as built-in commands since they are merely extensions of CP/M-80's built-in instruction set.

BUILT-IN COMMANDS SUMMARY

Only six built-in commands are recognized by CP/M-80 version 1.4, and seven are recognized by CP/M-80 version 2.2. CP/M-PLUS also recognizes six built-in commands:

CP/M-80 (1.4)	CP/M-80 (2.2)	CP/M-PLUS
DIR	DIR	DIR
ERA	ERA	ERA
REN	REN	REN
SAVE	SAVE	SAVE*
TYPE	TYPE	TYPE
	USER	USER
d:	d:	d:

*CP/M-PLUS's SAVE command is not built-in, but we cover it here for the sake of continuity.

In addition to the basic built-in commands, there are several immediately interpreted line-editing commands. For version 2.2 and unbanked versions of CP/M-PLUS they are

^C ^E ^H ^J ^M ^P ^Q ^R ^S ^U ^X

Banked versions of CP/M-PLUS add the following special control characters:

^A ^B ^F ^G ^K ^W

Each of these control-character commands is described in detail later in this chapter, but as you can see, you need to learn only a few built-in commands.

BUILT-IN COMMANDS DETAILED

Built-in commands have already been briefly mentioned. In the following section each built-in command is described in detail. Differences among usages with CP/M-80 version 1.4, CP/M-80 version 2.2, and CP/M-PLUS will be explicitly described.

DIR (CP/M-80, CP/M-PLUS, MP/M)

DIRSYS (CP/M-PLUS)

Display the System File Directory.

The DIR command displays a directory of files on a disk. Several forms of the command are allowed, with CP/M-PLUS and MP/M adding additional forms. All file names can be displayed, disk directories may be searched using the wildcard characters to select a group of similarly named files, or the user may specifically search for a single file.

Early versions of CP/M-80 (versions 1.3 and 1.4) provide directories in a single column, with one file name and type on each line, preceded by the drive specification:

```
A>DIR B:<cr>
B:DOCUMENT MAR
B:DOCUMENT APR
B:DOCUMENT JUN
A>
```

CP/M-80 version 2.2 and CP/M-PLUS display directories with as many as four files on a line, each separated with a vertical line:

```
A>DIR B:<cr>
B:DOCUMENT MAR : DOCUMENT APR : DOCUMENT JUN : DOCUMENT JUL
B:DOCUMENT AUG : DOCUMENT SEP
A>
```

Some CP/M-80 version 2.2 directories display only two columns due to reduced screen width (notably, the Osborne 1).

CP/M-PLUS also shows additional information when some of the options (see "Options") are chosen. One example of such a directory presentation for a standard CP/M-PLUS disk is the following:

```
A>DIR [FULL]<cr>

Scanning Directory...

Sorting Directory...

Directory for Drive A:  User  0

    Name       Bytes   Recs   Attributes      Name        Bytes   Recs   Attributes
------------ ------ ------ ------------ ------------- ------ ------ ------------

CPM      SYS    18k    138 Sys RO     DATE     COM      3k     22 Dir RW
DEVICE   COM     8k     58 Dir RW     DIR      COM     15k    114 Dir RW
ED       COM    10k     73 Dir RW     ERASE    COM      4k     29 Dir RW
HELP     COM     7k     56 Dir RW     HELP     HLP     62k    489 Dir RW
PIP      COM     9k     68 Dir RW     RENAME   COM      3k     23 Dir RW
SET      COM    11k     81 Dir RW     SETDEF   COM      4k     32 Dir RW
SHOW     COM     9k     66 Dir RW     SUBMIT   COM      6k     42 Dir RW
TYPE     COM     3k     24 Dir RW

Total Bytes     = 172k     Total Records =    1315   Files Found =    15
Total 1k Blocks = 172      Used/Max Dir Entries For Drive A:      19/  64
A>
```

File names
File sizes
File attributes

Information pertaining to the entire disk

The following are the forms of the directory command for CP/M-80 versions 1.4 and 2.2, which also work with CP/M-PLUS.

DIR d:

Displays the directory of all files present on the drive specified (d:). The drive specification may be omitted, in which case the default drive is used for the search.

DIR d:filename.typ

Displays the directory of all files present on the drive specified (d:) that match the file name and type specified. You may use the wildcard specifiers * and ? to search for groups of files.

CP/M-PLUS adds several distinct variations to the DIR command. First there is the "system directory" command, DIRSYS (sometimes abbreviated as DIRS), which lists all files considered to be system files by CP/M. A system file is one that is normally hidden from view of the user (in other words, normally used only by the system, not the user). In CP/M-PLUS, the actual CP/M program is kept as a system file (usually stored under the name CPM.SYS). If all system files were shown when you asked for a disk directory, you would get a cluttered list of files that included ones that you do not normally use directly (that is, the system files). By splitting the system files into a separate listing, you need not confuse the files you normally use with those making up the CP/M system. Designating a file as a system file is covered under the SET command, detailed in Chapter 6. DIRSYS works exactly like DIR, except that it shows a directory of only the system files.

DIRSYS d: or DIRS d: (CP/M-PLUS)
DIR d:[SYS] (MP/M)

Displays the directory of all system files present on the drive specified (d:). The drive specification may be omitted, in which case the default drive is used for the search.

DIRSYS d:filename.typ or DIRS d:filename.typ (CP/M-PLUS)
DIR d:filename.typ[SYS] (MP/M)

Displays the directory of all system files present on the drive specified (d:) that match the file name and type specified. You may use the wildcard specifiers * and ? to search for groups of files.

MP/M version 2.0 also recognizes the following commands:

DIR [G8]

Displays directory of user 8.

DIR file,file

Displays directory matching the file specifications of the first file or the second file. Each additional specification must be separated by a comma.

CP/M-PLUS allows an option list at the end of any directory command (DIR or DIRSYS). In MP/M, use the SDIR command. Options are enclosed in one set of square brackets ([ ]) at the end of the command, just prior to pressing CARRIAGE

RETURN. A series of options may be entered within the square brackets by separating each with a space or comma. (An aside: in CP/M-PLUS, the closing square bracket may be omitted if it is the last item on a command line.)

The format of this command is as follows:

DIR d:filename.typ d:filename.typ ... [option]
DIR d:filename.typ d:filename.typ ... [option, option]
Displays all matching files using the option(s) listed. Note that more than one file name and type may be matched against; each should be separated by a space, and a space must precede the start of the options portion of the command.

Options (CP/M-PLUS)

The available options are

[ATT]
Displays the four user-definable attributes (see SET command in Chapter 6 for a list of attributes).

[DATE]
Displays date and time stamps for files, if active.

[DIR]
Displays only files that are in normal directory.

[DRIVE=ALL]
[DRIVE=(d,d,d)]
[DRIVE=d]
Displays files on the drive or drives specified. Multiple drives may be searched by enclosing a list of them, separated by commas, within parentheses.

[EXCLUDE]
Lists all files except those matching the specified filename.typ.

[FF]
Sends a form feed character (0C hex, 12 decimal) to the printer before starting a listing, or, if the printer is not selected for output, disables the paged display on screen (same as [NOPAGE] if printer is not active).

[FULL]
Displays all information about matched files, including file sizes and attributes.

[LENGTH=n]
Displays n lines of output before inserting a new heading (where $5 < n < 65536$). The default is one screen length (usually 24 lines).

[MESSAGE]
Displays the names of the specified drives and user numbers being searched.

[NOPAGE]
Continuously scrolls directory on the screen; does not wait when screen is filled with information.

[NOSORT]
Does not alphabetize file names; instead presents them in the order they were found on the disk.

[RO]
Displays only files that have the read-only attribute.

[RW]
Displays only files that have the read/write attribute.

[SIZE]
Displays the file size in addition to the file name.

[SYS]
Displays only files with the system file attribute; same as typing DIRSYS or DIRS.

[USER=ALL]
[USER=(n,n,n)]
[USER=n]
Displays matching files of the user area(s) specified (where 0 <= n <= 15).

Note: You may abbreviate any option to its first one or two letters. (You must type enough of the option so that CP/M-PLUS can figure out what you want—typing F could stand for FF or FULL, so you must type two letters.)

Examples

The following are sample uses of the CP/M DIR command and the resulting directories:

```
A>DIR B:*.BAS<cr>
B:FRESHWTR.BAS
B:SALTWTR.BAS
A>
```

The above example shows a directory in version 1.4 format. The command used is DIR B:*.BAS (display a directory of all files with the type of BAS that are on drive B).

```
A>DIR FI??.*<cr>
A:FISH     TRT : FISH     BAS : FISH     CRP : FISH     ING
A:FISH     EEE : FILE     BAS
A>
```

The above example shows a directory in version 2.2 and CP/M-PLUS format. The command used is DIR FI??.* (display all files whose names start with FI and have any file type, all on the default drive).

```
A>DIR<cr>
A:TEE      COM : BEE      COM : ECTORY   COM : RED      COM
SYSTEM FILE(S) EXIST
A>
```

The above example shows a directory in CP/M-PLUS where system files exist.

```
A>DIRSYS<cr>
A:REENIE   TWO : LIZZIE   ONE : MARY     THR : EVA      ONE
A:CARLA    TWO
NON-SYSTEM FILE(S) EXIST
A>
```

The above example shows a directory of the system files in CP/M-PLUS (note that nonsystem files, i.e., directory files, exist). The example below shows a directory where options are requested.

```
A>DIR *.* [DRIVE=(A,B),SIZE]<cr>

Scanning Directory...

Sorting Directory...

Directory for Drive A:   User 0

A: WS       COM   16k : DS       COM   24k : CS       COM   26k
A: SB       COM   38k

Total Bytes    =     104k Total Records =    912 Files Found =    4
Total 1k Blocks =    104  Used/Max Dir Entries for Drive A: 4/ 64

Directory for Drive B:   User 0

NO FILE - *.*

A>
```

Error Messages

You can make several different errors in using the DIR command. The primary error messages CP/M might display are

NO FILE, NOT FOUND, or FILE NOT FOUND
: The disk does not contain the file(s) you specified. Make sure that you typed the command correctly; if you did type the command correctly, then the file(s) does not exist.

BDOS ERR ON d: (where d: is the drive identifier)
: CP/M cannot find a disk in the selected drive, the disk is improperly formatted, the power to the drives is off, or the drive door has not been closed. Check to make sure that a disk is properly inserted into the drive. If the above message is followed by a BAD SECTOR message, in all probability you either have a bad disk or inserted the disk upside down.

DIT?
: Any error message ending in a question mark indicates that CP/M could not find the command you typed. In this particular instance, you typed DIT

instead of DIR. Check carefully for typing errors when you see an error message ending with a question mark.

ILLEGAL COMMAND TAIL
The option list or the format of your directory command is incorrect (CP/M-PLUS only).

ERA

Erase a File (CP/M-80, CP/M-PLUS, MP/M)

ERASE

Erase a File (CP/M-PLUS)

ERAQ

Erase a File With Query (MP/M-80)

ERA stands for erase. To use the command, you must specify the file or files to be erased immediately after typing the command. Since it is extremely rare to remove all files from a disk, CP/M checks with you to make sure if you ask to erase all files from a disk (this is not true of version 1.3).

It is good to develop the habit of checking the directory before invoking the erase command. First verify that the file or files you wish to remove from the disk actually exist by using the DIR command. Next use the ERA command to perform the erasure. Last, use DIR again to make sure that CP/M correctly erased the selected file(s). If you do not use this procedure, you will normally not get any verification of when and what CP/M erases.

In CP/M-PLUS, the actual command to erase a file is ERASE, not ERA. However, to ensure compatibility between CP/M-PLUS and earlier versions, you may abbreviate ERASE to ERA. CP/M-PLUS does add one option to the standard CP/M erase command, the CONFIRM option. The CONFIRM option is similar to that of the ERAQ function of MP/M (described below) in that it presents the name of each file to be erased for user verification. It is suggested that you always use the CONFIRM option when erasing files under CP/M-PLUS.

Users of MP/M may use a special version of the ERA command, ERAQ, to force MP/M to query them before each file erasure. While ERA is also available under MP/M, if you use this CP/M cousin you should get into the habit of using ERAQ instead.

One form of the ERA command is allowed in versions 1.4 and 2.2:

ERA d:filename.typ
Erases all files that match the file name and type specified, on the disk specified (d:). The wildcard characters * and ? may be used to specify more than one file at a time. In CP/M-PLUS, any use of the wildcard characters results in CP/M-PLUS asking for a confirmation of the erasure request.

In addition to the above form, MP/M users may also use the form

ERAQ d:filename.typ
  Erases all files that match the file name and type specified on the disk specified (d:), but erases each file only after a user confirmation is entered.

CP/M-PLUS users may use the standard CP/M ERA command or add the CONFIRM option to the command

ERASE d:filename.typ [CONFIRM]
  Erases all files that match the file name and type specified on the disk specified (d:), but only after the user confirms the erasure of each file.

Examples

Here are some examples of the ERA command's use:

```
A>DIR C:<cr>
C: QUALITY  CTL : MIND     CTL : WEIGHT   CTL : THOUGHT  CTL
A>ERA C:QUALITY.CTL<cr>
A>DIR C:<cr>
C: MIND     CTL : WEIGHT   CTL : THOUGHT CTL
A>
```

In the above example we first ask for a directory of files on drive C; four files are listed. We then ask CP/M to erase the file named QUALITY.CTL on drive C. No message is presented (other than the A>) to confirm this action, so we ask for another directory to confirm the deletion.

```
A>DIR B:*.BAS<cr>
B: NOW      BAS : THEN     BAS : ALWAYS   BAS
A>ERA B:*.BAS<cr>
A>DIR B:*.BAS<cr>
NOT FOUND
A>
```

In this example we find three files on the disk in drive B with the type of BAS and then ask CP/M to erase all files on drive B with this type. Another directory command confirms that no files with the type of BAS are left on drive B.

```
B>DIR<cr>
B: SOHO     NY  : CHELSEA  NY  : UPPREAST NY : UPPRWEST NY
B>ERA *.*<cr>
ALL FILES (Y/N)?Y<cr>
B>DIR<cr>
NO FILE
B>
```

The above example demonstrates what happens when you ask CP/M to erase all files from a disk. Note the message ALL FILES (Y/N)? and the user response that follows it (CP/M-PLUS substitutes the message CONFIRM (Y/N)?). If you reply with anything other than a Y to the query, no files are erased from the disk. In this case, we replied with a Y to tell CP/M to proceed.

An MP/M example:

```
A0>ERAQ SNWAKEEN.*<cr>

A: SNWAKEEN VLY? Y
A: SNWAKEEN RVR? N
A: SNWAKEEN CTY? N
A0>DIR SNWAKEEN.*<cr>
A: SNWAKEEN RVR : SNWAKEEN CTY
A0>
```

Notice in this MP/M example that we have used the ERAQ (erase with query) option. Each file whose name and type match the one specified is presented one at a time for our consideration. We decided to erase the first one, but not the next two. A directory command confirms our actions.

```
A>ERASE TAPE.* [CONFIRM]<cr>
Erase A:TAPE    WRM (Y/N)? Y
Erase A:TAPE    MSR (Y/N)? N
Erase A:TAPE    URR (Y/N)? Y
A>
```

In this CP/M-PLUS example, the user asked the computer to confirm each file erasure, then proceeded to erase TAPE.WRM and TAPE.URR, but not TAPE.MSR.

Error Messages

The error messages that you may encounter when using the ERA command are basically the same as those described with the directory command.

NO FILE, NOT FOUND, or FILE NOT FOUND

CP/M or MP/M cannot find the file name and type you specified. For instance, if you type ERA KNOW instead of ERA NOW, this message may appear. But if you did have a file named KNOW, it would be erased! Do not count on this error message to catch your typing mistakes.

BDOS ERR ON d: (where d: is the drive identifier)

CP/M cannot find a disk in the drive you specified, the drive door is open, no disk has been inserted or it has been inserted improperly, or the power to the drive has not been turned on.

ERAQ?

Again, any error message ending in a question mark indicates that CP/M was unable to find the command you typed. If this particular error message appears, either you attempted to use an MP/M command with CP/M, or, if you are using MP/M, the file ERAQ.PRL is not on the default disk drive.

REN

Rename a File (CP/M-80, CP/M-PLUS, MP/M)

RENAME

Rename a File (CP/M-PLUS)

Files may be given new names with the REN, or rename, command. You must explicitly state the old name of the file and its new name in CP/M and MP/M; you cannot use the wildcard identifiers * and ? to rename a group of files at once. CP/M-PLUS allows use of the wildcard characters in renaming files. Renaming files does not make copies of them; instead, only the name kept in the directory is changed.

Almost universally, whenever the computer deciphers an equivalence statement—as in the rename command—the new formation or result is to the left of an equal sign, and the old formation or result appears to the right. This can be expressed as follows:

NEW = OLD

A disk drive specifier can be included with either or both file names when you use the rename command. If included with one name, it applies to both. If included with both file names, the same drive specifier must be used with both. If omitted, the default disk drive is used.

CP/M-PLUS's use of the REN command varies slightly from that of versions 1.4 and 2.2 and from MP/M. You may type either REN or RENAME under CP/M-PLUS. In addition, a variation in which the computer prompts you for information is also available (see formats below).

Here are the two formats of the REN command:

REN d:newfilename.typ=oldfilename.typ
REN newfilename.typ=d:oldfilename.typ

The rename command finds the file of name and type matching "oldfilename.typ" on the drive specified (d:), and then gives it the new name and type matching "newfilename.typ."

Note: You need to indicate the drive on which the renaming is being performed only once, since, by definition, you cannot rename a file on more than one disk. Thus, both of the above formats are equivalent. CP/M-PLUS users may type REN or RENAME in the first part of the command.

CP/M-PLUS users may also use the following form:

RENAME

The rename command prompts the user for the name of the file to rename and the new name to associate with the file.

Examples

Here is an example of the use of the REN command as it works in CP/M and MP/M:

```
A>DIR<cr>
A: HOLDEN   ONE : PHOEBE   TWO : 19EIGHTY FOR
A>REN NOVEL.ONE=HOLDEN.ONE<cr>
A>DIR<cr>
A: NOVEL    ONE : PHOEBE   TWO : 19EIGHTY FOR
A>
```

In this example we ask to change the file named HOLDEN.ONE to a file named NOVEL.ONE.

An example of CP/M-PLUS's RENAME (prompting for names) version of the rename command looks like the following:

```
A>RENAME<cr>
Enter New Name: NOVEL.ONE<cr>
Enter Old Name: HOLDEN.ONE<cr>
File HOLDEN.ONE is renamed NOVEL.ONE on drive A
A>
```

Error Messages

The rename command has several error messages associated with it:

filename?

You incorrectly used an ambiguous file reference in the rename command line. For instance, if you type REN TALL.CAR=SHORT???.CAR, the error message SHORT???.CAR? appears.

NO FILE

The file you specified does not exist. Check your typing.

FILE EXISTS

Not renamed: filename.typ file already exists, delete (Y/N)?

The new name you specified is the name of an existing file. You cannot use the CP/M-80 REN command to rename a file with a name and type that already exist on a disk; CP/M-80 considers this to be an error. If you wish to replace an existing file with a newer version of the same file, either rename or erase the existing file first or use the PIP utility described in Chapter 5. CP/M-PLUS is more forgiving and presents the second error message listed above, allowing you to press Y to confirm that you wish to delete the existing file with that name before you rename the one you requested.

BDOS ERR ON d: (where d: is the disk identifier)

CP/M could not find the disk or activate the disk drive you specified. Check to make sure the disk is inserted properly and that the disk drive is powered on with the door correctly closed.

SAVE

Save Memory Contents in a Disk File (CP/M-80, CP/M-PLUS)

One crude method used to save memory contents in CP/M is the SAVE command. This command is not applicable to MP/M.

SAVE places the contents of what is known as the Transient Program Area into a file on disk, using a name and type you choose. You must tell CP/M-80 how many pages (256-character blocks) of memory you wish saved and the name and type of the file you want the information stored in; CP/M-PLUS allows you to specify starting and ending memory locations to save. Select the file name carefully. SAVE erases any existing file of the same name before creating the new one.

You will use the SAVE command rarely if you use CP/M only to run off-the-shelf or "canned" application programs. On the other hand, assembly language programmers will use this command frequently. If you are not familiar with assembly language or if you want more background before tackling the particulars of SAVE, you should read Chapters 8 through 11 before proceeding with the rest of this description. Since DDT (or SID), the debugger utility program, is normally used in conjunction with the SAVE command, we have used DDT in our example. DDT is also examined in Chapter 8, while SID is discussed in Chapter 9.

In order to perform a SAVE in CP/M-80, you must know the number of "pages" of memory to be saved. A page of memory is a block consisting of 256 characters. The first page saved always begins at memory location 0100 hexadecimal. The number of pages to be saved must be expressed as a decimal number.

Beginners often encounter problems with the "page of memory" concept in which 256 decimal is equivalent to 0100 hexadecimal. The number conversion between decimal and hexadecimal is not an easy one for anyone with "math anxiety."

The hexadecimal numbering system (usually abbreviated as "hex") is equivalent to base 16. In other words, the one's place can have 16 digits, as opposed to the 10 digits in base 10. In base 10 we count

0 1 2 3 4 5 6 7 8 9

In base 16—hex math—we count

0 1 2 3 4 5 6 7 8 9 A B C D E F

The letter A represents our normal number 10, B represents 11, and so on. In everyday math we would interpret 111 to mean

1 in the 1's place	=	1
1 in the 10's place	=	10
1 in the 100's place	=	100
for a total of		111

In hex math 111 means

1 in the 1's place	=	1	
1 in the 16's place	=	16	
1 in the 256's place	=	256	
for a total of		273	(in base 10).

The two systems differ; so what does this have to do with the SAVE command?

Remember that 0100 hex equals one page of memory (256 decimal). Does 0200 hex equal two pages of memory? Yes. Since we are only concerned about the number of pages of memory to save, we can forget about the last two digits in converting computer memory addresses into the necessary information to fill out the SAVE command.

Let's calculate the number of pages to save if we wish to save information that resides from 0100 hex to 2785 hex in our computer:

1. First, forget the first address, 0100; the SAVE command always starts at this address.
2. Next drop the last two digits from the higher address. In our example, 2785 thus becomes 27.

3. Convert the remaining number to decimal. For our example

7 in the 1's place	=	7	
2 in the 16's place	=	32	
for a total of		39	(in decimal)

4. Step 3 always gives the correct result except for one special case. If the last two digits of the higher address in step 2 were 00 hex, you would have to subtract 1 from the result in step 3. For example, if the higher address were 2700 hex instead of 2785 hex, the correct result would be 39 minus 1, or 38 decimal pages to save.

This long, arduous process is not needed by CP/M-PLUS users, since SAVE merely asks for the starting and ending memory locations to save; CP/M-PLUS figures out how many "pages" of memory are involved.

One difference between the CP/M-80 and CP/M-PLUS versions of the SAVE command is that the CP/M-80 version is executed immediately, while CP/M-PLUS's SAVE command is not executed until the next ^C or program termination. Thus, in CP/M-80 you get the information you want to save into memory (usually with DDT), return to the A> prompt, and type a SAVE command to be immediately performed. In CP/M-PLUS you type SAVE *prior to* putting the information in memory, execute another program that puts the information in memory, and then exit that program normally, at which time SAVE becomes active and requests further information from you.

Another difference between CP/M-80 and CP/M-PLUS is that, if the file name you specify already exists, CP/M-PLUS will prompt you, asking if you wish to delete the existing file.

The one form allowed for the SAVE command in CP/M-80 is

SAVE ## d:filename.typ (where ## is the number of 256-character blocks of memory you wish to store on disk)

The one form allowed for the SAVE command in CP/M-PLUS is

SAVE

When the next CONTROL-C or program termination occurs, you will be prompted for the file name and type and the beginning and ending memory addresses to save.

Examples

Let us look at examples of SAVE's use:

```
A>DDT CURSEAND.HEX<cr>
DDT VERS 2.2
NEXT  PC
1100  0100
-
```

In this part of a CP/M-80 example we use DDT (discussed in Chapter 8) to load a file named CURSEAND.HEX into memory. As you will eventually learn, the numbers under the "NEXT" and "PC" are significant; the first indicates one more than the last memory address used by the file, while the second indicates the starting address of the file. If we use the rules given above for converting these numbers into the number of pages of information to save, we come up with the answer 16 (1 in the 1's place is 1, plus 1 in the 16's place equals 17; subtract 1 because the last two digits of the higher address are 00 hex). Therefore, we would use the following SAVE command in CP/M-80:

```
A>SAVE 16 CURSEAND.COM<cr>
A>
```

CP/M-PLUS users would use SAVE in the following manner:

```
A>SAVE<cr>
A>SID SEIZE.HER<cr>
SID VERS 3.0
NEXT MSZE  PC   END
0300 0300 0100 0300
#GO<cr>
SAVE Ver 3.0
File (or RETURN to exit)? GOT.HER<cr>
Delete got.her? Y
From? 100<cr>
To? 300<cr>

A>
```

In this example we first invoke SAVE to get it into memory. Next we use SID (see Chapter 9) to load a program named SEIZE.HER into memory. SID responds with some information and its prompt (#), to which we respond with a GO to leave SID. SAVE intercepts the program termination and prompts us for the name of the file in which we wish to save information and the beginning and ending memory addresses. After we respond to SAVE's prompts, we are returned to CP/M.

Error Messages

filename?

You failed to specify the number of pages to save, used a wildcard identifier, or misspelled the word SAVE. Check your typing for accuracy before going on. Unfortunately, because of a quirk in the way some CP/M-80 systems use memory during the SAVE process, you cannot assume that the data you wished to save is still valid. In short, you must first reload the memory with the information you wish to save before reattempting the command.

NO SPACE or DISK FULL

Too many files are already on the disk, or no room is left on the disk to save all the information you specified. Either erase unnecessary files on the disk before proceeding or use a different disk.

TYPE

Display a File Containing ASCII-Coded Information (CP/M-80, CP/M-PLUS, MP/M)

If you have a file that consists of printable characters (that is, data, as opposed to computer instructions), you may display the file's contents on your console display by using the TYPE command.

TYPE usually works for files with types of BAS, ASM, BAK, DAT, HEX, DOC, TXT, or any other files that contain ASCII text or data. ASCII is a character recognition and storage scheme for computers; each character has a unique representation that can be saved or used by the computer.

You could also use a text editor or word-processing program to look at the contents of a file, but not everyone using CP/M has such a program available. Also, if you merely want to take a peek at your program or data, why go to the trouble of using the text editor? The TYPE command is built into all versions of CP/M and is always available.

There is only one allowable form of the TYPE command in CP/M-80:

TYPE d:filename.typ
  Displays the contents of the specified file.

CP/M-80 and MP/M continuously list the file, not stopping when the display screen is filled up. In CP/M-PLUS, only 24 lines (or whatever has been set as the default size of the display by means of the DEVICE command) are displayed at one time. MP/M users may use an optional two-digit number with the TYPE command to specify the number of text lines to show on the console at one time:

TYPE d:filename.typ Pn   (where n is the number of lines to display at a time)

When the MP/M form of the TYPE command is used as shown above, the computer displays the specified number of lines (following the P in the command) of the file and then waits for the user to press the CARRIAGE RETURN key. In this fashion, an MP/M user may display a text file without worrying about text running off the screen before it can be examined. The normal specification would be P23 for 24-line terminals.

CP/M-PLUS users may also use the forms

TYPE d:filename.typ [NO PAGE]
  Displays the contents of the specified file, but lists the file continuously, as opposed to stopping every 24 (or user-specified number) lines.

TYPE d:filename.typ [PAGE]
  Displays the contents of the specified file one screen at a time; this is the default option, so it need not be explicitly requested.

TYPE

CP/M-PLUS prompts you for the filename to display with the prompt:

Enter filename:

Example

An example of TYPE's use would be

```
A>TYPE O.POS<cr>
Had Dick Seeker been present, and had he been able
to see inside the NASCOM Cray-1 computer, he would
have seen a string of bits spelling out his name,
computer style.  But the National Security Computer
Center was 1500 miles away; in fact, Dick wasn't
even aware of its existence.
```

In the above example, the user asked to see a text display of the file O.POS, and the computer complied. If this were a long file—longer than the console display could show at one time—a CONTROL-S could be typed to temporarily "pause" the display. (CP/M-PLUS and MP/M require a CONTROL-Q to resume displaying information, while CP/M-80 allows you to resume display by pressing any key.) To terminate a text display of a file, press any key or enter a CONTROL-C.

Error Messages

filename?

This error message appears when the file you named does not exist or you misspelled the TYPE command. Check your work and try again.

BDOS ERR ON d: (where d: is the disk identifier)

CP/M cannot find the disk or disk drive you specified.

No File

The file you requested cannot be found.

There is one final error situation that may occur, but a message will not be displayed. Instead, a meaningless display, sometimes accompanied by a bell, will appear. This happens when you try to use TYPE with a file that does not contain ASCII text or that includes machine language code within the text. If you accidentally displayed a file with machine language code in it, restart CP/M to make sure that you did not also accidentally change the contents of your computer's memory.

USER

Change the User Number (CP/M-80, CP/M-PLUS, MP/M)

Version 2.2, CP/M-PLUS, and MP/M all include a special command named USER. This command allows you to specify a number between 0 and 15, inclusive, that is to be kept with any files you create.

When you cold start CP/M, user number 0 is assumed; when you cold start MP/M, the user number is initialized to the console number. Your disk operations will reference files in user area 0 only (or another number in MP/M if you are using a different console number). Thus, if you save a new file called JUNK.AGN after a cold start, it will always appear in directories assigned to user area 0. If you type USER 2<cr> before you save the file, it will appear only in the user area 2 directory.

"User areas" are imaginary. Every file on a disk has a user number associated with it, stored on the disk as an additional piece of information about that file. Thus it is not necessary to set aside room on the disk for each user area.

The USER command is of minimal value in running canned programs on a floppy disk system. However, when several users share disk drives, as in MP/M, one user can save files in user area 1 and another in user area 2, and both can share files in user area 0. Another good use of USER comes when you have a hard disk system with lots of storage space. You might want to put all word-processing files in user area 1, data-processing files in user area 2, and so on.

When you utilize different user areas, most commands function differently. For example, ERA *.* <cr> only erases all files in the currently chosen user number. There is no way to erase all files on the disk with a single command unless they are all in the same user area.

Almost without exception, any disk you receive from software vendors will have all files in user area 0.

When you are in a user area other than 0 in CP/M-PLUS or any user area in MP/M, the user number area is displayed as a prefix to the normal CP/M prompt:

`3A>`	User area 3, disk drive A
`5B>`	User area 5, disk drive B
`C>`	User area 0, disk drive C.

The only form of the USER command allowed in CP/M-80 and MP/M is

USER n (where n is a number between 0 and 15, inclusive.)
This establishes the user area you wish to use.

CP/M-PLUS users may also use the following form of the USER command:

USER
The system prompts you for the user area number to use.

Error Messages

? or n?
You forgot to specify a number or specified a number greater than 15, or you misspelled the command name USER. Check your work and try again.

filename? or NO FILE
These messages may appear if you change user areas and attempt to access programs or data not in the current user area.

d:

Change Default Disk Drive (CP/M-80, CP/M-PLUS, MP/M)

On a CP/M system with two or more drives, change the currently active (default) drive by typing the letter representing the drive being logged into, followed by a colon and a CARRIAGE RETURN:

```
B:<cr>
C:<cr>
L:<cr>
```

To revert to drive A, type

```
A:<cr>
```

When you change the default drive, CP/M changes its prompt letter. Following B:<cr>, CP/M returns with a prompt of B>. MP/M would return with the prompt nB>, where n represents the user area. CP/M-PLUS would return either with B> if the user area was 0 or nB> if the user area was other than 0.

When selecting a file on the default drive, you do not have to type the drive letter with the file name; but in any reference to files on drives other than the default you must specify the desired drive.

Error Message

BDOS ERR ON d: SELECT

The above error message will appear if you attempt to change to a drive that does not exist or that CP/M cannot find (perhaps because the power is off or the door is left open).

CONTROL-CHARACTER (LINE-EDITING) COMMANDS DETAILED

Line-editing commands, which consist of control characters typed on the command line, let you correct typing errors while entering command lines and give you some control over the console display (output). The line-editing commands are grouped by function, as shown in Table 4-1.

The CONTROL-P and CONTROL-S commands are useful almost any time CP/M is in control of your system, as is—usually—the CONTROL-H command (some programs, most notably word-processing and spreadsheet programs, usurp this duty from CP/M). The other line-editing commands must normally be typed within a CP/M command line, that is, after the CP/M prompt appears and before you press the CARRIAGE RETURN key to process the command.

The line-editing commands can often be used when typing input requested by transient programs. Their usefulness in this case will depend on the program.

TABLE 4-1. Line-Editing Codes Grouped by Function

Function	Codes Sent to Computer	
Terminate command line	carriage return line feed control-J control-M	(<cr>) (<lf>)
Cancel command line	control-U control-X	
Recall command line	control-W	
Cancel portion of command line	backspace delete rubout control-H control-K	(<bs>) (<del>) (<rub>) (banked CP/M-PLUS)
Display control	control-E control-R control-S control-Q	
Printer control	control-P	
Cursor control	control-A control-B control-F control-G	(banked CP/M-PLUS) (banked CP/M-PLUS) (banked CP/M-PLUS) (banked CP/M-PLUS)
Restart CP/M	control-C	

If you use any of the control characters that are valid only for banked CP/M-PLUS (systems using more than 64K memory) in CP/M-80, nonbanked CP/M-PLUS, or MP/M, the system will ignore the character.

CONTROL-A

Advance Cursor One Space to Right (Banked CP/M-PLUS)

Pressing CONTROL-A while typing on the command line allows you to move the cursor one space to the right without affecting anything else that has already been typed.

CONTROL-A, in conjunction with CONTROL-B, CONTROL-F, CONTROL-G, CONTROL-K, and CONTROL-W, allows you to edit command lines without having to retype them.

CONTROL-B

Cursor to Beginning (or End) of Command Line (Banked CP/M-PLUS)

The CONTROL-B character moves the cursor to the beginning of the command line without changing anything already typed. If the cursor is already at the beginning of the command line, CONTROL-B moves the cursor to the end of the command line.

CONTROL-B, in conjunction with CONTROL-A, CONTROL-F, CONTROL-G, CONTROL-K, and CONTROL-W, allows you to edit command lines without having to retype them.

CONTROL-C

Restart CP/M

A *warm start* restores CP/M's internal information to a predefined state without destroying programs or data stored in memory. A *cold start* starts a system from scratch, destroying programs that were in memory before the cold start. A cold start is often called a *cold boot* and a warm start a *warm boot*. In CP/M the warm start command has two primary uses:

- To "log in" a disk when you insert a different disk into one or more drives.
- To interrupt the current transient program and return to the CP/M command level.

You can create problems if you do not "close a file" (tell CP/M that you are through with a file) at the proper time. You can avoid such problems by always allowing a program to end normally. If there is an option in the program to QUIT, use it rather than pressing RESET or CONTROL-C.

If you change disks without telling CP/M, strange things may happen. Always press CONTROL-C after you insert a different disk into a disk drive when you are using CP/M, unless the disk is specifically *requested* by the program. In this latter instance, you have to assume that the programmer knew that you were changing disks and that instructions were included to inform CP/M of the requested change.

MP/M works differently. CONTROL-C in MP/M only stops execution of the current program. Because multiple users may be logged onto a computer with MP/M, a special command is necessary to reset specific disks (that is, to restart one user, not all users). This command is DSKRESET, described in Chapter 12.

Error Message

BDOS ERR ON d: R/O (where d: is the drive identifier)

CP/M can usually detect a switched disk. When it does, it will set the read-only attribute for that disk. If any program subsequently tries to write information onto that disk, this error message appears. The only way to recover from this error and not destroy information on your disk is to type CONTROL-C.

For the experienced or brave: you will notice that the error message you receive when CP/M detects a switch in disks mentions the disk is "read-only." This error message implies that you can switch disks at any time as long as you only read from the disk. If you use your system like most users, it is rare for a disk to be read from, but not written to; thus this is a potentially dangerous suggestion.

CONTROL-E

Continue Typing on Next Line

To continue typing a long command on the next line of the console display, type CONTROL-E. This moves the cursor to the beginning of the next line. When you ultimately press the CARRIAGE RETURN key, the entire command line is used, even though it may appear as several lines on the display. The CONTROL-E character itself is not considered part of the resulting command line.

CONTROL-F

Insert a Space at Cursor Position (Banked CP/M-PLUS)

The CONTROL-F command inserts a single space at the current cursor position on the command line, effectively moving all characters from the cursor position to the end of the line one space to the right.

CONTROL-F, in conjunction with CONTROL-A, CONTROL-B, CONTROL-G, CONTROL-K, and CONTROL-W, allows you to edit command lines without having to retype them.

CONTROL-G

Move Cursor One Space to Left (Banked CP/M-PLUS)

Pressing CONTROL-G while typing on the command line allows you to move the cursor one space to the left, without affecting anything else that has already been typed.

CONTROL-G, in conjunction with CONTROL-A, CONTROL-B, CONTROL-F, CONTROL-K, and CONTROL-W, allows you to edit command lines without having to retype them.

CONTROL-H or BACKSPACE

Delete Last Character

Version 2.2 and CP/M-PLUS allow you to use CONTROL-H or BACKSPACE to correct simple typing errors before pressing the CARRIAGE RETURN key. If your keyboard has a key labeled BACKSPACE or BS, you can use it; in any case you can type CONTROL-H. The two are just different names for the same function.

CONTROL-H is similar to RUBOUT or DELETE; it differs in that it erases the unwanted character from the screen, while RUBOUT or DELETE leaves the unwanted character on the screen and repeats it.

CONTROL-H or BACKSPACE is intended for video displays rather than printers.

CP/M will respond correctly to CONTROL-H even if you are using a printer; the printer may respond strangely, however.

DELETE or RUBOUT

Cancel One Character and Echo It

The DELETE key cancels the last uncancelled character in the command line and echoes (repeats) it. Press the key marked DELETE, DEL, RUBOUT, or RUB to do this.

Versions 1.3 and 1.4 usually lack the true backspacing delete that we described in the section on CONTROL-H. Instead, these versions almost always perform the delete function that echoes, or repeats, each deleted character. Type BLA and then press DELETE or RUBOUT; you will see either:

BLAA   Deleted characters are echoed

or

BL   Deleted characters are erased (rubbed out).

Echoed characters may seem a little strange to computing novices. When CP/M was first designed, the primary console device on most microcomputers was a Teletype or similar printer. These printers cannot backspace. In order to show that a character was erased, Digital Research used echoing in the earliest versions of CP/M.

Today, most computers use high-speed video display consoles. Such consoles have the ability to backspace and erase characters. Digital Research will provide a patch to any user of version 1.3 or 1.4 who wants true backspacing deletions.

CONTROL-J and CONTROL-M

Line Feed and Carriage Return

If you are using version 2.2 or CP/M-PLUS, you can substitute CONTROL-J or the LINEFEED key (if your keyboard has one) for the CARRIAGE RETURN key. If your keyboard has a LINEFEED key, it may be marked LF.

Typing CONTROL-M is exactly the same as pressing the CARRIAGE RETURN key when typing CP/M commands.

CONTROL-K

Delete to End of Line (Banked CP/M-PLUS)

The CONTROL-K command erases all information on the command line from the current cursor position to the end of the line.

CONTROL-K, in conjunction with CONTROL-A, CONTROL-B, CONTROL-F, CONTROL-G, and CONTROL-W, allows you to edit command lines without having to retype them.

CONTROL-P

Assigning Output to the Printer

To turn on the printer, type a CONTROL-P. If your version of CP/M has been configured for a printer, all output going to the console display is now also sent to the printer.

CONTROL-P works like a push-on, push-off switch: type it once to turn the printer on; type it a second time to turn it off.

Remember to turn the printer on when you use CONTROL-P; the printer mimics the screen. Unless someone added a printer interface to your version of CP/M, you will most likely have to tolerate the following minor inconveniences:

- Your printer will not paginate; it simply types line after line, oblivious to page ends.
- Any control code embedded in the text may adversely affect the printer. For example, many computers use the ASCII Form Feed character to clear the screen; thus, every time your screen clears, the printer may skip to the next page.
- Unless you have a high-speed printer, output to your console display slows down. Every time the computer wants to send a character and finds the printer busy, it waits to send that character.

Some programs disable the printer automatically, whether or not you have selected it. These programs, such as WordStar, have other commands for sending information to the printer.

Likewise, if you purchased your programs as complete, prewritten (canned) packages, they may turn the printer on and off as necessary. Do not type a CONTROL-P before executing such a program unless directed by the manual; let the computer do this work whenever possible.

Error Messages

If you type a CONTROL-P and double characters appear on your screen but none appear on your printer, contact the firm that sold you the system.

```
A>DIR^P<cr>
AA:: SSTTUUTTTTEERR..TTXXTT  ::  RREEPPEEAATT..DDOOCC  ::
     etc.
AA>>
```

Repeating characters indicate that CP/M has not been told where to send characters destined for the list device (usually the printer). Instructions must be added to the input/output section of CP/M to send information to the printer properly.

Another problem that can occur is that, immediately after you type a CONTROL-P, the system can "lock up" or stop accepting characters from you. If this happens, it usually means that the printer is either not connected properly (check to see if it is unplugged) or not turned on.

CONTROL-Q

Unpause Display (CP/M-PLUS, MP/M-80)

Pressing CONTROL-Q causes the resumption of normal screen display ("unpauses" the screen) that has been paused with the CONTROL-S command.

CONTROL-R

Repeat Current Command Line

If you are a poor typist and have an early CP/M system that echoes deleted characters, you may find that the command

```
A>DIR B:BASIC???.*
```

looks more like:

```
A>DIBBR BAA:BASIXXC?????.*
```

Reading command lines like that may well make you hate your computer. CONTROL-R comes to the rescue. Type a CONTROL-R to display a new, correct line below the original command line. This new line deletes all the characters that were echoed instead of being erased. Here is an example:

```
A>DIBBR BAA:BASIXXC?????.*^R
  DIR B:BASIC???.*
```

The CONTROL-R command does not work with version 1.3. Users of version 2.2 and CP/M-PLUS will probably not find the CONTROL-R command useful.

CONTROL-S

Pause the Display

CP/M can pause the console display. Like a freeze frame in film, everything stops until you tell CP/M to begin again. Pause the screen by typing a CONTROL-S. Another CONTROL-S in CP/M-80 (or a CONTROL-Q in CP/M-PLUS and MP/M-80) resumes the output to your display. Actually, typing any character except CONTROL-C will resume the output to the display. CONTROL-S really pauses the computer, and as a result the display pauses.

Pausing the display is not the best possible answer to handling overflow on the screen, however. Generally you are surprised by the overflow or respond too slowly to pause the frame exactly where you want. "Good" programs use formatted screen output and never attempt to put more information on the screen than it can handle. Good programs also include an automatic stop at the end of each screen of information and wait for you to press the CARRIAGE RETURN (or some other key) before resuming output. In short, if you find yourself using the CONTROL-S key while executing a program, you might consider other programs with better human interfacing, or you could ask your vendor to modify your program.

CONTROL-U/CONTROL-X

Cancel Current Command

If you start typing gibberish, don't worry—it happens to all of us. Perhaps you typed

```
A>DIRG A:THOMKJLSK.SAB=SLIUF
```

which makes no sense whatsoever. Instead of using the BACKSPACE or DELETE key to get back to the first mistake, you may find it easier to start over by typing CONTROL-U. CP/M will ignore what you have already typed and move to the beginning of the next line. CP/M places a number sign (#) at the end of the cancelled line.

With version 1.3, use CONTROL-U. With all other versions of CP/M, use CONTROL-X if you want to erase the cancelled line or CONTROL-U if you want to keep the cancelled line on the screen.

CONTROL-W

Recall and Display Previously Entered Command Line (Banked CP/M-PLUS)

The CONTROL-W command, when entered as the first character on a line, will recall the most recent command line entered into the system, either at the system prompt or from within an executing program.

CONTROL-W, in conjunction with CONTROL-A, CONTROL-B, CONTROL-F, CONTROL-G, and CONTROL-K, allows you to edit command lines without having to retype them.

SUMMARY

This chapter introduced you to the built-in commands within CP/M and MP/M. You should now be familiar with the built-in commands

DIR ERA REN SAVE TYPE USER d:

and with the control commands

^A ^B ^C ^E ^F ^G ^H ^J ^K ^M ^P ^Q ^R ^S ^U ^X ^W

CHAPTER

5 Basic CP/M Transient Commands

In the last chapter we introduced CP/M's built-in commands. CP/M also allows you to expand the basic set of commands with additional programs that act like commands. This chapter will describe some of these additional programs, specifically those normally supplied with CP/M-80 only or with both CP/M-80 and CP/M-PLUS.

A PROGRAM IN THE CONTEXT OF CP/M

Recall from Chapter 4 that built-in commands are those words that CP/M can interpret using only the instructions already present in memory, while transient commands (usually referred to as programs) are invoked by typing a command-like phrase that tells CP/M to get further instructions from the disk.

How does CP/M know what other instructions are available on the disk? If you type something in response to the CP/M command prompt that CP/M does not recognize as a command, CP/M searches the disk directory for a file with the COM file type matching the first word you type. Suppose you type

```
A>BUY<cr>
```

After realizing that BUY is not a built-in command, CP/M looks for a file entitled BUY.COM on the current disk drive. If there is no such file, CP/M issues the error message BUY?. If such a file does exist, CP/M loads the contents of that file into memory and transfers control to the first instruction in it.

MP/M works virtually the same as both versions of CP/M, except that it will also accept file types of PRL as containing commands to execute. Thus, in our example, BUY.COM and BUY.PRL both contain valid MP/M commands and can be accessed simply by typing BUY. The PRL file type stands for "page relocatable" files; the only difference between these and COM files is that PRL-type files may be located anywhere in memory (a requirement for many MP/M systems), whereas COM-type files always are placed at a specific location in memory (0100 hex).

If you use a system that recognizes both 8- and 16-bit versions of CP/M, you should know that 16-bit CP/M command files are stored with the file type of CMD. The differences among command file types are necessary because it is quite common to have MP/M as well as 8- and 16-bit CP/M files on the same disk on some systems (most notably the CompuPro 816 and DEC Rainbow).

The value of the transient command facility in CP/M is that if the file contains instructions for the computer to do something, it will respond as if you had typed a valid CP/M command (although it might take a bit more time since the disk must be accessed before the program starts working).

What is this program that acts like a command? For the time being we will define the word *program* in the context of CP/M as a set of instructions that is stored on disk in a file with the COM type for 8-bit CP/M, the PRL type for MP/M, and the CMD type for 16-bit CP/M, and that is invoked by typing its file name. This program is often called a *transient program* or *transient command.*

Once a program is loaded from the disk into the memory of your computer, the computer temporarily ignores CP/M and obeys the instructions in the program. A hypothetical DISPLAY.COM/.PRL/.CMD program might instruct the computer to

1. Ask you for the name of the file you wish to display
2. Go to the disk and find the file you requested
3. Read a character from the file
4. Display the character on the console display
5. If there are more characters left, go back to step 3
6. Return to CP/M.

Invoking a Program

The command line is what you type after the CP/M prompt A>, up to but not including the carriage return. Quite different from the eight-character limitation on file names, command line in CP/M can be up to 128 bytes long—you can type up to 128 characters for a single command!

Just as you can add extra refinements to some built-in commands by typing further information, so too you can invoke programs with additional information. With DIR B:*.BAS, for instance, the built-in command is DIR, but B:*.BAS refines the command. For lack of a better name or even an established standard, we will call this additional information *parameters.* There can be more than one parameter in a command line.

Let us recap briefly. A generalization of the command line format looks like this:

```
A> COMMAND PARAMETERS <cr>
↑  ↑           ↑        ↑
└──┼─CP/M prompt └──────┼──Additional refinements
   └─Command to be executed └──Carriage return ends command line
```

Likewise, we can generalize the way a transient command, or program, is invoked:

```
A> FILENAME PARAMETERS <cr>
↑  ↑             ↑        ↑
└──┼─CP/M prompt └────────┼─Additional refinements
   └─File to be loaded and executed └─Carriage return ends command line
```

Now what are the parameters we give the program? There is no simple answer; some programs use no additional parameters, some have optional parameters, while some require parameters. You may give no parameters to the program or as many as the command line can hold.

You now have all the information you need to proceed. While we have exhausted the list of built-in commands that CP/M recognizes, we have barely hinted at the number of programs that may be loaded and executed as transient commands. In the remainder of this chapter, as well as in Chapters 6 and 7, we will deal with some important transient commands that Digital Research provides with CP/M as well as some manufacturer-provided programs that may be important to you.

Note: We have used examples from a variety of CP/M implementations, although we have restricted them to common ones. Your version of CP/M may not display messages or information in exactly the same manner as we show here; this is nothing to worry about, unless the information is so radically different that it does not seem related to our discussion. If you receive apparently meaningless or unusual messages that do not match our examples, consult with your dealer to try to resolve the discrepancy before proceeding.

Housekeeping Utilities

For computer users, housekeeping is the job of maintaining the environment in which a computer program and its data operate. A well-maintained environment ensures proper storage and retrieval of information; we place our information so we can find it easily later.

Consider a file cabinet in which we arrange files for easy access. What happens when the file cabinet becomes full? If we are in a hurry, do we still maintain everything in the proper order? How do we retrieve an item that temporarily resides not in the cabinet but on a desk? The answers to these questions suggest the routine housekeeping chores necessary to maintain the integrity of the information kept in the file cabinet.

Now consider the disk used to store information (and instructions) as an electronic file cabinet. Just like a regular file cabinet, this electronic one can become full, get out of order, or lack information that is stored elsewhere.

Clearly, we need a few housekeeping routines to maintain that electronic cabinet, our disks. These routines must perform the following housekeeping tasks:

- Ascertain the current status of a disk
- Rearrange the information on the disk
- Expand the filing capabilities.

"Aha," you say, "we already have some commands that perform these tasks." True, we could categorize the built-in commands presented in Chapter 4 by function, as shown in Table 5-1. However, these commands are not sufficient for usefully altering a disk or for doing major reordering. For instance, while you can use DIR to see which files are on the disk, you cannot use the built-in commands CP/M-80 provides to determine the size of those files (you can with CP/M-PLUS, however) or easily perform a number of other useful functions, such as copying a file from one disk to another. Fortunately, Digital Research provides a number of *housekeeping utilities* to help you keep your disk in order. These transient programs are shown in Table 5-2.

Like the built-in commands, the transient housekeeping commands can be categorized by function, as shown in Table 5-3.

- Chapter 5 (this chapter) will discuss the transient commands DUMP, ED, PIP, STAT, SUBMIT, and XSUB.
- Chapter 6 will talk about DATE, DEVICE, GET, HELP, INITDIR, PATCH, PUT, SET, and SHOW.
- Chapter 7 discusses COPYSYS, MOVCPM, and SYSGEN.
- Finally, Chapter 12 will discuss ABORT, CONSOLE, DSKRESET, GENHEX, GENMOD, PRLCOM, SCHED, SPOOL, STOPSPLR, and TOD.

The description of STAT in this chapter is divided into two sections because of the two distinct uses of this program. The "Statistics on Files" section tells how STAT is used in the housekeeping of files. The "Statistics on Devices" section tells how STAT is used in the housekeeping of devices. Devices were introduced briefly earlier in this book and are described in detail in the second STAT section and in the descriptions of the DEVICE and SET commands in Chapter 6.

DUMP

Displaying the Contents of a File

DUMP presents the contents of a file in hexadecimal form in CP/M-80 and in both hexadecimal and ASCII form in CP/M-PLUS.

TABLE 5-1. Built-in Commands by Use

Command	Status	Rearranging	Expansion
DIR	x		
ERA		x	
REN		x	
SAVE			x
TYPE	x		
USER		x	

TABLE 5-2. Transient Programs Supplied With CP/M and MP/M

CP/M-80	CP/M-PLUS	MP/M
STAT.COM	SHOW.COM	STAT.PRL
PIP.COM	PIP.COM	PIP.PRL
ED.COM	ED.COM	ED.PRL
DUMP.COM	DUMP.COM	DUMP.PRL
SYSGEN.COM	COPYSYS.COM	
MOVCPM.COM		
SUBMIT.COM	SUBMIT.COM	SUBMIT.PRL
XSUB.COM	GET.COM	
	DEVICE.COM	
	SET.COM	
	DATE.COM	TOD.PRL
	HELP.COM	
	INITDIR.COM	
	PATCH.COM	
	PUT.COM	
	SETDEF.COM	
		CONSOLE.PRL
		DSKRESET.PRL
		SPOOL.PRL
		STOPSPLR.PRL
		SCHED.PRL
		ABORT.PRL

TABLE 5-3. Transient Programs by Use

Command	Status	Rearranging	Expansion
STAT	x	x	x
DEVICE	x	x	x
SET		x	x
SHOW	x		
PIP		x	x
ED	x	x	x
DUMP	x		
COPYSYS		x	x
SYSGEN		x	x
MOVCPM		x	x
DATE	x	x	
GET		x	
HELP	x		
INITDIR		x	x
PATCH		x	
PUT		x	x
SETDEF		x	x
SUBMIT		x	x
XSUB		x	x

DUMP operates like the TYPE command discussed earlier. But instead of presenting the ASCII representations of the file, DUMP presents the contents of the file in hexadecimal form. Assembly language programmers use the DUMP command to check the contents of a program file, a binary data file, or any non-ASCII file.

The allowable forms for this command are

DUMP d:filename.typ

Displays the hex representation of each byte stored in the file with the name filename.typ on drive d:. CONTROL-S pauses DUMP; press any key to interrupt DUMP and return to A>.

DUMP d:*.*

Displays the hex representation of the first file that matches the *.* (or other ambiguous) filename. CONTROL-S pauses DUMP; press any key to interrupt DUMP and return to A>.

DUMP is used as shown below:

CP/M-80 DUMP:

```
A>DUMP B:PROGRAM.COM<cr>
0000 3A 07 00 FE C8 DA AC 03 21 00 00 39 22 25 07 31
0010 00 C8 3E 11 D3 FD 21 27 07 7D D3 FD 7C D3 FD CD
0020 3B 02 11 13 04 CD 28 02 CD 3B 02 11 55 04 CD 28
A>
```

CP/M-PLUS DUMP:

```
A>DUMP B:PROGRAM.COM<cr>
DUMP -- Version 3.0
0000: 3A 07 00 FE C8 DA AC 03 21 00 00 39 22 25 07 31 :.......!..9"%.1
0010: 00 C8 3E 11 D3 FD 21 27 07 7D D3 FD 7C D3 FD CD ..>...!'........
0020: 3B 02 11 13 04 CD 28 02 CD 3B 02 11 55 04 CD 28 ;.....(..;.....(
A>
```

In both CP/M-80 and CP/M-PLUS, the four-digit number that appears at the start of each line is the relative address of the first byte on that line. The pairs of hexadecimal digits represent each byte of the stored file, one pair for each byte in the file.

In CP/M-PLUS, a period in the ASCII display section indicates a nondisplayable character, such as the control characters (ASCII 20-7F hex are displayable characters).

ED

Context Editor

ED is a program with a number of built-in commands used to edit text files. You may have wondered how to put something new onto a disk. The answer is that you use an *editor.* The editor CP/M includes is ED, and you will find it saved in the file ED.COM.

The editor is a program that takes characters from the keyboard and puts them in a disk file. Since you may make entry errors or wish to make changes, the editor also includes a number of built-in commands that display, modify, delete, and add to the information you have typed.

The CP/M editor (called *context editor* by Digital Research) is both character- and line-oriented; commands operate on text either a character at a time or a line at a time. (A line is a block of characters ending in a carriage return.)

In CP/M-80, to edit the file filename.typ, type the following:

ED filename.typ

This form invokes the editor and searches for the input file. If filename.typ does not exist, a temporary file of that name will be created. If it does exist, a temporary file of filename.$$$ will be created. The temporary file is used to store the edited text.

In CP/M-PLUS, three possible input forms are allowed:

ED x:filename.typ

This form is the same as the CP/M-80 case, with the addition that a disk drive can be specified for input to come from and output to go to.

ED x:filename.typ y:

This form is the same as the first form, except the temporary output file is generated on drive y. This form is used when there is not enough room on the original disk to hold both the original file and the edited file.

ED x:i-filename.typ z:o-filename.typ

This form is the same as the first form, except that all input is from i-filename.typ (on drive x, if specified) and all output goes to o-filename.typ (on drive z, if specified). This form is used when the original file is read-only or resides on a write-protected disk.

For example, suppose the file MYFILE.TEX requires editing. To edit this file, type:

```
A>ED MYFILE.TEX<cr>
```

ED creates the temporary file MYFILE.$$$on the disk. This file contains no information; it contains only the structure of the file to be written.

In order to make changes to the original file MYFILE.TEX you must be able to see the text and manipulate it. ED's commands permit you to move text from the original file into memory, view the text that you have moved into memory, make the required changes, and move the text from memory back to the file. You can only edit a file while it is in memory. The area of memory ED sets aside to hold text is called the *edit buffer.*

As you progress in your editing, you will move more text from the original file into the edit buffer for editing. The edit buffer holds a limited amount of text; as it becomes full you must move the edited text to the temporary file MYFILE.$$$. The overall ED operation is shown in Figure 5-1.

Since movement through the entire text may require shifting bodies of text in and out of the edit buffer in the direction shown by the arrows above, you basically move forward through the text (the H command allows you to restart from the head of the

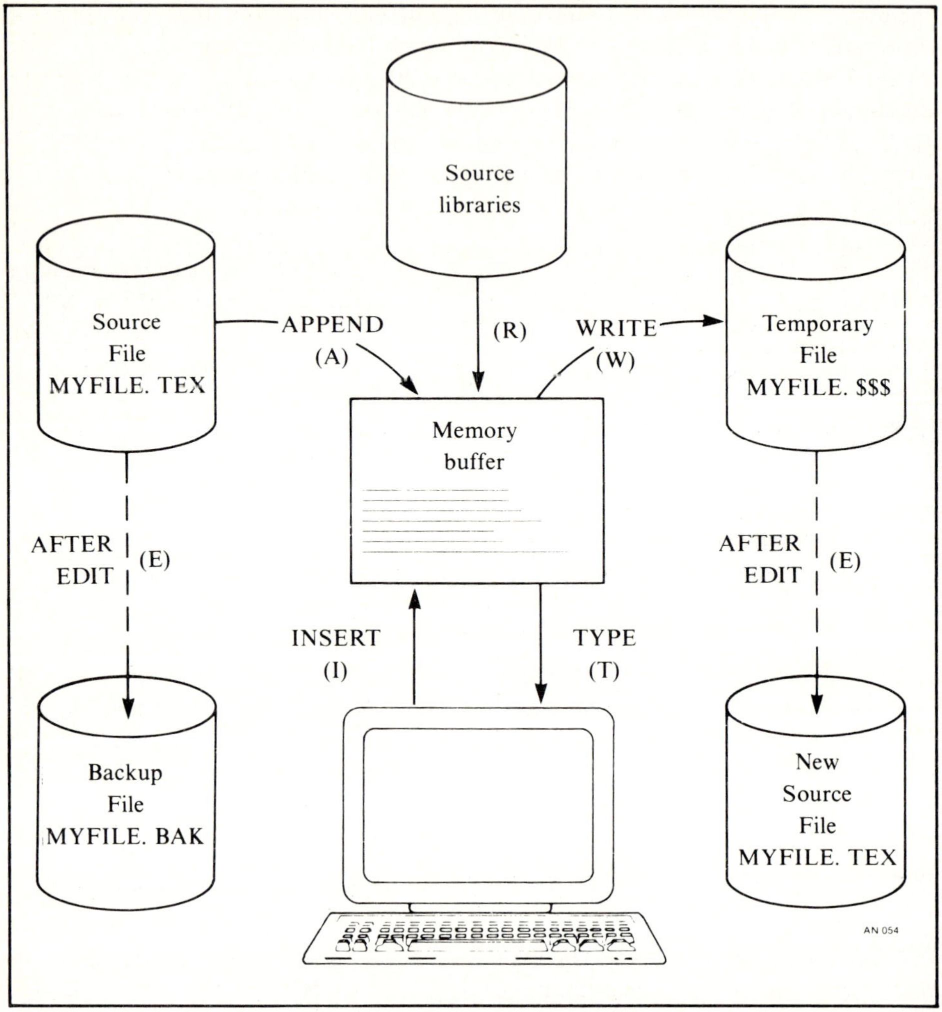

FIGURE 5-1. Overall ED operation

file). This will be explained in more detail later. Examine the ED commands on the following pages to learn how to perform the tasks we have described.

ED Commands

To use ED commands, invoke ED and follow ED's prompt (* or: *) with the proper command and a CARRIAGE RETURN <cr>, as follows:

```
A>ED filename.typ<cr>
*edcommand<cr>
```

We will use several abbreviation conventions in this section. Whenever a plus or minus sign can be typed, you will see the symbol +, which stands for plus (+) *or* minus (−); if you type neither + nor −, ED assumes you mean +. Whenever a number can be typed to give the command further information, you will see the symbol n. An "n" can be any decimal integer number in the range 0 through 65535, inclusive. Do not use a comma between digits. If you omit the number, ED assumes a value of 1. Typing a zero (0) has a special meaning for some commands. If you type a number sign (#), ED substitutes 65535.

For the purposes of ED, a line of text is a sequence of zero or more characters followed by a carriage return character and a line feed character. We will represent this character pair by the symbol [CRLF]. When you type a line of text for ED and then press CARRIAGE RETURN, ED adds the line feed character so that the line ends with [CRLF].

We can separate ED commands into four functions:

Transferring Text. These commands transfer by line or by blocks of text

- From the original file into the edit buffer.
- From the edit buffer into the temporary file.
- From the original file to the temporary file.
- From the edit buffer into another file (not the original or the temporary file but a distinct file on a disk).
- From another file (not original or temporary but a distinct file on the disk) into the edit buffer.

Working in the Edit Buffer. An imaginary character pointer (CP) locates the text in the edit buffer. These editing commands

- Insert text into the edit buffer
- Manipulate text within the edit buffer in relation to the CP
- Direct movement of the CP.

Searching and Changing Text. These commands work within the edit buffer to

- Search for a particular set of characters
- Substitute a set of characters
- Switch placement between sets of characters
- Move text from the original file through the edit buffer to the temporary file automatically while searching.

Combining Commands. A string of ED commands can be entered in one command line ending with a <cr> to permit a variety of editing functions and to repeat a command string a specified number of times.

Commands for Transferring Text

nA

Appends (copies) a number of lines from the original file to the edit buffer. To move a single line, enter only A; 1 is the default number of lines to move. To move the maximum number of lines into the edit buffer, include the number (nA). The nA command moves lines until the original file is exhausted or the edit buffer is full. To move a portion of the text into the edit buffer, enter 0A; this moves text from the original file until the edit buffer is at least half full. Once appended, lines in the original file are ignored by subsequent commands that read from the original file.

nW

Writes a number of lines from the edit buffer to the temporary file. To write a single line, enter only W; 1 is the default number of lines to write. To write the maximum number of lines into the temporary file, include the number (nW). The nW command moves lines until the edit buffer is exhausted. To write a portion of the text into the temporary file, enter 0W; this moves text from the edit buffer until the edit buffer is at least half full. Lines written are deleted from the edit buffer as they are written to the temporary file.

E

Ends the editing session. Text is transferred, and files are renamed as follows:

1. All text remaining in the edit buffer moves to the temporary file, as with the W command.
2. All text remaining in the original file is then appended to the temporary file.
3. The type of the original file becomes BAK.
4. The type of the temporary file is changed to the type of the original file.
5. The block move file X$$$$$$$.LIB, if present, is erased. (For more detail on the file X$$$$$$$.LIB, see the section on nX.)
6. The CP/M prompt returns.

Use the E command as the normal ending of an editing session. To work properly, E must be the only command on a line.

H

Moves to the beginning of the file being edited (moves to Head). Text is transferred, and files are renamed as follows:

1. All text remaining in the edit buffer moves to the temporary file, as with the W command.
2. All text remaining in the original file is moved to the temporary file.
3. The type of the original file becomes BAK.

4. The type of the temporary file is changed to the type of the original file.
5. A new, empty temporary file is created.
6. You are now ready to edit the new original file.

H must be the only command on the line. The H command has two uses: (1) Since the A, N, and W commands can move only forward, not backward, through the original and temporary files, you use the H command to save the editing done so far and return to the beginning of the file for more editing. (2) Use the H command every few minutes during editing of critical files to save your results on the disk. Text left in the edit buffer is generally lost if an operator error or equipment malfunction occurs, but text saved in the temporary file is easily recovered.

Frequent use of H is especially important when inserting a lot of text or making numerous changes. However, remember that the H command makes a new backup file; this means that after using the H command twice, the original file as it was before beginning the editing session is lost. For this reason, if you anticipate using the H command often, use PIP (see the PIP section later in this chapter) to make your own second copy of the original file. (Do not call it type BAK; use OLD or place it on a different drive to be safe).

O

Erases the edited file. Text is transferred as follows:

1. The contents of the edit buffer and the temporary file are deleted
2. You are returned to the beginning of the original file.

ED asks "O-(Y/N)?" before it proceeds, since all changes made to the text are erased when the O command executes. Press Y to return to the original file or N to continue editing.

O must be the only command on the line.

Q

Quits editing; does not institute any changes. ED asks "Q-(Y/N)?" before it proceeds, since all changes made to the text are erased when the Q command executes. Press Y to quit editing or N to continue the editing session.

Q must be the only command on the line.

R<cr> (CP/M-80)
R^Z (CP/M-PLUS)

Reads the file created by the X command into the edit buffer. R inserts the entire contents of the transfer file X$$$$$$$.LIB into the edit buffer immediately after the character pointer (CP). The transfer file is not affected; you can read it as many times as you want during an editing session. The transfer file is automatically erased when you leave ED with the E, Q, or CONTROL-C commands.

Rfilename<cr> (CP/M-80)
Rfilename^Z (CP/M-PLUS)

Reads the library file filename.LIB into the edit buffer. This command inserts the entire contents of the specified file into the edit buffer immediately after the character pointer (CP). The library file is not affected.

nX

Writes (Xfers, or transfers) lines from the edit buffer to a temporary file named X$$$$$$$.LIB. You may later transfer these lines back to the edit buffer by using the R<cr> command. With the X, R<cr> command combination you can move blocks of information. The file X$$$$$$$.LIB is erased when editing is completed with an E, Q, or CONTROL-C command. The X command copies the n lines that follow the character pointer in the edit buffer into the transfer file. The lines are not deleted from the edit buffer, and they are added to any previous contents of the transfer file.

In CP/M-PLUS you may also use 0X^Z to erase the library file X$$$$$$$.LIB, or 0Xfilename.typ^Z to erase any specified file.

Commands for Working in the Edit Buffer

±B

Moves the character pointer to the beginning (use a + or nothing before the B) or the end (use a − before the B) of the edit buffer. Notice that the direction implied by the sign in front of the B command is the opposite of that for all other commands.

±nC

Moves the character pointer by plus or minus n characters. The carriage return/line feed combination that terminates a line in ED is counted as two separate characters. Type +5C to move the character pointer five characters toward the end of the edit buffer.

±nD

Deletes n characters immediately before (−) or after (+) the character pointer.

For example, we have the line NOW IS THE TIME FOR ACTION with the character pointer pointing at the I in TIME. If we issue the command −3D<cr> the result would be NOW IS THIME FOR ACTION, with the character pointer still pointing to the I, now in THIME.

I

Enters the insert mode. ED accepts all characters you type and inserts them into the edit buffer after the character pointer. With certain exceptions, every character you type goes into the buffer until you press CONTROL-Z. CONTROL-Z terminates the insert mode and returns the ED prompt. If you enter an uppercase I, all inserted text will automatically be translated to uppercase-only characters.

There are some characters that perform differently in the Insert mode than you may expect.

Characters	Function
CONTROL-H or BACKSPACE	Deletes the last character typed
CONTROL-L	Inserts a carriage return/line feed
CONTROL-M or RETURN	Inserts a carriage return/line feed
CONTROL-R	Redisplays the current line
CONTROL-U	Deletes the current line
CONTROL-X	Deletes the current line
RUBOUT or DEL	Deletes the last character typed and redisplays it.

The *current line* consists of the characters that follow the last carriage return typed while in the insert mode.

Use the insert mode to type in a new file or to add several lines to an existing file. Remember to exit the insert mode and use the save command H often.

Istring^Z

Insert a string. This command inserts the character sequence "string" into the edit buffer following the character pointer. Use this command to insert short strings.

Istring<cr>

Insert a line. This command inserts the character sequence "string" into the edit buffer following the character pointer. A carriage return/line feed combination is inserted after the string. The carriage return/line feed is the difference between this command and the previous one. Use this command to insert a single line.

±nK

Kills (deletes) those lines from the edit buffer that you do not wish to appear in the final edited version. Lines referenced by the nK command are not transferred to the temporary file but remain in the original file, which later becomes the backup file. You may remove any number of lines from the edit buffer in either direction from the character pointer. + K or K erases all characters after the character pointer up to and including the current line's carriage return/line feed. − K erases all characters in the line before the character pointer, back to the first carriage return/line feed encountered, but not including it. If you still have some characters remaining in a line that you thought you had deleted using the K command, check to see if the character pointer was at the start of the line when you issued the command.

±nL

Moves the character pointer forward or backward n lines in the buffer. First the character pointer moves to the beginning of the current or next line (that is, if the character pointer is not currently at the beginning of a line). Subsequent moves encompass full lines; the character pointer moves n lines forward or backward. The 0L moves the character pointer to the beginning of the current line.

+nP

Moves the character pointer one page and displays the page following the character pointer. This command is repeated for a total of n pages. P is a convenient method of scrolling through the text in the edit buffer. A page is a fixed number of lines that varies with the version of CP/M, but usually is one screenful. +nP moves you forward through the edit buffer and −nP moves you backward. P operates by first moving the character pointer backward or forward one page and then displaying the page that follows the character pointer. 0P displays a page without moving the character pointer.

+nT

Displays lines of text that are in the edit buffer. To see the three lines before the character pointer, you would type −3T. To see the three lines after the character pointer, type +3T or just 3T. If the character pointer is positioned at the beginning of a line, type T to see that line. If the character pointer is positioned within a line, type 0T to see the part of the line before the character pointer, type *T* to see the part of the line after the character pointer, or type 0TT to see the whole line.

The T command does not move the character pointer; it displays lines of text in relation to the character pointer.

+U

Translates lowercase letters to uppercase. Type +U to begin translation and −U to end translation.

Ordinarily ED does not translate characters. After being given the command U or +U, however, ED translates characters that enter the edit buffer either from the keyboard or from the original file. Lowercase a through z is translated to uppercase A through Z. This translation continues until ED receives the −U command or the editing session is concluded. (Note that you can create a file of all lowercase characters by using the PIP [L] parameter, discussed later in this chapter.)

+V

Displays line numbers. Line numbers are useful in identifying text and moving the character pointer. (V stands for verify line numbers, by the way.) Type −V to suppress display of line numbers.

0V

Indicates how much of the edit buffer is in use and how much is still available for use. The result is shown by the editor in the form

xxxxx/yyyyy

The first number ED reports (xxxxx) is the amount of available memory in the edit buffer; the second (yyyyy) is the maximum possible size of the edit buffer. Subtracting the first from the second, we find out how many characters of the file being edited are currently in the buffer.

n:

Moves to line number n. When line numbers are being displayed (see V), you can use this command to move the character pointer directly to the beginning of a specific line. The n: command can be used as a command prefix, making commands start at a particular line number. For example, 75:0P will make ED move to line 75 and display a page of text.

:n

Starts at the character pointer and continues through line number n. This is not really a command by itself, but a prefix to a command. For example, if you type :75T, ED will type lines (T) beginning at the character pointer (currently in line 55) and ending at line 75.

Notice that you can use this command together with the previous one to perform an operation on a specified range of lines. For example, to delete lines 20 through 30, no matter where the character pointer is, type 20::30K.

±n

Moves forward or backward and displays one line. This is an abbreviated form of the command nLT, where the character pointer is moved forward or backward by n lines, whereupon the line then at the character pointer is displayed.

The simplest form of this command is just a carriage return and is equivalent to LT, which moves the character pointer to the next line and displays it.

Commands for Searching and Changing Text

In this section on searching and changing text the following rule applies: you must use lowercase commands to search for uppercase and lowercase matches; an uppercase command means that ED will only search for uppercase matches to your string.

nFstring^Z

Finds a particular unique sequence (string) of characters. If the search is successful (the string is found the specified number of times), the character pointer is placed immediately following the "n" th matching string. If you were searching for the first chorus of "Row, Row, Row Your Boat" with the command 3fRow, the character pointer would come to rest between "w" in the last "Row" and the space preceding "Your" if its original position was before the first letter of the first "Row." If the search cannot satisfy the command given, the character pointer does not move.

The search begins at the location of the character pointer, so be sure it is positioned well before the string to be found when using the F command.

Also remember that the F command searches only within the text in the edit buffer; it cannot look through text still in the original file or already saved on the disk — to do so, see the N command, described next.

nNstring^Z

Looks for the string in the edit buffer and on the disk. This command automatically loads the next portion of the original file into the edit buffer and writes lines from the edit buffer to the temporary file as necessary. The N command (called *autoscan*) acts on the entire document, beginning at the character pointer, even if portions of it are still in the original file, while F looks only in the edit buffer for the string.

Remember to position the character pointer properly before issuing the N command. (See the F command described earlier.)

Use CONTROL-L to represent the carriage return/line feed pair if it is part of the string.

nSfindstring^Zreplacestring^Z

Substitutes information in the edit buffer. The substitute command finds one string and replaces it with another. As shown, the command would search for "findstring" and replace it with "replacestring." The searching begins at the character pointer and ends at the last character in the edit buffer. The substitution is performed a total of n times.

As in all substitution commands, be sure the strings you want to replace are unique.

Use CONTROL-L to represent the carriage return/line feed pair in the string.

nJfindstring^Zinsertstring^Zendstring^Z

Juxtaposes two or more unique strings one or more times. This command combines the insertion and deletion operations.

To use this command, first find "findstring." Immediately following "findstring" insert "insertstring," and then delete all characters from the end of "insertstring" to the beginning of "endstring." Repeat a total of n times. The character pointer, assuming that the operation was successful, is placed at the end of the final "insertstring."

For example, we have in text the line

WHEN IN ROM DO AS THE ROMANS DO, AND BE ROMANTIC

with the character pointer at W in WHEN. By means of the juxtaposition command, JROM ^ZDON'T ^Z AS^Z would result in

WHEN IN ROM DON'T AS THE ROMANS DO, AND BE ROMANTIC

with the character pointer at A in AS.

Be careful when using multiple repetitions of the juxtaposition command, as you can often change information you do not mean to change.

Combining Commands

ED lets you group some commands in one command line to save typing time. You can cascade ED commands one after another and follow the last command with the carriage return. For example, the commands 0A<cr>, B<cr>, and T<cr> could be typed as 0ABT<cr>, all on one line.

There are a few simple rules to follow when typing several commands on one line.

- Some commands must be typed alone in a command line; these commands are E, H, O, and Q. This is done to prevent the disastrous consequences of certain typographical errors.
- When typing commands that use strings, use CONTROL-Z, rather than <cr>, to end the strings. Commands that use strings are F, I, J, N, and S. Use <cr> only at the end of the command line.

You can create a command sequence for frequently used commands. The format is

nMcommand1command2command3<cr>

For example, if you type

MROM^Z-3DIRAM0TT<cr>

the command line says to perform the following sequence of steps repeatedly:

1. Find ROM (the character pointer is placed after the M)
2. Delete the three previous characters (ROM)
3. Insert RAM
4. Show each line as it is changed (0TT).

This macro command will change all occurrences of ROM to RAM. If used on the previous example in the J commands, the resulting line would read: WHEN IN RAM DO AS THE RAMANS DO, AND BE RAMANTIC .... If n is absent or is equal to 0 or 1, the command sequence repeats until an error condition develops. Striking any key aborts the macro command.

PIP

Copying Information

PIP, or Peripheral Interchange Program, copies information from one place to another. The names of the files you wish to copy can be ambiguous, and a number of optional parameters are available for use. PIP can also copy information from and to devices.

PIP can be invoked in one of two ways. If you want to perform only one operation with PIP, invoke it as follows:

```
A>PIP pipcommandline<cr>
```

If you have several operations to perform, use this second method to invoke PIP:

```
A>PIP<cr>
*pipcommandline<cr>
*pipcommandline<cr>
*^C
A>
```

No matter which method you use, there is no significant difference in the manner in which PIP performs the operation requested by pipcommandline. One minor difference is explained under the discussion of the Q parameter later in this section. Another difference is PIP's response to errors. If the first invocation method, above, is used, errors cause a return to CP/M. If the second method is used, errors cause a return to the PIP prompt.

The PIP command line (pipcommandline in our examples) usually takes the form of

destination = source[parameters]

where destination is the name of the new file, source is the name of the old file, and parameters are the optional parameters you select for the copying process.

If there is already a file with the same name as your destination filename, the existing file is erased after successful completion of the copy. The previous contents of the destination file are lost.

PIP command lines and special parameters specify the transfer made between two files or two groups of files. In every instance, the original file remains intact; we can duplicate an entire disk or only a portion of a file without changing the original. We can specify that certain characteristics of the new file be changed from the original without changing the original. When used with files, PIP can do the following:

- Copy a file from one disk to another
- Create an identical file with a different name
- Copy several files from one disk to another
- Copy all files from one disk to another
- Create one file from the concatenation of several
- Copy a portion of a file
- Copy from a system file
- Copy onto an R/O file
- Display the contents of a file while it is being copied.

PIP also copies data from a file to a device, from a device to a file, or between devices; you simply substitute a device name for a file name in either the destination or source position, or both. When you read from or write to a device, as opposed to a disk file, make sure you can terminate the copying process. Some devices do not emit an end-of-file marker (^Z) as CP/M does at the end of every disk file.

When used with devices, PIP can do the following:

- Send the contents of a file to a device, such as a printer.
- Pass the data from a device, like paper tape reader or modem, into a file.
- Send data from one device to another.
- Print the contents of a file, formatting it for a special printer or paper size.
- Display on the console selected data arriving at an input device.
- Convert uppercase letters to lowercase or vice versa.
- Save in a file all the data arriving at an input device.

PIP has five "special" device names in addition to the ones that will be explained in the section on STAT.

NUL
A source device that sends 40 nulls (do-nothing characters—00 hex) to the destination specified.

EOF
A source device that sends an end-of-file marker (^Z or a 1A hex) to the destination.

OUT
A user-created custom destination device. PIP must be modified to include this device. (CP/M-80 only)

INP
A user-created custom source device. PIP must be modified to include this device. (CP/M-80 only)

PRN
A special form of the LST: device that expands tabs, numbers lines, and paginates the copy (the same as LST:[NPT8]).

Like the devices discussed earlier, these device names are used as sources and destinations in the command line.

Variations in Using PIP

The following is a summary of the varieties of PIP commands that you may enter.

PIP
Loads PIP into memory for use; PIP commands entered individually at PIP prompt (*) with the format destination = source. A RETURN or CONTROL-C at the PIP prompt cancels PIP and returns you to CP/M.

PIP d:new.typ[Gn]=d:old.typ[options]
Copies the file old.typ on the drive specified to the file new.typ on the drive specified using the options specified ([options]). A single option is permitted in CP/M-PLUS only for the destination file, that of the G (get from user area) option (see "PIP Options," below).

PIP d:new.typ[Gn]=d:old1.typ[options],d:old2.typ[options]
Creates a new file on the drive specified, the new file consisting of both files old1.typ and old2.typ. In other words, a comma on the PIP command line indicates concatenation. Multiple files may serve as the source, but each must be set apart from the others with a comma on the command line. Selected options apply only to the file immediately preceding the option list. A single option is permitted in CP/M-PLUS only for the destination file, that of the G (get from user area) option (see "PIP Options," below).

PIP dev:=d:filename.typ[options]
Sends the contents of a file on the drive specified to a device. You may stop the PIP-to-device process by pressing any key while the copying is in progress.

PIP d:filename.typ[Gn]=dev:[options]
Copies input from a device to the filename specified. Special Input: Both a carriage return (CONTROL-M) and a line feed (CONTROL-J) must be entered at the end of each line from the source device. A CONTROL-Z terminates the transfer and signifies the end of the file. You may stop the PIP-to-device process by pressing any key while the copying is in progress. A single option is permitted in CP/M-PLUS only for the destination file, that of the G (get from user area) option (see "PIP Options," below).

PIP destinationdev:=sourcedev:[options]
Copies data from one device to another. Special Input: You may stop the PIP-to-device process by pressing any key while the copying is in progress.

PIP Options

This section describes each of PIP's options. You will probably use only one or two of these options frequently; you may never use some of them. You may combine two or more options between the square bracket characters (e.g.,[BEU]) for source files; destination files can only use the G option (CP/M-PLUS).

[A] Transfer only modified files (CP/M-PLUS only)
The A option specifies that the PIP transfer should occur for the matching files *only* if they have been modified since the last time they were copied. (CP/M-PLUS keeps an "archive bit" in the directory entry for every file, clearing the bit each time the file is copied and resetting the bit each time the file is modified.)

[B] Block transfer option (CP/M-80 only)
[B] designates the "block mode transfer." In Block mode, PIP transfers information from the source to a buffer until the ASCII character DC3 (53 hex, or CONTROL-S, sometimes called *XOFF* or *reader off*) is received. Once this character is received, PIP takes the information it has received so far and sends it to the destination device specified. Then PIP returns to the source for more data. We use [B] for source devices that transfer data continuously and would fill up PIP's buffer area (where it stores information before processing to the specified file or device) if the buffer were not periodically purged. For normal file-to-file operations, [B] is not necessary. [B] is normally used to read a paper tape into a file. Whatever the source device, it must send the DC3 character often enough to avoid filling the buffer, and then it must wait for PIP to empty the buffer.

[C] Prompt for confirmation (CP/M-PLUS only)
Use of the C option causes PIP to prompt the user for confirmation before each separate copying operation is performed. (In the case of ambiguous file names, a confirmation is asked for each matching file name before copying it.)

[Dn] Delete all characters after the nth column

[Dn] tells PIP to delete any character received that extends past a column number, which must be specified immediately following the D, as in [D20]. This type of transfer will work only for line-oriented data (data which contains periodic carriage return characters). After each carriage return is detected, PIP counts and processes characters up to and including the column number specified and then ignores all remaining characters sent until the next carriage return is received. (**Note:** Line feed characters are interpreted the same as carriage returns for this operation.)

The [Dn] option is primarily used to send wide-lined output to a device that handles only narrow lines (like a printer or CRT terminal). For file-to-file transfers, this option is rarely used.

The value n is a decimal integer in the range 1 through 255, inclusive. Input lines longer than 255 characters are not truncated properly by the [Dn] option.

[E] Echo the copying to the console as it is performed

The characters sent to the destination device are echoed to the console display during the copying process. This is a handy method of reviewing exactly what is being copied.

[F] Filter form feeds from the original file

The [F] option "filters" form feed characters (0C hex) from the data flow; PIP ignores the ASCII-defined character for form feeds and copies without it. Form feeds are often embedded in files for correct pagination of the printed output. You may wish to eliminate form feeds to conserve paper, to display a file on your console screen, or to use a printer that improperly interprets the form feed character.

The ASCII form feed character is called "FF" and is equivalent to hexadecimal 0C and CONTROL-L.

The form feed character is a format character that controls the layout or positioning of information in printing or display devices. Thus, a printer would normally respond to this character not by printing it, but by advancing the paper to the top of the next form or page.

Use [F] if your printer does not respond properly to form feed characters, or if you are sending a file to a device other than a printer. (See also the [P#] parameter.)

[Gn] Direct PIP to copy files from other user areas

The [Gn] option allows PIP to copy files from another user area to the current one. A decimal number (between 0 and 15, inclusive) represents the source user area and should immediately follow the G in the command line. This option is helpful in setting up a user area with files that may be needed later. The [Gn] parameter is not available in version 1.3 or 1.4.

[H] Check data transfer for proper Intel hex format

[H] specifies that the data to be transferred is in the special Intel hex format rather than in the normal ASCII or binary formats. The Intel format is usually used with paper tape punch and reader devices. Most users do not utilize this option. When PIP detects errors in the hex format, a prompt will ask what corrective action to take. (See also the [I] parameter.)

[I] Ignore any null records in Intel hex format transfers
The [I] option also applies to Intel hex format records (see [H]). The [I] option tells the PIP program to ignore any data that appears in a null record (00: in Intel format). Again, this option is rarely of use to end users, as it applies primarily to paper tape reader and punch devices. If the [I] option is specified, then the [H] option is automatically set by PIP. Thus the PIP command line of

PUN:=PROGRAM.HEX[I]

is equivalent to

PUN:=PROGRAM.HEX[HI]

[L] Convert uppercase letters to lowercase
The [L] option allows you to change the letters A through Z to their lowercase equivalents during the copying process. Be extremely careful in using this option, as it should never be used with files that contain instructions to the computer. If you do happen to use it on a program file, you may find that some important instructions that happen to look to PIP like the letters A-Z are changed when they should not be.

[N] Add line numbers to each line during the data transfer
The [N] option adds a line number to each line of data transferred. Each time a carriage return (or line feed) is detected by PIP, the line number counter is incremented. [N] is of particular use when transferring a file to the printer. If a 2 is appended to the [N] option (i.e., [N2]), leading zeroes are added, and the number is printed in a six-character field followed by a three-character blank buffer. Here is the difference between files transferred using these options:

Original	**File Using [N]**	**File Using [N2]**	
Now is the	1: Now is the	000001	Now is the
time for all	2: time for all	000002	time for all
good persons	3: good persons	000003	good persons
to come to	4: to come to	000004	to come to
the aid of	5: the aid of	000005	the aid of
their party.	6: their party.	000006	their party.

[O] Transfer object code files or other non-ASCII files
Use the [O] option when copying from non-ASCII files (such as program, object code, or binary data files) or from devices sending non-ASCII data. Specifying the [O] option is not necessary when copying from files with the COM type, because PIP assumes that COM-type files are non-ASCII (non-text) files.

Use of [O] tells PIP to treat CONTROL-Z (1A hex) just like any other character it receives from a source device or file; PIP would otherwise interpret CONTROL-Z as signaling the end of the transfer from that source.

The following paragraphs contain more detailed information about ASCII files, non-ASCII files, and end-of-file markers. Read on if you are interested in these details.

PIP assumes that a CONTROL-Z character received from an ASCII source (device or file) is an end-of-file marker or data terminator, meaning that all the data has been transferred. PIP sends a CONTROL-Z character to an ASCII destination (file or device) to indicate that all the data has been sent.

CP/M uses different methods for marking (and detecting) the end of ASCII and non-ASCII files. CP/M marks the end of an ASCII file by placing a CONTROL-Z character in the file after the last data character, unless the file happens to contain an exact multiple of 128 characters, in which case adding the CONTROL-Z would waste 127 characters, so CP/M does not do so. Use of the CONTROL-Z character as the end-of-file marker is possible because CONTROL-Z is seldom used as data in ASCII files.

In a non-ASCII file, however, CONTROL-Z is just as likely to occur as any other character. Therefore, it cannot be used as the end-of-file marker. CP/M assumes it has reached the end of the file when it has read the last record (basic unit of disk space) allocated to the file. The disk directory entry for each file contains a list of the disk records allocated to that file. This method relies on the size of the file, rather than its contents, to locate the end of the file.

[Pn]   Issue a form feed after the nth line

Use [Pn] when the destination is the LST: device and the current LST: device (usually a printer) does not print the source data in the following format:

- Top margin is blank
- Bottom margin is blank
- Top and bottom margins together total six lines
- Text fills the space between top and bottom margins.

Deviation from these conditions usually occurs when the current LST: device has one of the following characteristics:

- Does not understand the form feed character (see [F])
- Does not insert top and bottom margins
- Is printing on a different length page than that assumed by the source data.

[Pn] tells PIP you want it to insert a form feed after each n lines of data. Enter the desired number of lines in place of n in the PIP command line option [Pn]. Here n is a decimal number in the range 1 through 255, inclusive. If you do not enter a number or if the number is 1, PIP assumes you want a page eject after each 60 lines.

If [F] is also present in the option field, all form feeds detected during the transfer will be removed, and PIP will then insert new form feeds as specified by [Pn]. In other words, [F] and [Pn] used together will override the paging implied by the presence of form feed characters in the source data.

A printer that understands the form feed character responds to it by immediately advancing the paper to the top of the next page, whether or not the current page is full. Printers that do not understand the form feed character may perform erratically.

(See the section on the PIP PRN: device.)

[Qstring^Z] Copy a portion of the file up to the string listed

Use of the [Q] option allows you to tell PIP to look for a set of characters and terminate the copying of data when the set is encountered. Select the terminating string of characters carefully; they must be unique to ensure that you are copying the exact portion of the file desired. Q marks the beginning of the string, and CONTROL-Z marks the end of the string.

The string following the Q option is converted to uppercase if the command line is typed after the CP/M prompt (A>). If the command is typed after the PIP prompt (*), then the automatic conversion does not occur. To include lowercase letters in the string, your command line must follow the PIP prompt. (See also the [S] parameter.)

[R] Allow PIP to copy a system file

Only by appending the command line with [R] can we copy system files. The system file attribute, if present, is copied. This option does not apply to versions 1.3 and 1.4.

[Sstring^Z] Copy the portion of data beginning with string

Like the [Q] option, the [S] option specifies that you wish to copy only a portion of a file using PIP, this time beginning at the point where PIP detects the string of characters specified immediately following the S, where "string" is the sequence of characters to search for and ^Z is a CONTROL-Z used to terminate the string. Both the [S] and [Q] options may be present on the same command line.

See the important explanation of automatic lowercase-to-uppercase conversion under the [Q] option, above.

[Tn] Set tab stops every nth column

[Tn] tells PIP to expand any tab character (09 hex or CONTROL-I) it detects to the number of spaces necessary to reach the next tab stop. This is useful as some editor programs do not save tabs as spaces but as tab characters, and not all printers or terminals are set up to detect tab characters and expand them to the number of spaces they represent. Use [Tn] to change the standard tabbing from eight characters (or whatever your console or printer defaults to) to a number you define.

[U] Translate lowercase to uppercase

The U option causes all information in lowercase characters to be translated into uppercase characters during the transfer process.

[V] Verify the copy is correct by comparing the memory buffer with the newly created file(s)

The destination must be a disk file; if it is not, [V] is ignored. After the transfer is complete, the destination is reread and compared to the data in PIP's memory buffer. This means that the [V] parameter will catch errors in writing the file but not in reading it.

When concatenating several sources, the [V] option must follow the first source name; only one [V] is necessary.

(Note that Gary Kildall, creator of CP/M, never uses the [V] parameter, and members of the Digital Research staff indicate that in four years they have yet to see a verify error that is not accompanied by a BDOS ERR ON d: BAD SECTOR error. Therefore, it is doubtful that the [V] parameter will prove effective in catching otherwise unseen errors.)

[W] Allow PIP to copy into a file with the R/O attribute
Since [W] permits you to write to an R/O file, verifying this attribute is no longer required before proceeding. If you attempt to write to an R/O file without using the [W] attribute, you receive the message: DESTINATION FILE IS R/O, DELETE (Y/N)? The [W] parameter is not available in CP/M-80 versions 1.3 and 1.4.

[Z] Zero the parity bit during the transfer
Use the [Z] option to set the unused eighth bit of a character to zero when receiving ASCII characters from a device. Each ASCII character uses seven of the eight bits that are processed by the computer. The eighth bit is sometimes called the *parity bit*. To avoid mysterious problems when processing ASCII data, you will usually find it wise to set the unused bit to zero.

Special PIP Devices

EOF: Send an end-of-file marker to the destination device
When copying between two ASCII-type disk files, an end-of-file marker is automatically sent to the destination device. In some special instances EOF: can be used to terminate the transfer. When sending files from one computer to another, it is often necessary to terminate the transfer by sending the EOF: device character.

NUL: Send 40 null (do-nothing) characters to the destination device
NUL: was originally used to terminate punched output with a blank section of paper tape; it provided a header or trailer to the actual information, useful for threading purposes. NUL: will produce a 4-inch length of blank paper tape. The ASCII null character is called "Null" and is equivalent to 00 hex, or CONTROL-@.

PRN: Send data to LST: device with special instructions
The PRN: device specifies additional instructions to the LST: device. It expands tabs, numbers lines, and paginates the copy. Tab stops are assumed at every eighth column. Every time a tab character is detected, PIP inserts spaces instead; all lines are numbered (beginning at 1 and continuing sequentially throughout the transfer); page ejects are sent to the printer every 60 lines (giving a margin of three lines at the top and bottom of a normal 11-inch piece of paper). PRN: is used for program development and for listing the contents

of an ASCII-type file; the line numbers provide recognizable reference points within the file. PRN: is equivalent to [NPT8].

INP: and OUT: Special device drivers for PIP (CP/M-80 only)
INP: retrieves information from a special user-created PIP input source. OUT: sends information to a special user-created output destination. You can add special input and output routines (in machine language) to PIP. Hexadecimal locations 103, 104, and 105 are reserved for a jump instruction to your special input routine. PIP calls location 103 hex to input a character and, upon return, expects to find the character in location 109 hex. Hexadecimal locations 106, 107, and 108 are reserved for the jump to your special output routine. PIP loads Register C with the character to transmit and then calls location 106 hex. In addition, the area from 10A to 1FF hex is free for you to insert your routines. It is rare for a user to use this option.

Examples of PIP Use

On the following pages each PIP command line parameter and option is illustrated with an explanation of the computer display. You may want to explore the possible combinations of PIP command lines and options and the resulting variations on the uses we have listed.

When you see the PIP prompt (*), you may enter a valid PIP command line or press RETURN or CONTROL-C to return to CP/M.

```
A>PIP<cr>
*
```

In the following example we show a simple use of the PIP command to copy a file into a new file with a new name.

```
B>PIP LETTER2.DOC=LETTER1.DOC<cr>
B>
```

Here is another simple use of the copying aspect of the PIP command, here used to copy a file between disks A: and B:.

```
B>PIP A:LETTER2.DOC=B:LETTER1.DOC<cr>
B>
```

In the example below we show the use of an option, in this case the V (Verify) option.

```
B>PIP LETTER2.DOC=LETTER1.DOC[V]<cr>
B>
```

The next two examples use the shorthand method of specifying a file name when the same name will be used on both drives. Either side of the equal sign may be abbreviated to just the drive identifier.

```
A>PIP B:=A:DOCUMENT.LET[V]<cr>
A>
```

```
A>PIP B:DOCUMENT.LET=A:[V]<cr>
A>
```

This example uses both the abbreviation method (B:=) and ambiguous file references (A:*.*). When ambiguous file references are used, PIP reports the names of the files that match your request as it copies them.

```
A>PIP B:=A:*.*[V]<cr>

COPYING-
DOC.ONE
DOC.TWO
LET.ONE
A>
```

The preceding example combines the data in the files JUNE and JULY (in that order) into a new file named DOC.

```
A>PIP B:DOC=A:JUNE[V],A:JULY<cr>
A>
```

The following example would send a copy of the file LAFFERTY.RT to the LST: device. **Note:** You may not use ambiguous file references to send a series of files to the LST: device.

```
B>PIP LST:=B:LAFFERTY.RT<cr>
B>
```

Acceptable CP/M-80 destination devices are

Device	Description
CON: PUN: LST:	Logical
TTY: PTP: LPT: CRT: UP1: UP2: UL1: UL2:	Physical
OUT: PRN:	Special

Acceptable CP/M-PLUS destination devices are

Device	Description
AUX: CON: LST:	Logical
(varies with implementation)	Physical
PRN:	Special

```
B>PIP<cr>
*B:DOCUMENT.MAY=CON:<cr>
*^C
B>
```

The above example creates a file directly from information typed at the console device (up to and including the terminating CONTROL-Z).

Acceptable CP/M-80 source devices are

Device	Description
CON: RDR:	Logical
TTY: PTR: CRT: UR1: UR2: UC1:	Physical
NUL: EOF: INP:	Special

Acceptable CP/M-PLUS source devices are

Device	Description
AUX: CON:	Logical
(varies with implementation)	Physical
NUL: EOF:	Special

```
A>PIP CON:=PTR:[U]<cr>
THIS IS A PAPER TAPE READING DATA
INTO THE SYSTEM, WHICH DISPLAYS IT
ON THE DESTINATION DEVICE, THE CONSOLE.
A>
```

In the above example, we asked for the data being read from the paper tape reader to be copied to the console display. In addition, we specified the option of converting information to all uppercase characters ([U]).

STAT

Statistics on Files

(CP/M-PLUS users should see the SHOW (Chapter 6) and DIR (Chapter 4) commands for the equivalent command to STAT—Statistics on Files.)

STAT commands either provide information on the size and attributes of a file or files on a disk, or they change the attributes of a file or files on a disk. The command line parameters specify which files are to be included. File size refers to the amount of space (in bytes) occupied by a file. Free space refers to the amount of unused space (in bytes) still available on a disk for storage of files. File or disk attributes are a specific set of characteristics we can assign to a file or a disk.

Introduction to STAT and Its Terminology

The size of a file or the amount of storage that is currently unused on a disk is always reported by STAT in bytes. As we discussed earlier, a byte is a memory unit capable of storing a single character. Also recall that 1K byte equals 1024 bytes, a quantity which is universally (but incorrectly) called a kilobyte.

If STAT tells us that we have 34K of space remaining on our disk, we can store an additional 34,816 (1024 $\times$ 34 = 34816) bytes of information on that disk.

Experience is the best guide for interpreting what STAT tells you about your files. If you use STAT often and compare its reports, you will develop a sense of what 34K represents. For your reference, 34K bytes is the equivalent of ten single-spaced pages of typewritten material (assuming 65 characters per line and 54 lines per page).

Users of version 2.2 and MP/M may assign two pairs of file attributes: R/O or R/W, and DIR or SYS.

R/O
: Read-only file. You may not update an R/O file nor erase it by using the ERA command. You may not write to or enter information on an R/O file. R/O status protects against accidental erasures of valuable files.

R/W
: Read/Write file. You may update or erase an R/W file; it is not protected (unless the disk is write-protected). This is the normal attribute of a file and is the default attribute (i.e., you do not have to set it explicitly).

SYS
: System file. An SYS file does not appear in the display of a disk directory. You may retrieve information from an SYS file or store new information in it, erase it, or use it in any other normal manner, but it will not appear in any directory. It will appear, however, when you use STAT to review the status of files. SYS files are available to all user areas in version 2.2, but only SYS files in user area 0 will be available to other user areas in later versions.

DIR
: Directory file. A DIR file appears in all directory displays for the current user area. This is the normal attribute given to a file.

The members of each pair of attributes are mutually exclusive; files cannot be both R/W and R/O, nor can they be both SYS and DIR.

If you try to save information on an R/O disk or write on an R/O file, the error message BDOS ERR ON d: R/O will appear (where d: is the drive identifier). Even if a disk is not write-protected, it may still appear as an R/O type using STAT; this means that you exchanged disks without telling CP/M, but CP/M recognized the swap. To restore the new disk to R/W status, simply type a CONTROL-C.

If a disk is protected with the write-protect notch covered, it will still appear as R/W in the STAT report, as CP/M has no way of detecting the physical status of the write-protect notch until you actually attempt to write on the disk.

You use the information STAT gives you on file size, file attributes, and disk space to

- Examine how much space is left on a disk
- Examine how much space is occupied by a group of files
- Examine how much space is occupied by a single file
- Assign R/O or R/W attributes to a group of files

- Assign R/O or R/W attributes to a single file
- Assign DIR or SYS attributes to a group of files
- Assign DIR or SYS attributes to a single file.

To determine which STAT command line to enter for each of the uses listed above, study the next few pages carefully. Examine each command line, its purpose, and the computer display results. Try these examples at your computer. Try to generate the error messages. Consider how you might use the information displayed, given the uses of STAT we have just listed.

Using STAT on Files

STAT
: Displays the attributes and the amount of free space left on the disks accessed since the last cold or warm start.

STAT d:
: Displays the amount of free space available on the disk in drive d:.

STAT d:filename.typ
: Displays the amount of space occupied by the file(s) filename.typ on drive d:. The file name and extension may contain the CP/M ambiguous characters (* and ?). The drive identifier is optional; if omitted, the current drive is assumed.

STAT d:filename.typ $atr
: Assigns the attribute atr (which can be R/O, R/W, DIR, or SYS) to the file(s) filename.typ on drive d:. The filename.typ file(s) may be ambiguous. The drive specification d: is optional; if omitted, the current logged drive is assumed.

Examples of STAT Used for Files

In the following examples the write-protection status of the disk is reported first, and then the amount of free space remaining is reported.

```
B>STAT<cr>

B: R/O, SPACE: 120K

B>A:<cr>
A>STAT<cr>
A: R/W, SPACE: 2K
B: R/O, SPACE: 120K
A>
```

Version 1.3 only reports the status of the current logged disk drive.

```
A>STAT B:<cr>
BYTES REMAINING ON B: 170K
A>
```

Statistics were requested for the second drive, drive B:.

```
A>STAT JOAN.ARC<cr>
RECS BYTS EX ACC D:FILENAME.TYP
  5   2K   1 R/W A:JOAN.ARC

A>STAT B:JOAN.ARC<cr>
RECS BYTES EX ACC D:FILENAME.TYP
 10    4K    1 R/W B:JOAN.ARC

A>STAT *.COM<cr>
RECS BYTES EX ACC D:FILENAME.TYP
  4    2K    1 R/W A:DUMP.COM
 48    6K    1 R/W A:(ED.COM)
 56    8K    1 R/O A:PIP.COM
 24    4K    1 R/W A:STAT.COM
 10    2K    1 R/W A:SUBMIT.COM
BYTES REMAINING ON A: 218K

A>STAT B:EXAMPLE.?X?<cr>
RECS BYTES EX ACC D:FILENAME.TYP
 48    6K    1 R/W B:EXAMPLE.TXT
 24    4K    1 R/W B:EXAMPLE.EXT

A>
```

In the above examples new terminology is introduced in the headings STAT prints out:

RECS
: The number of 128-byte records used by the file. CP/M stores information in 128-byte units.

BYTES
: The length of the file in bytes. 2K represents 2048 characters of information; a kilobyte is 1024 bytes since computers use the binary numbering system.

EX
: The number of physical extents occupied by the file. Extents are another part of the way CP/M maintains files, but for most users they can be ignored.

ACC
: The file access attribute, R/W or R/O. Versions 1.4 and earlier did not include this function.

D:FILENAME.TYP
: The heading for the drive and file-name column on the display. The heading is absent for versions 2.2 and later.

A:(ED.COM)
: Parentheses surrounding a file mean that the SYS file attribute has been set. The SYS file attribute is only available on versions 2.2 and later.

```
A>STAT BROTHER.AND $R/O<cr>
BROTHER.AND SET TO R/O
A>

A>STAT B:BROTHER.AND $SYS<cr>
B:BROTHER.AND SET TO SYS
A>

A>STAT *.* $R/W<cr>
BROTHER.AND SET TO R/W
SISTER.TOO SET TO R/W
A>
```

In these examples STAT is used to change the attributes of files. Remember, a file may be SYS (system) or DIR (directory), R/W (read/write) or R/O (read-only). The default setting for files is DIR and R/W; you must use STAT to change these file attributes in CP/M-80.

STAT

Statistics on Devices

(For equivalent functions, CP/M-PLUS users should consult the explanation of DEVICE and SET transient commands detailed in the next chapter.)

STAT also provides information about CP/M's physical and logical devices. Earlier we briefly introduced physical units as the devices you may choose to make up your microcomputer system. A logical device denotes a general function of your microcomputer, while a physical device is the specific piece of equipment you choose to perform that function. CP/M requires us to select a physical device to perform the function of each logical device. We convey our choices to the computer by using the STAT (on devices) command.

There are four logical devices in CP/M-80.

Device	Function
CON:	Enters commands and displays information; operator console function
RDR:	Receives information; paper tape reader function
PUN:	Sends information; paper tape punch function
LST:	Lists (prints) information; list function.

There are 12 possible physical devices.

Device	Function
TTY:	Slow console display (teletypewriter)
CRT:	Fast console (cathode-ray tube display)
BAT:	Batch processor
UC1:	User-defined console
PTR:	Paper tape reader
PTP:	Paper tape punch.

Device	Function (*continued*)
UR1:	User reader #1
UR2:	User reader #2
UP1:	User punch #1
UP2:	User punch #2
LPT:	Line printer
UL1:	User list device.

Sixteen physical-to-logical device assignments are possible.

Logical		Physical
CON:	may be performed by	TTY:, CRT:, BAT:, or UC1:
RDR:	may be performed by	TTY:, PTR:, UR1:, or UR2:
PUN:	may be performed by	TTY:, PTP:, UP1:, or UP2:
LST:	may be performed by	TTY:, CRT:, LPT:, or UL1:

Your microcomputer may be programmed for physical devices other than the default TTY:. This programming was most likely performed by the vendor who supplied your CP/M system. If you have two printers, one may be programmed to be the LPT: device and the other as the UL1: device. Once made, such arrangements are generally constant; they reflect the distinct programming required to connect each device to the microcomputer. In our example, both LPT: and UL1: are physical devices that can perform the function of the logical device LST:.

Unfortunately, most computer manufacturers have not followed the original recommendations of Digital Research in assigning physical devices, and Digital Research steadfastly maintained the original device names up through version 2.2, despite major changes in the technology of terminals, modems, and printers. Here is the normal (and confusing) setup of a typical microcomputer:

Logical	Physical	Actual Device
CON:	TTY:	High-speed video terminal
RDR:	PTR:	Modem receive line
PUN:	PTP:	Modem send line
LST:	LPT:	Printer

Notice that the above table does not seem to match the descriptions we gave for each device above (i.e., TTY: is supposed to be a slow console device, not a high-speed video terminal). Paper tape reader and punch devices are not widely used anymore; the abbreviations PUN:, RDR:, PTR:, and PTP: reflect an earlier time when paper tape was commonly used.

When your computer is first started, the default values of the device assignments are made. These default assignments vary from system to system and are programmed into your CP/M by your vendor. The default values should be the assignments you most often use. A cold start changes the device assignments to their default value, but a warm start does not affect the assignments in any way.

We use STAT on devices to

- Learn the current device assignments
- Learn the possible device assignments
- Assign physical devices to logical devices.

A few STAT-on-devices command lines request information on the disk drives. Specifically, we use these special command lines to

- Learn the current status of a drive
- Learn the current status of user areas on the disk
- Protect a disk from accidental "writes."

To determine which STAT-on-devices command line to enter for each of the uses listed above, consider the following pages carefully. Examine each command line, its purpose, and the computer display results. Consider how you might use the information displayed, given the uses of STAT on devices we have just listed.

Using STAT on Devices

STAT DEV:
: Displays the current device assignments.

STAT VAL:
: Displays the possible assignments of physical-to-logical devices and an abbreviated STAT command line summary.

STAT log:=phy:
: Assigns the physical device specified to the logical device specified.

STAT USR:
: Displays the current user number and lists all user numbers for which there are files.

STAT d:DSK:
: Displays information on how data is stored on the disk in drive d:.

STAT d:=R/O
: Assigns a temporary write-protect (read-only) status to the disk in drive d:.

Examples of STAT Used for Devices

The following is an example of using STAT to find out the current device assignments.

```
A>STAT DEV:<cr>
CON: IS CRT:
RDR: IS UR1:
PUN: IS UP2:
LST: IS UL1:
A>
```

Notice that the left-hand entry reflects the logical device; the right-hand entry is the current physical device assigned to it.

```
A>STAT VAL:<cr>
TEMP R/O DISK: D:=R/O
SET INDICATOR: D:FILENAME.TYP $R/O $R/W $SYS $DIR
DISK STATUS  : DSK: D:DSK:
USER STATUS  : USR:
IOBYTE ASSIGN:
CON:=TTY:CRT:BAT:UC1:
RDR:=TTY:PTR:UR1:UR2:
PUN:=TTY:PTP:UP1:UP2:
LST:=TTY:CRT:LPT:UL1:

A>
```

Note: Only the last four lines appear if you are using version 1.3 or version 1.4. The first several lines STAT presents tell you the possible STAT device commands.

Command	Function
STAT D:=R/O	To make a temporary receive-only disk
STAT D:FILENAME.TYP $ATR	To set an attribute
STAT D:DSK:	To see the statistics on a disk drive
STAT D:USR:	To see the statistics on user area use.

The next lines from STAT set forth the possible device assignments.

You may want to think of this version of the STAT command as being a "help" facility. If you are trying to remember what you can assign to what, or what form of the STAT command to use for a particular device, simply type STAT VAL:, and the above display is presented.

```
A>STAT CON:=CRT:,LST:=UL1:<cr>
A>
```

In the preceding illustration we assign two devices. First CRT: is assigned to CON:, and then UL1: is assigned to LST:.

Notice that more than one device setting can be made by separating each with a comma. In addition, note that CP/M does not issue any message to inform you that the assignment has been made. If your system no longer works after you make a new device assignment, it is possible you have assigned the console function to a nonexistent device.

```
A>STAT USR:<cr>
ACTIVE USER: 0
ACTIVE FILES: 0 1 3
A>
```

The above use of the STAT command allows you to inquire as to the current user area as well as what other user areas have files in them. The messages from CP/M-80 in the example indicate that you are currently in user area 0 but have files on your disk in areas 0, 1, and 3. This function is not available in version 1.3 or 1.4.

```
A>STAT B:DSK:<cr>
B: DRIVE CHARACTERISTICS
4096: 128 BYTE RECORD  CAPACITY
512: KILOBYTE DRIVE  CAPACITY
128: 32 BYTE  DIRECTORY ENTRIES
128: CHECKED  DIRECTORY ENTRIES
128: RECORDS/EXTENT
 16: RECORDS/BLOCK
 58: SECTORS/TRACK
  2: RESERVED TRACKS
A>
```

Here we use the STAT command to find out some statistics on the disk drive. The d: (drive identifier) is optional; if omitted, information is displayed for all disks accessed since the last cold or warm start.

The most relevant information in the display is "KILOBYTE DRIVE CAPACITY," which is the amount of free space on an empty disk, and "32 BYTE DIRECTORY ENTRIES," which is the maximum number of files you can store on the disk (this number will be reduced if you have any files that are larger than one extent).

The information in the STAT d:DSK: display will not change unless you modify CP/M. This static information reflects design decisions about how to arrange data on the disks.

The following definitions explain each of the STAT responses presented in the above example.

128 BYTE RECORD CAPACITY
: The maximum number of 128-byte records you may store on the disk.

KILOBYTE DRIVE CAPACITY
: The maximum number of kilobytes you may store on a single disk in that drive.

32 BYTE DIRECTORY ENTRIES
: The maximum number of files you may store on the disk.

CHECKED DIRECTORY ENTRIES
: Usually the same as "32 BYTE DIRECTORY ENTRIES" for drives with removable media (diskettes); usually "0" for drives with nonremovable media (sealed hard disks).

RECORDS/EXTENT
: The maximum number of records per directory entry.

RECORDS/BLOCK
: The minimum amount of disk space that may be allocated to a file.

SECTORS/TRACK
: The number of sectors into which a track is divided (see Chapter 1).

RESERVED TRACKS
: The number of disk tracks not available for storage of files (CP/M-80 and the directory are stored on tracks reserved for only their use.)

```
A>STAT B:=R/O<cr>
A>SAVE 2 B:JUNK.FIL
BDOS ERR ON B: R/O
```

In the above example we first set drive B: to read-only status using STAT. Note that STAT does not provide any confirmation of our request. Next we attempted to save a new file on the disk and received a BDOS ERR message indicating that CP/M considers the disk to be write-protected. A warm or cold start cancels the temporary R/O status.

BATCH-PROCESSING UTILITIES

Your computer is far more sophisticated than the mammoth beasts used in the 1960s. Almost all of the original computers operated primarily in the batch mode. A batch is a group of things; in the case of computers, it is a sequence of commands and/or data.

Most microcomputers in use today are interactive machines. This means that you input something, the computer responds, you input something else, the computer responds again, and so on. Interactive processing is appropriate for small business accounting, word processing, and other tasks for which microcomputers are used. However, it is sometimes faster and more efficient to submit a group of commands to be processed sequentially without your presence. The SUBMIT and XSUB commands fulfill these functions in CP/M-80, while CP/M-PLUS users can use SUBMIT, GET, and to some degree, PUT for batch operations. GET and PUT are described in Chapter 6.

SUBMIT

Command Line Automation

SUBMIT directs the sequential entry and execution of a number of CP/M commands without additional operator response. To utilize SUBMIT, you must first create a file with the SUB file type, using the CP/M editor or another editor. The file you create should contain the list of CP/M commands to be executed, in the order you wish them performed, one to a line.

SUBMIT can provide a link to the BACKUP or DISKCOPY program, for instance every time you finish using a program. First create a SUBMIT file named ORREPENT.SUB that has only two commands in it:

RUN YOURPROG.RAM<cr>
BACKUP<cr>

(The RUN YOUR PROG.RAM can be any valid CP/M command, you should substitute the name of your copying program for BACKUP.)

Next run YOURPROG.RAM by typing SUBMIT ORREPENT<cr> instead of the usual RUN YOURPROG.RAM<cr>; when you finish using your program and attempt to return to CP/M, the SUBMIT facility will whisk you to the BACKUP program, forcing you to duplicate your disk every time you run YOURPROG.RAM.

Program developers often use a compiler rather than an interpreter to write programs. A compiled program requires an extra process: the actual compilation. In small business packages there may be five, ten, or more related program modules, all of which need compiling. The compilation process could take as much as an hour or more; the SUBMIT facility performs this function and frees the programmer from having to sit and type each compilation command individually.

SUBMIT sequences can be chained (linked together) by including a normal SUBMIT command line as the last line in a SUB-type file.

SUBMIT filename
: Creates a file $$$.SUB that contains the commands listed in filename.SUB and executes commands from this file rather than from the keyboard.

If you have created a file named NUCLEAR.SUB that contains

STAT *.BAS<cr>
ERA *.BAS<cr>
DIR *.BAS<cr>

when you submit this file for execution, the dialog will look like this:

```
A>SUBMIT NUCLEAR<cr>
A>STAT *.BAS
RECS BYTS EX D:FILENAME.TYP
 2     4K    1 A:PORGY.BAS
 4     8K    1 A:PORKY.BAS
 8    17K    2 A:PORTLY.BAS
BYTES REMAINING ON A: 151K

A>ERA *.BAS
A>DIR *.BAS
NO FILE
A>
```

The commands following SUBMIT are not underlined, since CP/M is doing the typing, not you. The only thing you typed in the above sequence is

```
A>SUBMIT NUCLEAR<cr>
```

Press any key to stop the execution in between SUBMIT file commands; that is, just before the prompt is displayed.

SUBMIT filename A B C
: Creates a file $$$.SUB that contains the commands listed in filename.SUB and executes commands from this file rather than from the keyboard.

This form of the SUBMIT command differs from the previous one in that you may include incomplete CP/M command lines in the file filename.SUB when you create it. SUBMIT fills in the missing information using the A, B, C, and so on from the command line you type when you start SUBMIT. These parameters can be file names or any other information needed by the commands in filename.SUB. The symbols $1, $2, $3, and so on should be used in your SUBMIT file to hold the place for the missing parameters. Up to nine parameters may be used.

Suppose that you are editing a file on drive A and you want to copy it to drive B, then check disk space each time you finish an editing session. Without SUBMIT, you would enter the following command lines in the course of your work (intervening ED commands and other dialog are omitted for clarity):

```
A>ED MYFILE.DOC<cr>
A>PIP B:=A:MYFILE.DOC[V]<cr>
A>STAT B:MYFILE.*<cr>
```

Suppose also that you use this method with every file you edit, not just with MYFILE.DOC. To make SUBMIT do the typing for you, first create a SUB-type file named WORKON (for example) containing the incomplete commands listed below.

ED $1.$2<cr>
PIP B:=A:$1.$2[v]<cr>
STAT B:1$.*<cr>

To use this SUB file as outlined above, type the command line below:

```
A>SUBMIT WORKON MYFILE DOC<cr>
```

SUBMIT will create $$$.SUB from WORKON.SUB by substituting the first parameter, MYFILE, for $1 each time it appears and the second parameter, DOC, for $2 each time it appears. SUBMIT then initiates a warm start, and CP/M looks for the file $$$.SUB. It then executes the commands listed in $$$.SUB.

CP/M-PLUS Users Only

CP/M-PLUS looks for a special file, named PROFILE.SUB, which will be automatically executed after every cold boot or system reset. By placing commands in PROFILE.SUB you can tailor a series of routines that are automatically triggered each time you start the computer. Many users put a DATE and SETDEF command in their PROFILE.SUB file, since these commands are usually only used once at the beginning of each computer session.

XSUB

User Input Automation: A Subset of SUBMIT

It is possible to put more than commands in a SUB-type file. In fact, it can respond to questions a program might ask or add other variables when you invoke SUBMIT. This is done using the XSUB command. XSUB is available only in version 2.2.

XSUB must precede the program name and program response in the SUBMIT file you create; it is a command that is not typed when you see the CP/M prompt, but instead is used only within a SUB-type file as a command to SUBMIT.

When SUBMIT encounters the XSUB command, a special set of instructions is loaded into CP/M's memory space, and whenever a program requests console information, the SUBMIT file is used to input it.

As discussed earlier, you may use $1, $2, and so forth to indicate last-minute submissions of information to SUBMIT, which will pass them on to XSUB if needed.

The symbols in your SUB-type file are replaced with the parameters you type in the actual SUBMIT command.

XSUB is most often used in program and system development. But you may find that programs you purchase use XSUB for a portion of their input. You may also use XSUB to provide an addition to the automatic backup system we discussed in the section on SUBMIT. For example, assume &BEFREE.SUB contains

RUN YOURPROG.RAM<cr>
XSUB<cr>
BACKUP<cr>
A<cr>
B<cr>

The following process occurs when you SUBMIT this file:

```
A>SUBMIT &BEFREE<cr>
A>RUN YOURPROG.RAM<cr>
      .
      .                 } Program runs until completion
      .
A>XSUB<cr>
(XSUB ACTIVE) <---- System message
A>BACKUP<cr>
DRIVE FOR SOURCE DISKETTE?  A<cr>
DRIVE FOR DESTINATION DISKETTE?  B<cr>

PUT BLANK DISKETTE IN B AND PRESS RETURN WHEN READY<cr>
```

In this example, everything that happens from your original SUBMIT command until you are prompted to put a blank disk in drive B and press RETURN is done automatically by the computer. XSUB supplies the A<cr> and B<cr> in response to the BACKUP program's request for information, for example.

The overriding implication of the use of SUBMIT and XSUB together is that the process of computing can be standardized to the point where actions are repeated in exactly the order you specify, without requiring a computer operator to type in each individual command. For some computing jobs such automated standardization makes sense; for others, especially those that have unpredictable or changing input needs, SUBMIT and XSUB offer little help.

CP/M-PLUS users do not need XSUB, since they may enter individual characters directly into their SUBMIT file without invoking XSUB. This is done by preceding the characters with a < in the SUB file. Here is a comparison of the same SUBMIT file in CP/M-80 and CP/M-PLUS:

CP/M-80	**CP/M-PLUS**
RUN YOUR PROG.RAM<cr>	RUN YOURPROG.RAM<cr>
XSUB<cr>	BACKUP<cr>
BACKUP<cr>	<A<cr>
A<cr>	<B<cr>
B<cr>	

CP/M-PLUS also allows individual control characters within a SUBMIT file

(CP/M-80 users can get a program patch from Digital Research or the CP/M User Group that will allow your SUBMIT to do the same thing) by prefacing the character with a ^ (caret) sign. For instance,

```
PIP $1.$2=CON:
I am typing this automatically, even though PIP would normally require I type this at the
keyboard. Remember, PIP needs an END-OF-FILE character to terminate console input,
like this:
  ^Z
```

is an example of a SUBMIT file that would start up the program PIP, enter information into the file named using SUBMIT parameters, and then complete the file entry with a ^Z. If you need to enter the $ or ^ symbol by itself, precede the symbol with itself ($$ or ^^).

SUMMARY

In this chapter you learned some of the basic CP/M transient commands. In the next chapter we will round out our investigation of transient commands supplied only with CP/M-PLUS.

You should now know how to use the following CP/M commands:

Built-in Commands:	DIR	(CP/M-80, CP/M-PLUS)
	DIRSYS	(CP/M-PLUS)
	ERA	(CP/M-80, CP/M-PLUS)
	ERASE	(CP/M-PLUS)
	REN	(CP/M-80, CP/M-PLUS)
	RENAME	(CP/M-PLUS)
	SAVE	(CP/M-80, CP/M-PLUS)
	TYPE	(CP/M-80, CP/M-PLUS)
	USER	(CP/M-80, CP/M-PLUS)
	d:	(CP/M-80, CP/M-PLUS)
Transient Commands:	DUMP	(CP/M-80, CP/M-PLUS)
	ED	(CP/M-80, CP/M-PLUS)
	PIP	(CP/M-80, CP/M-PLUS)
	STAT	(CP/M-80)
	SUBMIT	(CP/M-80, CP/M-PLUS)
	XSUB	(CP/M-80)

CHAPTER

6 Additional CP/M-PLUS Transient Commands

Since CP/M-PLUS has so many more transient commands than CP/M-80, this chapter examines the remaining commonly used transient commands that Digital Research supplies only with CP/M-PLUS.

DATE

Set or Display the Date

CP/M-PLUS keeps track of the time and day. This process is done automatically on some systems (those with built-in battery-operated clocks), while on others you have to manually enter the time and date each time you start up the system. The DATE command allows you to do so.

Forms of the DATE Command

The forms of the DATE command are

DATE CONTINUOUS
DATE C
Causes the system to display the date and time continuously until any key is pressed.

DATE SET
DATE mm/dd/yy hh:mm:ss

where	mm	represents a month (1–12)
	dd	represents a day (1–31)
	yy	represents a year (00–99); the 19 is assumed
	hh	represents an hour (0–23) (military time)
	mm	represents a minute (0–59)
	ss	represents a second (0–59).

Allows the user to set the date and time, with the first version prompting the user for the date and time and the second simply setting it. **Note:** The time and date are not actually set until the user presses a key in response to the prompt "Press any key to set time."

Examples Using DATE

The following example shows the continuous display of the time. Observe how pressing key interrupts the display.

```
A>DATE C<cr>
Mon 10/03/83 10:30:01
Mon 10/03/83 10:30:02
Mon 10/03/83 10:30:03 Q

A>
```

This example shows the prompting for the date and time that CP/M-PLUS displays when you ask to set the time:

```
A>DATE SET<cr>
Enter today's date (MM/DD/YY): 10/01/83<cr>
Enter the time (HH:MM:SS): 04:10:00<cr>
Press any key to set time Q
A>
```

This last example shows how to set the time without prompting from CP/M-PLUS:

```
A>DATE 10/01/83 04:10:00<cr>
Press any key to set time Q
A>
```

DEVICE

Display and Assign Devices

The DEVICE transient command is CP/M-PLUS's equivalent to the use of STAT for displaying the current status of devices and assigning them.

CP/M-PLUS's logical device names are similar to those of CP/M-80, but the physical device names under CP/M-PLUS are assigned by the system implementor, not Digital Research. The following is a table of the logical device names under CP/M-80 and CP/M-PLUS:

CP/M-80 Name	CP/M-PLUS Name
CON:	CON: or CONSOLE:
n.a.*	CONIN: or KEYBOARD:
n.a.	CONOUT:
n.a.	AUX: or AUXILIARY:
RDR:	AUXIN:
PUN:	AUXOUT:
LST:	LST: or PRINTER

*not applicable

Physical device names in CP/M-PLUS vary from system to system. The manufacturer of the system generally provides physical device names (and the drivers in BIOS) for each of the actual physical devices on the machine. The Osborne Executive, for example, includes the following physical devices:

Name	Device
CRT:	CRT display
PRNTR:	Printer connected to serial port #1
CEN:	Centronics-compatible printer
IEEE:	IEEE-compatible printer
MODEM:	Modem connected to serial port #2

In addition to being able to assign any logical device to a particular physical device, as in CP/M-80, CP/M-PLUS allows you to assign certain parameters to each of the devices:

Parameter	Device
I	Device is input
O	Device is output
S	Device is serial
X	Device uses X-ON/X-OFF communications protocol

Some assignments would not make sense, of course (for instance, assigning a Centronics parallel printer as a serial device; it communicates with parallel, not serial, data exchange). If you have problems with an assignment, first make sure that what you typed makes sense.

Forms of the DEVICE Command

The following are the allowable forms of the DEVICE command:

DEVICE

Displays the current assignments and then prompts for a new assignment.

DEVICE NAMES

Displays the allowable physical device names.

DEVICE VALUES

Displays the current logical device assignments.

DEVICE CONSOLE [options]

Displays the current console page width in columns and the page length in lines if the option is PAGE; sets the number of columns to the number indicated if the option is COLUMNS=n; sets the number of lines assumed to be on the console device if the option is LINES=n.

DEVICE device

Displays the current assignment for the device requested.

DEVICE logicaldevice = physicaldevice[options]
Assigns the logical device to the physical device indicated, with the options in effect as specified.

DEVICE logicaldevice = physical1[options], physical2[options]
Multiple physical devices can be attached to a single logical device by separating each assignment with a comma on the command line.

DEVICE logicaldevice = NULL
Unassigns the logical device from its previous physical device assignment.

DEVICE Options

[XON]
Sets the device to communicate using a standard data exchange protocol known as XON/XOFF. Before each character is output from CP/M-PLUS to the device, CP/M-PLUS checks to see if there is any incoming data from the device. If there is, and if that data corresponds to the XOFF character, CP/M-PLUS stops sending information until it sees an XON character from the device.

[NOXON]
Indicates that no protocol is to be used; CP/M-PLUS will send data whether or not the device is ready to receive.

[n]
A baud rate (for serial-type devices only) that indicates the speed at which information is to be sent and received. The number (n) must be one of the following to be valid:

50	75	110	134	150	300	600	1200
1800	2400	3600	4800	7200	9600	19200	

Examples Using DEVICE

In the following example, DEVICE first gives a summary of the current devices and their assignments and then prompts the user for a new assignment; the user indicates that the LST: device should be attached to the CEN: physical device instead of its current setting, PRNTR.

```
A>DEVICE<cr>
Physical Devices:
I=Input,O=Output,X=Serial,X=Xon-Xoff
CRT      NONE IO    CEN  NONE O     MODEM  300   IO
PRNTR    9600 IOSX IEEE NONE IO
```

```
Current Assignments:
CONIN:   = CRT
CONOUT:  = CRT
AUXIN:   = MODEM
AUXOUT:  = MODEM
LST:     = PRNTR

Enter new assignment or hit RETURN: LST:=CEN:<cr>
```

The following illustration shows two forms of assigning devices with the DEVICE command. The first attaches both the PRNTR and CRT physical devices to the CONOUT: logical device (output will go to both display and printer); the second attaches the physical device, MODEM, to the logical device, AUXIN:, setting MODEM for 300-baud transmission and no XON/XOFF protocol.

```
A>DEVICE CONOUT:=PRNTR,CRT<cr>
A>DEVICE AUXIN:=MODEM[NOXON,300]<cr>
```

In the following example we first examine the console setting to see the number of columns and lines CP/M-PLUS is currently using when outputting information to the console. Next we reset these parameters, in this case to 52 columns of 24 characters each.

```
A>DEVICE CONSOLE [PAGE]<cr>
Console: Columns = 80, Lines = 25
A>DEVICE CONSOLE [COLUMNS=52,LINES=24]<cr>
A>
```

GET

Get Program Input From Disk File

The GET command is similar in some respects to SUBMIT, but unlike SUBMIT, it represents what is known as true *I/O redirection* (input comes from a source other than the keyboard, in this case, a disk file). The practical differences between batch processing and I/O redirection are few; the primary difference CP/M-PLUS users will observe is that SUBMIT builds an extra, temporary file, while GET does not require the extra file.

GET is handy for automatically running programs, or portions of programs, that require the same input each time they are used. GET is especially handy for getting past annoying or repetitive requests that sometimes occur at the beginning of many programs (see "Examples Using Get").

GET CONSOLE INPUT FROM FILE filename.typ

GET FILE filename.typ

These two forms of the GET command are the same, since the words "CONSOLE INPUT FROM" are optional. Console input from the file begins immediately after the next system command is typed and terminates when the end of the input file is reached or the next CP/M-PLUS system prompt appears (for instance, A>).

GET CONSOLE INPUT FROM FILE filename.typ[options]
GET FILE filename.typ[options]
Invokes GET, as above, but with a specified option or options.

GET Options

[ECHO]
All input from the file will be displayed on the console, as if you had typed it. ECHO is the default setting.

[NO ECHO]
No display of information from the input file will be made on the console.

[SYSTEM]
Indicates that all input, both at the CP/M-PLUS system level and the program level, is to be taken from the file. If not specified, GET only retrieves information from the file at the program level and terminates execution at the system level. The SYSTEM option takes effect immediately; you are not returned to the CP/M-PLUS prompt until all the information in the input file is exhausted or until a GET instruction is read from the input file (which cancels the SYSTEM option).

Examples Using GET

The following is a simple example of using GET in the usual, default fashion:

```
A>GET CONSOLE INPUT FROM FILE FOLDER.1<cr>
A>PIP<cr>
PIP 3.0
*B:=A:*.BAS<cr>
*B:=A:*.BAK<cr>
*<cr>
A>
```

The file FOLDER.1 contains the following:

```
B:=A:*.BAS<cr>
B:=A:*.BAK<cr>
<cr>
```

In the next example, we use the instructions in FOLDER.2 to initiate a WordStar editing session, first starting the program, then logging onto drive B, then getting to the "Name of document file to edit?" prompt. All we have to do is supply the name of the file, and we can begin editing immediately.

```
A>GET FILE FOLDER.2 [SYSTEM]<cr>
A>WS<cr>

    [WordStar signs on and displays menu]

L
```

```
The logged disk is now A:

New logged disk drive (drive, colon, RETURN)? B:<cr>

   [WordStar redisplays menu]

D

Name of document file to edit? _
```

The FOLDER.2 file looks like this:

```
WS<cr>
LB:<cr>
D
```

Since it is exhausted after the D, we are left to use WordStar in our normal fashion (from the keyboard).

Even more cleverly, the GET command could be made part of a PROFILE.SUB file that is invoked upon starting the system.

HELP

Display Information About Various Subjects

The HELP transient command is really a program that allows you to receive information about most CP/M-PLUS subjects—it is an on-line reference manual. HELP can present general information or specific information, depending on how you phrase your help request. Digital Research supplies a basic HELP file (HELP.HLP) that covers CP/M-PLUS, but you may add help information of your own by using the special features of HELP.

HELP
: Invokes HELP and presents a menu of topics to choose from. HELP displays a prompt of HELP>, to which you may reply with a topic name or a subtopic name preceded by a period.

HELP topic
: Invokes HELP and presents information on the chosen topic.

HELP topic subtopic
: Invokes HELP and presents information on the chosen subtopic within the topic. Additional subtopics may be added following the first, each separated by a space.

HELP Options and Commands

Each form of the HELP program can be used with the following options (appearing at the end of the command line).

[NO PAGE]

Disables the default paged display of information. To stop the display, use CONTROL-S; to resume, use CONTROL-Q. NO PAGE may be abbreviated to N.

[LIST]

Is the same as NO PAGE except that extra lines between topic headings are removed. This option is useful for conserving paper if you are also printing out the HELP using CONTROL-P.

Other forms of the HELP command are

HELP [EXTRACT]

Takes data from the HELP.HLP file and copies it into a file named HELP.-DAT, which may be edited using ED or any other text editor. EXTRACT may be abbreviated to E.

HELP [CREATE]

Performs the reverse process of the EXTRACT option, taking information from HELP.DAT and creating a new HELP.HLP file. CREATE may be abbreviated to C.

HELP Data Files

HELP.DAT files have the following form:

- Topics are placed in alphabetical order.
- Subtopics are in alphabetical order within topic.
- Topic and subtopic levels are indicated with a number from 1 to 9.
- Each topic and subtopic text is preceded by a topic heading, in the format nTOPIC<cr>, where n is the topic level (1 being a topic, 9 being the lowest subtopic) and TOPIC is the topic name you select.
- Each topic name should be unique.
- Topic names can be up to 12 characters in length.

Examples Using HELP

This example shows how to invoke HELP without asking for a specific topic:

```
A>HELP<cr>

Help is available for:

DIR DIRSYS RENAME ERASE SAVE TYPE

Help>DIR<cr>

DIR is the directory command....
```

This example shows how typing a topic name takes you directly to the information for that topic:

```
A>HELP DIR<cr>

DIR is the directory command....
```

INITDIR

Initialize Time and Date Stamping

The SET command, described later in this chapter, allows time and date stamping of files under CP/M-PLUS. The INITDIR command is initially used to modify the directory entries so they are capable of storing the time and date stamping.

INITDIR is a simple program that performs only a single function: rearranging the directory for use with or without time and date stamping.

The allowable form of the INITDIR command is

INITDIR

or

INITDIR d:

If time and date stamping has not been activated for the disk in the drive you specify, INITDIR asks if you want to reformat the directory for time and date stamping.

```
A>INITDIR B:<cr>

INITDIR WILL ACTIVATE TIME STAMPS FOR SPECIFIED DRIVE.
Do you really want to re-format the directory: B (Y/N)? Y<cr>
```

If the time and date stamping option has already been invoked for the disk in question, INITDIR asks if you want to reformat the directory without time and date stamping.

```
A>INITDIR<cr>
TIME AND DATE STAMPING IS ACTIVATED FOR SPECIFIED DRIVE.
Do you want the existing date/time stamps cleared (Y/N)? N<cr>
```

PATCH

Modify and Update System or Command Programs

The PATCH transient command displays or installs patches (machine language modifications) to the CP/M-PLUS system or command files. You use PATCH to make simple modifications (supplied by Digital Research or the manufacturer of your system) without having to learn assembly language programming. Generally the patches are provided to you on disk, and you must first copy the patch files over to the disk you wish to modify.

The form of the patch command is

PATCH filename.typ n

The file name is the program to be patched, which must be of type COM if no file type is specified, or types COM, PRL, or SPR if the type is specified. The patch number (n) is optional and must be a number between 1 and 32, inclusive.

An example of the use of PATCH looks like this:

```
A>PATCH PIP 1<cr>
Do you want to indicate that Patch #1
has been installed for PIP.COM? Y<cr>

Patch Installed

A>
```

PUT

Place Program Output in Disk File

PUT is the corollary to GET. Instead of retrieving input from a file, PUT writes console or printer output to a file for later use. We suggest that you use PUT in conjunction with GET, so that if anything unusual happens during a GET-automated session you will be able to go back and review what happened from the file that PUT created.

PUT CONSOLE OUTPUT TO FILE filename.typ[options]
PUT CONSOLE FILE filename.typ[options]

The above are two equivalent PUT commands that direct all console output to the named file. Console output is redirected to the file until the program terminates.

PUT CONSOLE OUTPUT TO CONSOLE
PUT CONSOLE CONSOLE

Redirects console output to the console instead of a file (restores normal operations).

PUT PRINTER OUTPUT TO FILE filename.typ[options]
PUT PRINTER FILE filename.typ[options]

Sends all output normally destined for the list device to the named file. Printer output is redirected to the file until the program terminates.

PUT PRINTER OUTPUT TO PRINTER
PUT PRINTER PRINTER

Redirects printer output to the printer instead of a file (restores normal operations).

PUT Options

The allowable PUT options are

[ECHO]
Indicates that all output is to be sent to the console as well as the file. This is the default setting.

[NO ECHO]
Indicates that all output is to be sent to the file only; no output is directed to the console.

[FILTER]
Tells PUT to translate all control characters into readable form (a CONTROL-C, for instance, is saved in the file as ^C).

[NO FILTER]
Tells PUT not to translate any control or special characters it sends to the file. This is the default option.

[SYSTEM]
Like GET, the SYSTEM option indicates that I/O redirection is to take place immediately and to continue until a subsequent PUT CONSOLE command is encountered. SYSTEM SENDS both system and program output to the file, whereas the default sends program output only.

Example Using PUT

Here is an example using the PUT command:

```
A>PUT CONSOLE OUTPUT TO FILE CABINET.1[ECHO]<cr>
A>PIP<cr>
*AUXOUT:=CON:<cr>
This is an example of sending something from the<cr>
keyboard to the AUXILIARY device and to a file at<cr>
the same time.  Isn't this fun?<cr>
^Z
*<cr>
A>TYPE CABINET.1<cr>
*AUXOUT:=CON:
This is an example of sending something from the
keyboard to the AUXILIARY device and to a file at
the same time.  Isn't this fun?
^Z
*
A>
```

This routine shows how the console output was saved by the PUT command in the file specified. We have redisplayed it by using the TYPE command to verify that PUT did save the output.

SET

Assign Password, Time Stamping, Disk Label, File and Drive Attributes

The SET command provides CP/M-PLUS with some of the same capabilities as STAT does for CP/M-80. Specifically, the SET transient command allows the user to do the following:

- Set the file type attribute to DIR or SYS
- Set the file type attribute to R/O or R/W
- Label a disk
- Set a password for disk or files
- Set password protection to ON or OFF
- Set the time and date stamping option to ON or OFF
- Set the archive attribute ON or OFF
- Set user-definable attributes ON or OFF.

Obviously, CP/M-PLUS provides far more file and disk attribute options than does CP/M-80, which is perhaps the reason Digital Research chose to separate CP/M-80's STAT command into three distinct CP/M-PLUS commands (DEVICE, SHOW, SET).

Uses of the SET Command

The following are possible uses of the SET command:

SET
  Initiates the SET program and prompts user for a valid setting.

SET[options]
  Performs a setting assignment based upon the options the user types (see "SET Options").

SET d:[options]
  Performs a setting assignment on the indicated disk based upon the options the user types (see "SET Options").

SET d:filename.typ[options]
  Performs a setting assignment for the specified file based upon the options the user types (see "SET Options").

SET Options

The allowable options for SET are

[DIR]
  The DIR option is used with a file specification to set the file type attribute for the file (or files, if ambiguous references are used) to DIR, short for Directory.

DIR files appear in normal directories, but they do not appear when DIRSYS is used.

[SYS]

The SYS option is used with a file specification to set the file type attribute for the file (or files, if ambiguous references are used) to SYS, short for System. SYS files do not appear in normal directories; they appear when DIRSYS is used.

[RO]

The R/O option is used with a file specification to set the file type attribute for the file (or files, if ambiguous references are used) to R/O, short for Read-Only. Read-Only files cannot be written to or erased under normal circumstances.

[RW]

The R/W option is used with a file specification to set the file type attribute for the file (or files, if ambiguous references are used) to R/W, short for Read/Write. Read/Write files can be written to or erased under normal circumstances.

[ARCHIVE=s]

The ARCHIVE option is used to set the archive file attribute to the state (s) indicated, which must be ON or OFF. Files that have the archive bit set to ON have not been modified since they were last copied (using PIP); files with the bit set to OFF have not been copied since they were last modified.

[F1=s]
[F2=s]
[F3=s]
[F4=s]

CP/M-PLUS allows four user-definable file attribute bits to be set to the state (s) indicated, which must be ON or OFF. The user may use these bits to indicate any desired attribute of the file; CP/M-PLUS does not use these bits for any other function.

[NAME=labelname.typ]

The NAME option assigns a label (name) to the disk specified (if no disk is specified, the default disk is used). The naming conventions for disk labels are the same as those of file names: eight characters in the name and an optional three-character type. Label names can be used to keep track of disks and, with proper assembly language programming, can be used within programs to check that the appropriate disk is in the drive before a function is invoked.

[PASSWORD=password]
[PASSWORD= (**Note:** No closing bracket.)

CP/M-PLUS allows the user to set passwords for an entire disk or to individual files on the disk. Passwords should be unique and should contain eight characters or less. If you use passwords, be careful to remember what they are, since CP/M-PLUS does not allow you to look them up once they are assigned. Should you forget a file's password, you will not be able to use that file anymore. Pressing CARRIAGE RETURN removes any current password from a file or disk.

[PROTECT=s]
[PROTECT=t]

This option has two forms. The first form allows you to set password protection for all files on the disk by indicating the password status (s), which must be ON or OFF. The second form allows you to set the type (t) of password protection for files, where t is one of the following:

READ	Password is required to read from file.
WRITE	Password is required to write to file.
DELETE	Password is required to delete the file.
NONE	No password is required for the file; any current password is deleted.

[DEFAULT=password]

This option sets a default password for the system to use during the current session (it is temporary, unlike the other password options).

[CREATE=s]
[ACCESS=s]
[UPDATE=s]

Date and time stamping is controlled by three options that may be set ON or OFF as desired. CREATE=ON turns on time stamping for the disk. CREATE=OFF turns the time stamping off. ACCESS=ON time stamps files each time they are accessed; ACCESS=OFF disables this feature. **Note:** If CREATE is ON, then ACCESS must be OFF, and vice versa. Either CREATE or ACCESS can be ON, but not both. UPDATE=ON turns on the time stamping function each time a file is modified; UPDATE=OFF disables this feature.

Note: You must use INITDIR on a disk before activating the time and date stamping options. INITDIR is described earlier in this chapter.

Examples Using SET

The following example sets all COM-type files to be read/write and system files:

```
A>SET A:*.COM[RW SYS]<cr>
```

The following example turns on the archive attribute and user-definable attribute 1 for all files:

```
A>SET A:*.*[ARCHIVE=ON F1=ON]<cr>
```

The following example labels the disk in drive B with the name MYDISK.1:

```
A>SET B:[NAME=MYDISK.1]<cr>
```

In the example we set the password for the default disk to "opnsesme."

```
A>SET [PASSWORD=opnsesme]<cr>
```

We have combined two options in the next example. First we set the password for all files to DOIT. Next we tell the system that the password should be required every time we delete a file. (This is a good idea—you will never accidentally erase a file if you require a password for deletion on every disk.)

```
A>SET *.* [PASSWORD=DOIT PROTECT=DELETE]<cr>
```

In the following example we tell CP/M-PLUS to turn on the date and time stamping for any access or update of a file:

```
A>SET[ACCESS=ON UPDATE=ON]<cr>
```

SETDEF

Set Default Definitions

One problem that first-time users often have in CP/M-PLUS occurs when they log on to another drive (say B:) and then type a built-in CP/M-PLUS command that has information stored in a file on drive A. The result is an error message, since CP/M-PLUS looks for that file on drive B. The SETDEF command corrects this problem by allowing the user to specify which disk drives are to be searched, for what, and in what order.

SETDEF allows the user to define (either for the entire computer session or until the next SETDEF instruction) the following:

- Which drives to search for files and in what order
- What types of files to search for and in what order
- Where to place temporary files (used by ED and SUBMIT, among others)
- Whether to display information about a file before executing its instructions
- Whether to display information on the console in a paged or nonpaged fashion.

Forms of the SETDEF Command

The allowable forms of the SETDEF command are

SETDEF
: Displays the current defined settings for disk search order, drive to store temporary files, and file type search order.

SETDEF [TEMPORARY = d:]
: Tells the system to store all temporary files on the disk drive specified.

SETDEF d:
SETDEF d:,d:,d:,d:
: Tells the system to search for files on the drive specified (in the first case) or on the drives specified (in the second case). An * can be substituted for d: to

represent the default drive. The order in which drive names are listed indicates the order in which to search.

SETDEF [ORDER = typ,typ]
This command tells CP/M-PLUS to search for the file types in the order indicated. The file types can be COM or SUB only. This facility is useful for automatically invoking the SUBMIT facility if a user types the name of a SUB-type file.

SETDEF [DISPLAY]
SETDEF [NO DISPLAY]
DISPLAY indicates that CP/M-PLUS is to show the file name, the drive on which it was found, the file type (if any), and the user number (if not the current user area) of the file before accessing the file. This is useful for validating that the file accessed is the one intended. NO DISPLAY, the default setting, turns off this facility.

SETDEF [PAGE]
SETDEF [NO PAGE]
The PAGE and NO PAGE options control whether CP/M-PLUS stops after displaying one full page of information or continues to scroll the screen when full. The default setting is PAGE.

Examples Using SETDEF

The following example sets the default search order to the default drive, drive A, and drive B, in that order. CP/M-PLUS will search each of these for any future file references.

```
A>SETDEF *,A:,B:<cr>
```

This example shows how the DISPLAY option shows the name and location of the file before executing its instructions:

```
A>SETDEF [DISPLAY]<cr>
A>COPY
B:COPY      COM (User 1)
The Whiz-Bang Four COPY Program...
```

This next example tells CP/M-PLUS to look first for a COM-type file when interpreting command lines and then to look for a SUB-type file if no COM-type file is found.

```
A>SETDEF [ORDER=COM,SUB]<cr>
```

SHOW

Displays Information on Disks

The SHOW program provides CP/M-PLUS with some of the same capabilities as

STAT does for CP/M-80. In particular, SHOW allows the user to see the following information concerning a disk:

- Access mode (R/W or R/O) and free space
- Disk label (user-supplied name for disk)
- Current user number
- Number of files for each user on disk
- Number of available directory entries left on disk
- Drive characteristics.

The SHOW command has one form:

SHOW d:[options]
This command displays information where d: is an optional disk drive specifier and options are one or more of those in the following section (each separated by a space).

SHOW Options

[SPACE]
The SPACE option displays the drive name, its access status, and the remaining space in Kbytes. If no drive specifier was typed, SHOW displays the information for all logged-in drives in the system. The SPACE option is the default and need not be explicitly typed unless another option is requested.

[LABEL]
The LABEL option displays the disk's label information: the directory label (name) given the disk, whether passwords are required, whether the date stamping option (see the SET command section in this chapter) is turned on, and the dates when the label was created and last updated.

[USERS]
The USERS option displays the current user number and all the users on the drive specified, as well as the number of files assigned to each user. In addition, it displays the number of free directory entries.

[DIR]
The DIR option displays the number of free directory entries on the specified drive.

Examples Using SHOW

The following example shows the simplest use of the SHOW command: the user has asked for the status of all logged-in disk drives (in this case, A and B). Note that the access mode of drive A is read/write, while that of drive B is read-only. Note that CP/M-80 uses R/W for read/write and R/O for read-only, while CP/M-PLUS uses RW and RO, respectively.

```
A>SHOW<cr>
A: RW, Space:      24k
B: RO, Space:     128k
A>
```

The next example shows the label for the disk in drive B. The name of the disk is THOM15; the password, date stamping on creation, and date stamping on file updating options are ON. The label was created at 12:01 on July 22, 1983, and was updated a week later.

```
A>SHOW B:[LABEL]<cr>

Label for drive B:

Directory  Passwds   Stamp  Stamp  Label Created  Label Updated
Label      Reqd      Create Update
---------- --------- ------ ------ -------------- --------------
THOM15     on        on     on     07/22/83 12:01 07/29/83  1:23

A>
```

In the next example the SHOW command is used to find out what other users are on the system (note that the prompt shows we are in user area 5). The number of active files in each user area is displayed immediately below the user area number, and the number of available directory entries is displayed at the end of the report.

```
5A>SHOW [USERS]<cr>
Active User:   5
Active Files:   0    1    2    3    4    5    6
A: # of files 82   10    1    2    1   42   12
A: Number of free directory entries: 156
5A>
```

In the following example we have combined two options, SPACE and DIR, to determine the space left on the disk and in the disk's directory.

```
A>SHOW B:[SPACE DIR]
B: RW, Space:    1,433k
B: Number of free directory entries: 221
A>
```

SUMMARY

In this chapter you have learned nearly all of the built-in and transient commands that Digital Research supplies with CP/M. At this point you should be relatively proficient at using the system and should understand how to use each of the commands presented. The next chapter will discuss some disk-related commands and the ways other programs you purchase relate to CP/M.

CHAPTER

7 Other Transient Programs and CP/M

You will use many different types of programs in conjunction with CP/M: programs to help you develop your own software (utilities and programming languages) and user application programs (word processors, number processors, database programs, and so on). Digital Research provides language and utility programs, but markets few application programs; you will have to approach vendors for these. Remember, CP/M is not the entire solution. Application programs from vendors contribute significantly to reaching your end goals. This chapter addresses five classes of "solution" programs:

- Utilities
- High-level languages
- Editors and word processors
- Number processors
- Database programs.

In Chapter 5 we used the term *housekeeping* to describe programs that help you keep your disks and their files clean. We refer to another class of related programs as *utilities.* A utility disk contains programs that maintain your disk collection. Such utility programs are

- Disk copy programs
- Disk format programs
- CP/M system generators
- Disk viewers.

Before we proceed with a description of the utility, language, and application programs you will use with CP/M, it will be helpful to back up a step and review the hierarchy that software follows.

PROGRAM DEVELOPMENT

Assembly language — which will be discussed in later chapters — is one of several layers of software existing between the computer and the user. In the past, software was frequently designed to facilitate the subsequent development of microcomputer programs. Thus several layers of software developed, each directly dependent on an earlier one.

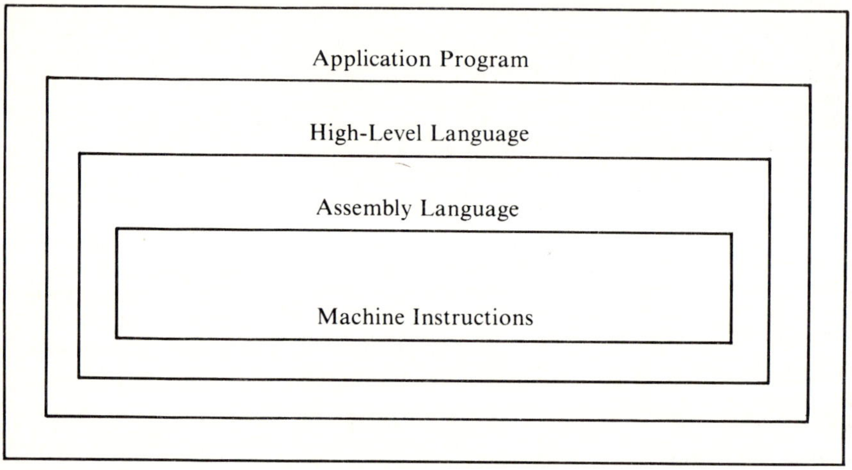

At the "lowest" level of programming are machine instructions. These are the binary 1's and 0's the CPU interprets. Each different pattern of 1's and 0's causes the CPU to perform a unique task. Each CPU model has a particular set of machine instructions it understands, one of the reasons that 8- and 16-bit versions of CP/M differ. Both CP/M-80 and CP/M-PLUS use the same CPUs and thus can share a particular set of instructions.

To program (instruct) a computer at the machine instruction level, you need a method of entering the machine instructions. CP/M does not provide this facility directly, but you may do this indirectly with DDT (Chapter 8) and SID (Chapter 9). Two conceptual problems are apparent with machine language programming, however.

First, a machine instruction (such as 11000011) bears little resemblance to the computer's response to it. This is true of any code or language that does not use hieroglyphics. While the 1's and 0's represent various ON and OFF states to the computer, we must further translate the 1's and 0's so we can understand them. In human languages, number strings do not form basic components of meaning; a series of numbers may represent something, but we require an intermediate translation. Computers likewise need a translation, and therefore the 11000011 translates for 8080-based computers to an instruction to "jump" to an address. This is typically done with assemblers, interpreters, and compilers.

Second, machine instructions perform operations that are firmly rooted in computer architecture and terminology. The task you wish to perform may be difficult to describe by means of machine instructions. For example, if you want to print a character, you might use some of these instructions:

Hexadecimal Representation	Binary Machine Representation
3E	00111110
58	01011000
DB	11011011
03	00000011
E6	11100110
01	00000001
C2	11000010
00	00000000
D3	11010011
02	00000010

Assembly language is a level above machine instructions, providing an English-like mnemonic that describes the action of each machine instruction. Using the above 8080 example (sending a character to the printer) we now get

```
MVI     A,58h
IN      03
ANI     01
JZ      0000
OUT     02
```

If you know what MVI, IN, ANI, JZ, and OUT mean, then the instruction is now represented in a shorthand that is more easily translated into human-readable language than are machine instructions. Unfortunately, these five assembly language program lines convey only the meaning of each single instruction. What do the five lines together, as a program, accomplish?

At one step above assembly language, the computer interprets a high-level language. Here assembly language instructions are combined into larger building blocks. Our program now becomes

```
LPRINT "X"
```

which sends the character X to the printer. The concept of what the program does is now evident. LPRINT "X" may actually trigger the execution of several (or several hundred) machine instructions, but the phrase LPRINT "X" gives us an immediate understanding of the program's function. Thus, as we get closer to understanding the computer's task, we get farther from the machine instructions the CPU actually executes. The first high-level languages were based on the next most sophisticated method, in this case, assembly language. And the first assembly language programs were written in machine language.

The last level we will consider is the application program. An application program causes a computer to execute a specific task, for example, to create and maintain a list of names and addresses. Most computer users run application programs unaware of any lower level of program operation.

Now that we have introduced the levels of program instructions, let us look in more detail at each of the five types of programs you may use with CP/M.

UTILITY PROGRAMS

Several utility programs are provided with almost every CP/M system. It is important to be aware of these utilities and to learn how to use them. This is particularly true of the disk-formatting and copying programs. As you read the following sections, consult the manuals that accompany your version of CP/M. Compare the material in your manuals with our discussion so you may determine how to use your own versions of these utility programs.

FORMAT

Preparing a Disk for Use

Before any operation can begin, the computer must know where to put information on the disk. You may recall that a disk is laid out in sectors and tracks. How does the computer distinguish between the sectors and tracks of a disk? How does it assign information within a sector or track?

Part of this job is done by the hardware (equipment) and CP/M, but you will first have to prepare the disk. Almost any CP/M system includes a format or initialization type of program. The names of these programs vary because Digital Research did not include an initialization program with CP/M. An efficient initialization program must be written specifically for each hardware system; manufacturers and distributors generally provide custom versions of this program. Among others, the following names have been given to initialization programs:

```
FORMAT     INIT       IN
DSKFMT     FMT        CREATE
INITDSK    INITDISK   FORMT#
FORMTHD    MFORMAT    HDF
HARDFMT    HDFORMAT
```

The exact name of your formatting program depends on your CP/M source. In some rare instances there may be no initialization program; instead, the accompanying documentation describes how to initialize a disk.

Every blank disk must be formatted before you can put data onto it. This is a good practice even if your disk vendor claims to have formatted your disks.

Assume your initialization program is called FORMAT. A FORMAT program session might look like this:

```
A>FORMAT<cr>
DISK TO FORMAT? (A,B,C,D) B<cr>
PRESS RETURN TO BEGIN FORMATTING <cr>
DISK FORMATTED.  MORE?  (Y/N) N<cr>
A>
```

While the exact syntax of the messages may differ, these steps normally occur in any format program:

1. Run the program (type its name and then press RETURN).
2. Tell the program which drive contains the disk to be formatted.
3. If your system runs both single- and double-density disks, you must specify a density.
4. Tell the program to start formatting.
5. Tell the program whether you want to quit or format another disk when it finishes.

The program may direct you to remove any disk you are not formatting so as to prevent accidental formatting of a disk that contains valuable, irreplaceable information.

The format program may or may not obey the write-protect notch on the disk. To determine this, try to format an expendable protected disk. If the format program ignores the write-protect mechanism, then you must be extra careful not to inadvertently format a disk containing useful information.

Initializing a disk only prepares it for use. If you ask for a directory of the disk after initializing it, messages like NO FILE or NOT FOUND appear, since no files are yet present. Also, initializing a disk does not mean that the disk can be used to boot (start) the system; the disk does not yet contain the CP/M system (see SYSGEN and COPYSYS).

The format program moves the magnetic head of the disk drive to the first sector of the first track. The program then writes some known dummy information and moves on. Each sector of a track is written into, and the head moves to the next track. Most programs fill the disk with the hexadecimal byte E5. You probably will not care what is done, or how, so long as the disk is properly formatted.

Note that the amount of time a formatting program takes is directly proportional to the storage capacity of the disk drive. Formatting a small-capacity disk may take only 30 seconds, while formatting a hard disk drive may require as much as 30 minutes.

COPY

Transferring Information From One Disk to Another

Suppose you want to make a copy of an entire disk. You could use PIP, as described in Chapter 4, but this method is slower and does not initialize a blank disk. Instead, you will normally use a copy program.

Like initialization programs, the programs used to copy entire disks have different names. Again, these depend on the CP/M implementation used because Digital Research did not include a copy program with CP/M. Among the various copy program names you may encounter are

COPY	DISKCOPY	COPYDISK
DSKCPY	BACKUP	COPYATOB
COPY1D	SDCOPY	MCOPY
FCOPY	FASTCOPY	DUPE

All of these programs are used much like the formatting program we discussed.

```
A>DISKCOPY<cr>
SOURCE DRIVE? A<cr>
DESTINATION DRIVE? B<cr>
PRESS RETURN TO BEGIN COPYING <cr>
COPY COMPLETE.  MORE? (Y/N) N<cr>
A>
```

Most copy programs function similarly, but yours may not conform exactly to the prompts in our example. You usually follow these steps:

1. Execute the copy program by typing its name.
2. Indicate which drive contains the original disk (the one to be copied *from,* known as the *source disk*).
3. Indicate which drive contains the disk you want the copy placed onto (the *destination disk*).
4. Begin the copying process by pressing CARRIAGE RETURN.
5. When the copy is complete, indicate whether you wish to quit or make more copies.

Check the manuals accompanying your CP/M to determine whether or not your copy program requires an initialized disk as the destination disk. Most do not, but a few do. If you attempt to use the copy program with a blank disk and get an error message, try initializing the destination disk first. Most good copy programs initialize the disk.

Disk copying generally takes longer than just formatting a disk, since most copying programs first format the disk being copied to.

Organization of Files on Disk

Remember that copying a disk results in an *exact duplicate* of your source disk. Your source disk, like most disks, may store its information in a rather haphazard order if it has been used for any length of time. This is a result of erasing files or adding information to several files a piece at a time, practices that occur with regularity in the actual use of a computer system. The reason files become disorganized over time is that CP/M allocates space for them on a variation of the first-come–first-served basis.

As an example, assume that you have three files on a disk:

FILE.ONE
FILE.TWO
FILE.THR

and the three files take up all the available room on the disk.

The way CP/M would originally allocate space (assuming the files were created in the order their names indicate) might be like this:

FILE.ONE	FILE.TWO	FILE.THR
start————>end	start————>end	start————>end

If you erase FILE.TWO from the disk, the space is now divided like this:

FILE.ONE		FILE.THR
start————>end	empty	start————>end

Now let us add information to FILE.THR. Here is what the disk's storage looks like:

FILE.ONE	FILE.THR		FILE.THR
start————>end	———>end	empty	start——>middle

Note that FILE.THR is no longer one continuous entity on the disk. Fortunately, CP/M keeps track of where it puts the various pieces of the file. But it should be obvious that the more you erase and add to files, the more disorganized the internal structure of the disk.

Now what does this have to do with disk copying? Because all disk copy programs exactly duplicate disks, including any "scattering" of files, the more scattered a file is, the longer it takes the computer to retrieve its information. However, there is a way to copy a disk and restore an efficient, sequential organization. Instead of using the copy program to create a copy of your disk, first format a disk and then use PIP to copy files from your original to the freshly formatted disk. As you have already learned, PIP copies files one at a time and restores them to a logical, sequential order if they have been split up. Using the PIP method instead of the copy program on your imaginary disk would result in the following data structure on the new copy:

FILE.ONE	FILE.THR	
start————>end	start————————>end	

Other considerations enter into the disk-copying process, most notably, how often you make copies. Generally, before ending a session at the computer you should make copies of any disks you have changed or updated. This practice is called *backup*.

Suggestions for Backing Up Disks

Label all disks. Distinguish the original disk from the copy. One way is the *father-son method.* The original disk is labeled "father," and the copy is labeled "son." If you maintain a third copy of the disk for archival purposes, the original is the "grandfather," and the "father" and "son" disks are copies. However, this may not be the best way to maintain copies as you can easily slip into the habit of making infrequent backups.

A far better method is the *rotating backup* procedure. You have one data disk for each day you use the computer. At the end of Monday's processing, you copy the Monday disk onto the Tuesday disk. At the end of Tuesday's processing you copy Tuesday's information onto Wednesday's disk. Using this method (assuming that you have carefully labeled each disk), you know immediately if you are working on the right disk, and there is a natural backup sequence.

Copy all disks. No disk will last forever. The reason for this fact is simple: there is a great deal of physical contact between the disk's surface and the inside of its sleeve. Also, the head of a poorly aligned drive will wear away the disk's surface.

Estimates of a disk's life can range over an extraordinary time span. One manufacturer claims its disks will endure a year of continuous use. In any case, do not expect disks to last forever. If you use the rotating backup procedure, retire disks some time between 6 and 12 months of use. This is a conservative practice, since each disk has been used for only 30-50 days. But if you compare the price of a disk to the cost of reentering data, backup will be a wise practice.

Never use programs on their original disks. When you receive a new program (or CP/M update) on disk, make a copy of it, label the original "master," and safely store this master disk. Using an original disk is foolhardy. Someday your computer may sit idle while you wait for a replacement disk. Most software vendors provide an update only on return of the original disk, so be sure to store it in a safe place.

MOVCPM

Adjusting CP/M to Memory Capacity (CP/M-80)

When you first receive your CP/M-80 disk, it is usually ready to operate in a 16K or 24K computer. This means you need only 16 or 24K of RAM to use CP/M-80. You will quickly find this is not enough memory to execute most programs, especially when you use a high-level language like BASIC or Pascal. In this case you need to make CP/M-80 aware of the maximum amount of memory available in your system. If you have 48K of memory and you receive a CP/M-80 expecting only 24K, you waste 24K of memory. CP/M-PLUS does not use MOVCPM, as it normally uses the top portion (or second bank) of memory and leaves the rest available to you.

The MOVCPM command provides a simple method of changing CP/M-80's memory-size expectations. Changing CP/M-80 to expect a different quantity of memory is called *moving*. There are two ways to move CP/M-80: (1) move CP/M and immediately execute it, but do not save it on disk; or (2) move CP/M and save the new configuration on disk.

The first possibility is perfect for the day you borrow an extra 8K of memory from another system to learn what you can do with more memory. To move CP/M and immediately execute it, use MOVCPM or MOVCPM #.

MOVCPM
: Makes use of all existing memory.

MOVCPM #
: In this form # is the decimal number of kilobytes of memory you want CP/M-80 to recognize. Use this command when you want to reserve some room for a special program or utility above CP/M.

For example, if you want to create and execute a 48K CP/M-80 system (one that makes use of 48K of your available memory), type MOVCPM 48<cr> or just MOVCPM<cr> if you have only 48K of RAM. After a few moments you see a message followed by the A> prompt; you are now using the 48K CP/M system you created.

Most of the time, however, you will want a more permanent solution. To move CP/M-80 and then save it on disk, use one of the following forms of MOVCPM:

MOVCPM * *
: Makes use of all existing memory.

MOVCPM # *
: In this form # is the number of kilobytes of memory you want CP/M-80 to recognize.

The # in the above command forms must be

- A decimal number from 16 to 64 for versions 1.3 and 1.4
- A decimal number from 20 to 64 for versions 2.0 and newer
- Less than or equal to the number of kilobytes of memory in your computer.

Saving your new-sized CP/M system on disk requires another step. MOVCPM prompts you for this step by displaying

```
READY FOR "SYSGEN" OR
"SAVE 32 CPM##.COM"
```

This cryptic message means that you will save the CP/M you just created by typing SYSGEN<cr> or SAVE 32 CPM##.COM<cr> (## is the size of the new CP/M-80 system given in the MOVCPM command). Unless you are an experienced CP/M-80 user or a brave soul, you should immediately execute the SYSGEN program by typing SYSGEN<cr> (see next section).

MOVCPM is sometimes called by another name, such as CPM, NEWCPM, MAKECPM, CPMGEN, or MOVECPM. MOVCPM does not affect any files on a disk.

If MOVCPM does not work properly, your computer may "die" (fail to operate properly). Press the RESET button to recover. If the computer dies, the portion of

CP/M-80 that customizes it for a particular computer (BIOS) has not been placed in the MOVCPM program (see Chapter 7), or you specified a greater amount of memory than your system contains. This last possibility can often be overlooked: the Osborne 1 computer and most computers that use memory-mapped video utilize the top 4K of memory for video displays, meaning you can only create a 60K—not a 64K—CP/M-80 system.

SYSGEN

Placing the CP/M System on Disk (CP/M-80)

SYSGEN is short for System Generation. *System* refers to the CP/M-80 operating system. Placing a copy of the operating system on disk is system generation, which is the purpose of SYSGEN. (The parallel in CP/M-PLUS is the COPYSYS command.)

Why not copy the CP/M-80 system just as you would copy a file? Because the system is not stored as a file. The details of this oddity are explained at the end of this section. For now, remember that SYSGEN copies the CP/M-80 operating system from one disk to another.

System generation is accomplished in one of three ways:

- By using SYSGEN alone to copy the system from a disk, without change, and by placing it on a new disk.
- By using MOVCPM and then SYSGEN to place the new system on a disk.
- By using MOVCPM, saving the result on disk, reloading the result for modification by DDT, and then using SYSGEN to save it on a disk.

Modifying the system is described in later chapters. Here we will describe the use of SYSGEN alone and then describe its use in conjunction with MOVCPM. SYSGEN does not affect any file on either the source or destination disk.

When copying the system from one disk to another, your dialog with the computer looks like this:

```
A>SYSGEN<cr>
SYSGEN VER 2.2
SOURCE DRIVE NAME (OR RETURN TO SKIP) A
SOURCE ON A:, THEN TYPE RETURN <cr>
FUNCTION COMPLETE
DESTINATION DRIVE NAME (OR RETURN TO REBOOT) B
DESTINATION ON B:, THEN TYPE RETURN <cr>
FUNCTION COMPLETE
DESTINATION DRIVE NAME (OR RETURN TO REBOOT) <cr>
A>
```

Let us examine each step a little more closely. First, type SYSGEN<cr> in order to load and execute the SYSGEN program. It requests the source location; you type the letter A. That tells SYSGEN to get the system from the disk in drive A. Next, SYSGEN asks where to put the system; you specify drive B. SYSGEN then tells you to put a disk in drive B (DESTINATION ON B:) and to press CARRIAGE RETURN when you are ready. After you press CARRIAGE RETURN, the drives whir and clack for a few moments while the system is written onto the disk in drive B, and then the process starts again (DESTINATION DRIVE NAME...). A CARRIAGE RETURN ends the process, or another drive specifier tells SYSGEN that you wish to place the same system onto another disk.

If you want to save the larger CP/M-80 system you created by using MOVCPM on the disk in drive A, you could specify this drive instead of drive B. But when you press the CARRIAGE RETURN key at the end of the program, you may discover something is wrong. Usually you must exit from SYSGEN using the disk with which you first started the system.

When saving the new-sized system you created with MOVCPM, your dialog with SYSGEN differs slightly. Assume you type MOVCPM * *<cr> or MOVCPM ## *<cr>, and now MOVCPM is ready for a SYSGEN or a SAVE. Proceed as follows:

```
READY FOR "SYSGEN" OR
"SAVE 32 CPM##.COM"
A>SYSGEN<cr>
SYSGEN VER 2.2
SOURCE DRIVE NAME (OR RETURN TO SKIP) <cr>
DESTINATION ON B:, THEN TYPE RETURN <cr>
FUNCTION COMPLETE
DESTINATION DRIVE NAME (OR RETURN TO REBOOT) <cr>
A>
```

As the example shows, SYSGEN continues to ask for a destination disk until you respond with a CARRIAGE RETURN. Using this method, you can update many disks in one session.

The SYSGEN command can also include the name of a CP/M-80 system that has been saved as a file, for example, SYSGEN CPM48.COM<cr>. This form of the SYSGEN program loads the system file into memory and then asks only for the destination drive.

Why SYSGEN Is Necessary

The first two tracks, tracks 0 and 1, of every CP/M-80 disk do not contain files. Instead, this (normally) 6656-byte space is reserved for bootstrap (cold start) loaders and the CP/M-80 operating system. These programs are not stored as files, they do not appear in the file directory, and they are not accessible as files. However, it is occasionally necessary to read or write to these tracks.

Disk tracks 0 and 1 are always set aside, whether or not they contain the loader and system programs. It is not necessary to keep these programs on every disk; they are required on a disk only if you do a cold or warm start with it.

Most disk-copying programs copy the system, or lack of it, from one disk to another. Disk application programs you receive from software companies rarely contain CP/M-80 on the system tracks. That is why SYSGEN is needed to place a new or modified operating system on disk. Only by using this special program can you save your changed CP/M-80.

One last word on the subject of system generation: MOVCPM moves only the raw, bare bones of the CP/M-80 operating system. Any additional special printer drivers or other changes you have made to the BIOS section of CP/M (see Chapter 10) are not moved by MOVCPM. If you use MOVCPM and then the printer (or any other special device you may be using) refuses to work, you may need to re-add the special drivers for those devices. SYSGEN, on the other hand, always copies the entire operating system, including all of BIOS. In fact, SYSGEN copies all of tracks 0 and 1.

COPYSYS

Placing the CP/M System on Disk (CP/M-PLUS)

CP/M-PLUS owners do not use SYSGEN. Instead, the distributor of your CP/M-PLUS operating system has provided (usually) a computer-specific program named COPYSYS, which performs the same function in CP/M-PLUS as SYSGEN does in CP/M-80.

Unlike CP/M-80, the actual CP/M-PLUS program information is stored as a file on disk (named CPM.SYS or CPM3.SYS on most systems). On the special "boot" tracks at the beginning of the disk (described in the SYSGEN section) a "loader" program is stored. The loader program's purpose is to take control of the system when it is started, load CPM.SYS into the proper position in memory, initialize some parameters CP/M-PLUS will be using, and pass control to CP/M-PLUS.

Since COPYSYS is not supplied by Digital Research but by the distributor of your CP/M-PLUS system, it is impossible to show exactly how COPYSYS works on your system. Normally, the following steps occur in the COPYSYS program:

1. Identification of the program.
2. Program asks user for name of disk that contains a valid CP/M-PLUS system. User responds with drive letter.
3. System prompts user to place disk in drive and press RETURN.
4. Program asks user for name of disk on which to place copy of the system. User responds with drive letter.
5. System prompts user to place disk in drive and press RETURN.
6. Program repeats last step until user enters RETURN instead of drive letter.

In this most simple form, the computer/user dialog may look something like this:

```
A>COPYSYS<cr>

COPYSYS for CP/M-PLUS -- by Your Computer Co.

Drive to get CP/M-PLUS from (A:-P:)? A:<cr>
Place disk with CP/M-PLUS on it in drive A
and press RETURN when ready. <cr>

Drive to put CP/M-PLUS on (A:-P:)? B:<cr>
Place disk to receive CP/M-PLUS in drive B
and press RETURN when ready.  <cr>
```

```
Drive to put CP/M-PLUS on (A:-P:)? <cr>

Returning to CP/M-PLUS...

A>
```

Error messages vary among COPYSYS programs, but the following types of messages may occur:

FILE NOT FOUND:
The CPM.SYS (or CPM3.SYS) file was not found on the disk you indicated.

NO SPACE: or DIRECTORY FULL:
There is not enough room on the disk you specified to store the copy of CP/M-PLUS.

HIGH-LEVEL LANGUAGES

As we mentioned earlier, program developers use high-level languages in writing computer programs. There are three main reasons:

- High-level languages are easier to use since one high-level instruction conveys the meaning of many machine-language instructions. Thus, high-level languages make programming faster and programs easier to understand.
- It is easier to conceptualize the executed process when the command resembles human communication. For example, PRINT is understandable in both human and computer languages.
- High-level languages have been designed for particular computerized tasks (computer control of machines, emphasis on numerical calculations, and so on).

A History of High-Level Languages

CP/M became a standard operating system because it was one of the first operating systems available. An operating system acts as the scheduler and arbitrator of the various tasks a computer must perform. In other words, to use disk drives you must have a disk operating system. But the disk operating system is only a go-between; it is not an end in itself.

Soon after CP/M became available to the general public, Gordon Eubanks, Jr. released EBASIC, a high-level language that he developed as part of his Ph.D. dissertation. (EBASIC is sometimes called BASIC-E.) EBASIC was written using another high-level language called PL/M. While other languages could be used with CP/M, EBASIC became available relatively early and made good use of CP/M's logical and physical device handlers (see the descriptions of STAT in Chapter 5 and DEVICE in Chapter 6). EBASIC was written at government expense, which automatically placed the software in the public domain; no copyright privileges could accrue to Eubanks, nor could EBASIC be sold for more than a "reasonable copying charge." In fact, the PL/M instructions (the source code) that make up EBASIC are available from the CP/M Users' Group (1651 Third Avenue, New York, New York 10028).

EBASIC is a type of compiler BASIC. You enter BASIC language instructions with an editor, and then EBASIC creates an intermediate file of instructions. But let us back up a step and describe what happens inside the computer when a program or high-level language is executed.

The computer executes only machine language instructions, those 1's and 0's that keep popping up in this book. BASIC is a computer language developed at Dartmouth to help beginners use computers. It has instructions like

PRINT
GOTO
LET
IF

How do these instructions translate into 1's and 0's? In EBASIC, when you have entered a set of BASIC instructions in a file with an editor, you have a file of text. We call this file the *program source code.* The source code consists of recognizable letters and numbers. Using other CP/M programs, you can manipulate the source code text. For example, you can use PIP to copy the text to a device like a printer and thus create a printed copy of the text.

Your BASIC disk contains a file named EBASIC.COM. Use that file to create an intermediate code file from the source code file. If you have a BASIC program in a file named SOURCE.BAS, type

EBASIC SOURCE<cr>

The conversion from text to a more compact form the computer uses occurs automatically. When complete, your disk has a file named SOURCE.INT. This new file contains no text; instead, each BASIC instruction has been *compacted* into a one-byte representation. For instance, a PRINT instruction from the source code file (SOURCE.BAS) is stored as hexadecimal 1A in the intermediate code file (SOURCE.INT). A number of advantages result from this compacting process (often called *compiling,* although a true compiler generates real machine instructions, not representations of high-level language instructions). The most significant advantages are a reduction in the file size and a faster execution speed. It takes less time to interpret one byte, such as 1A, than it does to interpret a series of letters, as in the PRINT instruction.

To execute a program written in EBASIC, you use another portion of EBASIC called RUN.COM. This program interprets compacted instructions in the file SOURCE.INT. RUN.COM is loaded into memory and begins execution, and then SOURCE.INT is loaded into memory and is interpreted by RUN.COM. While this sounds confusing, EBASIC takes care of the details. You only need to

1. Write (or purchase) an EBASIC program
2. Use EBASIC to create the intermediate file
3. Use RUN to begin interpretation of the intermediate file.

Although EBASIC is actually an extension of the standard Dartmouth BASIC, it lacks several features of a suitable business processing language. But because it was one of the first high-level languages available on CP/M and because of its low cost, EBASIC was quickly adopted by those supplying CP/M with systems.

Fortunately Eubanks did not stop with EBASIC. Using his experience in writing and developing EBASIC, he formed a small firm and developed CBASIC (and later, CBASIC2). CBASIC is an upward enhancement of EBASIC; many EBASIC programs will run using CBASIC, but not necessarily vice versa. Many program developers have used CBASIC and CBASIC2 to write programs, and you may find application programs that only use CBASIC. (CBASIC, by the way, uses the same three-step process as EBASIC. The program used to run the CBASIC intermediate file is named CRUN.)

While EBASIC/CBASIC was developing as a primary high-level language for CP/M, two young men from the state of Washington, Paul Allen and Bill Gates, began supplying another version of BASIC under the company name of Microsoft. Microsoft's clients have included MITS—the company that started the personal computer revolution—Radio Shack, Apple, Texas Instruments, Exidy, Ohio Scientific, Osborne, IBM, and other microcomputer manufacturers. What began as a cassette-based BASIC interpreter of modest size has grown into a comprehensive, disk-based language. The primary versions of Microsoft BASIC have been

- 8K BASIC—usually for cassette; used in various forms by MITS, Ohio Scientific, Apple, Radio Shack, and Exidy.
- DISK BASIC—originally developed for MITS, also modified for Radio Shack and CP/M systems.
- Extended Disk BASIC—the current version of the interpreter, used with all versions of CP/M.

Until 1980, all versions of Microsoft BASIC were interpreter high-level languages, as opposed to compiler languages like CBASIC. Rather than using an editor to enter programs, with an interpreter BASIC you enter programs directly into the computer's memory. The interpreter BASIC has a built-in line editor; type a command to load BASIC into memory (MBASIC<cr>, for instance), and the interpreter BASIC accepts valid statements thereafter. These statements are immediately interpreted as you enter them. (Actually, they are interpreted once you press CARRIAGE RETURN.) Each line is processed when completed.

Again, a compacting scheme saves both space and time in the actual execution of a program. For immediate execution, the statement is compacted as soon as it is entered.

Unlike compilers, interpreter languages allow you to develop and test each piece of a program individually. You may stop entering instructions at any time and begin executing the partial program by typing RUN<cr>. If an instruction error is present, the line on which it occurs is identified and a message details the type of error encountered. You can immediately edit the offending line, correct the error, and run the program again.

Compare this to the method of program development you must use with a compiler. You must leave BASIC, return to CP/M, invoke the editor, edit the program file, and then re-compile it, all before you get another chance to run it. An interpreter performs these same tasks, but the interpreter handles most of the details for you. This advantage has made Microsoft BASIC a popular language even though it largely duplicates features and instructions available in EBASIC and CBASIC.

In 1980 Microsoft released a compiler version of their Extended Disk BASIC, usually referred to as BASCOM (for BASic COMpiler). A unique feature of Microsoft BASIC allows you to use the interpreter for program development and then use BASCOM to compile the final version. Many people believe Microsoft's compiler BASIC provides the fastest execution of any BASIC currently available.

More recently, Digital Research acquired the rights to CBASIC and released another compiler version of it, CB-80. A unique aspect of Digital Research's new CB compiler is that it is part of a series of CBASIC compilers. All versions of the CB compiler, whether for 8-bit or 16-bit versions of CP/M, use the same syntax and perform exactly the same.

Choosing a Language

When choosing a language, you should remember the following two rules:

RULE #1

Many application programs require run-time modules in order to operate. Vendors may supply the necessary software, but they usually assume you will supply it yourself. A typical example would be programs written in many of the BASIC dialects, especially CBASIC. Many excellent accounting programs available today are written in CBASIC, but CBASIC programs require the CRUN module (CB-80 corrects this problem, but not all program suppliers have converted from CBASIC to CB-80). Therefore, before you can run a program written in CBASIC, you need to purchase the CBASIC language if the vendor did not supply CRUN with the software package.

RULE #2

If you are already familiar with a high-level language, choose a similar language available for operation under CP/M. Why buy Pascal if you are already well versed in COBOL?

If your expertise with computers is limited, or if you are interested in acquiring another language to satisfy your curiosity or to expand your knowledge, read the next section thoroughly. Brief explanations are given that will help you decide which language or languages to explore further.

A Dictionary of Languages

Following are short descriptions of currently available languages that operate under CP/M. This list is by no means complete, since companies are continually forming and existing companies keep expanding their lines of available software.

Reading trade hournals, such as *Byte* and *Personal Computing,* keeps you abreast of the latest software available. An important point to remember is that Microsoft, unlike most companies, only sells its manuals with its software; you cannot purchase them separately.

Note also that a particular language's inclusion or exclusion from this list does not reflect an endorsement or condemnation of the software by the author or publisher, nor are the relative merits of any given package to be inferred.

Ada

Ada is a new language developed by the U.S. Department of Defense. It is named after Augusta Ada Byron, who is thought of as the "first programmer." Ada was developed because all other languages evaluated by Defense (Pascal, PL/I, COBOL, FORTRAN, and so forth) failed to meet the needs of military software systems. All programs now written for the department's equipment or computers, with some exceptions, must be written in Ada. It is a highly structured and sophisticated language usable for all types of programs, from simple applications to highly technical systems programming. Ada resembles Pascal in many respects but incorporates many additions, particularly in the area of shared modules for multiple programs.

The most popular versions of Ada for CP/M are SuperSoft Ada and JANUS, both subsets of the full Ada language.

Assemblers

In addition to the assemblers that Digital Research supplies with CP/M (see Chapters 8 and 9), several advanced assemblers are now available. If you are well versed in assemblers, a more advanced product could be well worthwhile. If your system is a Z80 rather than an 8080 machine, investigate them; assemblers allow you to program directly in Z80 and 8080 codes, letting you take advantage of the Z80's more powerful instruction set.

The most popular assemblers for CP/M systems include Microsoft's M80, Digital Research's MAC and RMAC, Phoenix Software's PASM, and Sorcim's ACT I assemblers.

BASIC

BASIC stands for Beginner's All-purpose Symbolic Instruction Code. This language was developed at Dartmouth College in the 1960s to teach computer use and programming. Although BASIC is partially derived from FORTRAN, it has simpler syntax; BASIC is more understandable to the casual program reader.

Unfortunately, it is difficult to generalize about BASIC. There is an American National Standards Institute (ANSI) definition of the BASIC instructions set, but this standard was defined after the language had established itself as the most popular microcomputer programming language. By the time the standards were set, almost every extant version of BASIC deviated from them. In fact, language developers frequently add instructions from other languages to BASIC (most notably from Pascal) to overcome deficiencies.

Some of BASIC's advantages are these:

- It is widely available. Almost every microcomputer uses a version of BASIC.
- BASIC is easy to learn. Hundreds of books, many schools, and most computer retailers use BASIC to teach introductory programming.
- Because BASIC uses words and phrases, it is simple to understand. As Radio Shack, Commodore, and Apple have shown in computer sales to grade schools, with proper instruction children can learn the commands and write programs.
- A great number of the programs published in computer magazines are written in BASIC. These articles provide samples of programming style and logic to the BASIC user.
- Most BASICs are interpreters. The user can type in instructions and immediately see the results. That makes BASIC an excellent learning tool.
- BASIC has more dialects than any other language used in CP/M systems. You will probably find a BASIC dialect that suits your style and personality.

Some of BASIC's disadvantages are these:

- There is no standardization. While the frequently used instructions remain essentially the same in all BASICs, there are many extensions and added instructions. Extensions may please individual programmers, but they frustrate standardization.
- BASIC programs execute slowly compared to programs in other languages. Notwithstanding the occasional compiler versions of BASIC, the fact that most BASICs are interpreters immediately adds an extra level of execution (the interpretation). Even BASIC compilers can generate programs that execute slowly. The structure of the language and the resulting program do not make good use of memory space.
- You can write a sloppy BASIC program and still have the program work. BASIC does not impart much structure to programs. Unfortunately, the slack that BASIC allows in programming style often encourages programming "off the top of the head."
- Standard BASIC has not kept pace with other developments in the computer industry. BASIC is over 20 years old, and computers have changed radically in that time. The versions of BASIC that accommodate these changes inevitably suffer from the lack of standardization.

Overall, BASIC is probably the most approachable language available to CP/M users. The number of programs written in BASIC, the number of books written about it, and its wide application all suggest you will find help in understanding the language if you need it.

The most popular versions of BASIC for CP/M are Digital Research's CBASIC and CB-80 and Microsoft's BASIC and BASIC Compiler (BASCOM).

C

Bell Laboratories developed C; it is an integral part of the Bell operating system, UNIX. Currently, C is one of the more popular languages among CP/M programmers, and many software manufacturers have turned to it for use in development projects.

C, ALGOL, PL/I, and Pascal are relatively similar. These four languages all require *structured programming techniques.* In terms of instruction execution order, structured programs are easy to trace and are not easily written without careful planning.

The C language differs from these other languages in a number of ways. C often uses abbreviations or shorthand instructions while Pascal and the others use complete words or phrases. C programming emphasizes economy of effort. For instance, C uses the instruction

```
int x;
```

while Pascal expands that same concept in an instruction like

```
X: INTEGER;
```

C demands more understanding and memorization from its users, but it requires less typing. And although it is succinct, C is not difficult to learn. Where C clearly excels other languages, however, is in its instruction set extensions, which make it capable of many tasks normally reserved for assembly language. Indeed, C has been called a "high-level assembly language."

Users can use C to develop modules that can be used repeatedly in other programs without reentering instructions. This can be done both internally in a program (using user-defined macro definitions) or externally (using the #include function built into C). If programmed in C, repetitive tasks do not require the same amount of programming each time they occur as they do in some other languages.

Above all, C programs are transportable. Since it was specified and created by Bell Laboratories, C remains fairly standardized. Your C programs are likely to run on a larger variety of microcomputers than programs written in any other language.

Besides its other advantages, C executes programs extremely fast and creates extremely compact program code (it is, in fact, a compiler). Its features allow easy access to peripheral devices at a machine language level.

The primary disadvantage of C is its newness. Few resources for learning C are available. Nevertheless, there are a number of excellent C compilers for CP/M. The most popular are Software Toolwork C/80, BDS C, Supersoft C, and Aztec C. Small C, a public-domain version of C, is available from most CP/M users' groups.

COBOL

COBOL is an acronym for Common Business-Oriented Language. COBOL program statements look much like written English. In fact, programmers refer to

COBOL statements as sentences and use a number of predefined words. Here is a short section of COBOL program code:

```
PROCEDURE CALCULATION.
DETERMINE-COST.
     COMPUTE OUR-COST=LIST-PRICE - 10.05
     IF OUR-COST > ZERO
          SET PRICE-TO-US TO OUR-COST
          MOVE "OK" TO VALID-PRICE-CODE
     ELSE
          MOVE "NO" TO VALID-PRICE-CODE.
```

Notice that the sentences end with a period. By reading the sentences aloud, you learn what the program does. Little unintelligible computer code is built into the language.

The origin of COBOL is unique in the computer world. COBOL is a committee-designed computer language. A group named CODASYL (Conference On Data Systems Languages) established the COBOL language and also defined a standardized database structure for business computing. Unlike the other languages described in this book, COBOL is extremely standardized. A program written in ANSI COBOL (the standardized definition) should run on any computer utilizing the language. The United States government recognizes the standard COBOL version and periodically accepts new versions as meeting the accepted minimum standards. At present COBOL is one of the few languages the U.S. government checks to ensure a standard definition is met.

Since COBOL was developed for business applications, you would expect it to be used primarily by business. This is true for the large-computer environment, but several factors have minimized COBOL's impact in the microcomputer world.

First, COBOL is a "large" language. COBOL uses full sentences to indicate the task to be performed, and it is a carefully structured language. Statements must appear in a certain order, and a number of system-specific statements must also be included. Consequently, COBOL is not well suited to microcomputers. This was especially true when memory was a relatively expensive component of microcomputer systems and it is still the case today. But now that memory prices have decreased and 64K microcomputers are commonplace, several microcomputer versions of COBOL have appeared.

Second, COBOL is not very efficient; a microcomputer CPU takes a long time to decipher its lengthy program statements. This applies primarily to compilation rather than to program execution. In addition, batch-processing methods usually make COBOL a relatively slow language compared to others. On larger computer systems there is plenty of execution speed to spare, and tasks are often handled in a batch mode rather than as an interactive process. Microcomputers, however, are often taxed by the number of internal manipulations that COBOL must make.

Finally, COBOL was designed at a time when interactive computing was relatively unknown. It cannot efficiently utilize the console device in a CP/M system. Most microcomputer COBOLs offer extra (and thus, nonstandard) instructions to utilize the high-speed console devices featured on most microcomputers, but these vary from compiler to compiler.

The most popular CP/M versions of COBOL are Microsoft's COBOL-80, Digital Research's CIS COBOL and Level II COBOL, Micro Focus's COBOL, and Nevada COBOL.

FORTH

FORTH is one of the more misunderstood microcomputer languages. A relatively new language (invented in the early 1970s by Charles Moore), FORTH has been described as everything from "an assembly language like BASIC" to "a religion."

A FORTH program is not easily deciphered. It is a *threaded* language. You use its basic building blocks to make larger ones. In fact, it is extremely difficult to describe just how to program in FORTH. Consider the following program fragment (reprinted from *Byte,* August 1980, page 158):

```
( BREAKFORTH/MMSFORTH, BY ARNOLD SHAEFFER, PART 5 OF 6 )
: CLR
 XPOS @ 2- 124 AND 2+ DUP 4 + SWAP DO YPOS @ I DCLR LOOP
 YPOS @ 27 - ABS SCORE+ ! 0 32 PTC SCORE ? BOP
 YDIR @ MINUS YDIR !
;
: BALLCHKY DIR @ YPOS+ ! XDIR @ XPOS + XCHK YCHK PCHK
                YPOS @ XPOS @ D? IF CLR THEN
;
: BALL YPOS @ XPOS @ DCLR
                BALLCHK DUP 0= IF YPOS @ XPOS @ DSET THEN ;
: GAMECHK SCORE @ 1800 MOD 0= IF 191 15616 320 FILL THEN ;
```

Pretty intimidating, right? FORTH includes many aspects a beginner prefers not to find in a computer language. It frequently uses abbreviations; numeric manipulations are done in Reverse Polish Notation (the same as some pocket calculators; for example, 2 2 + rather than 2 + 2); and FORTH allows the user to invent new commands (BALLCHK is one such invention in our small sample).

If FORTH has so many apparent disadvantages, why does it exist? First, it is fast and well suited to applications that require quick screen or disk manipulations. Second, the machine language code created by FORTH is generally much smaller than other languages (another factor in its speed advantage). And finally, FORTH is the language you make it. The fact that the programmer can extend the language at will is a strong asset; programs can be tailored to the task.

If you are interested in getting a clearer description of FORTH's virtues, see *Discover FORTH* (Hogan, Berkeley: Osborne/McGraw-Hill, 1982).

The most popular versions of FORTH for CP/M are Laboratory Microsystem's FORTH, Micromotion's FORTH-79, Software Toolwork's FORTH, and various versions of a public domain FORTH provided by the FORTH Interest Group, dubbed FIG-FORTH.

FORTRAN

FORTRAN is another acronym; it stands for FORmula TRANslator language. It was designed for complex numerical calculations where speed is the primary factor. FORTRAN is not good at manipulating characters like letters of the alphabet; it does not handle input/output devices efficiently; and it was not designed for interactive use (although interactive programs are possible).

In many ways FORTRAN is the parent of BASIC; many BASIC statements are FORTRAN descendants. Their primary differences lie in BASIC's efficient input and output to the console and its ability to manipulate strings. In FORTRAN the FORMAT statement, which is difficult to understand, must be used to prepare information for transfer to the console or other devices.

FORTRAN, like C and COBOL, is a true compiler. Programs are input with an editor and then reduced to machine instructions.

The most popular versions of FORTRAN for CP/M are Microsoft's FORTRAN-80, Supersoft's FORTRAN, and Nevada FORTRAN.

Pascal

Like C and COBOL, Pascal is a structured language; programs must follow a particular structural concept. Statements must be executed in a specified order, and blocks of program code are identified to make them easy to use elsewhere. The same block may even be used in several different Pascal programs. In contrast, BASIC, FORTRAN, and several other languages allow the programmer to jump program execution from one set of statements to another set in an entirely different area, subject only to the programmer's whim. The logical grouping of program statements into subroutines (sections of code that perform one function and then return control to the calling statement) is possible in BASIC, but not with the flexibility offered in Pascal.

Developed in Switzerland in 1968 by Nicklaus Wirth, Pascal is very similar to Algol. Here is a typical section of a Pascal program:

```
VAR HOUR, MINUTES, SECONDS: INTEGER;
BEGIN
      HOURS:=1;
      MINUTES:=1;
      SECONDS:=15;
      REPEAT
            WRITELN('TIME LEFT = ');
            WRITE(HOUR,':');
            WRITE(MINUTES,':');
            WRITE(SECONDS);
            WHILE SECONDS>=0 DO
                  SECONDS:=SECONDS-1;
            END;
            IF SECONDS=-1 THEN
                  SECONDS:=59;
                  MINUTES:=MINUTES-1;
                  IF MINUTES=-1 THEN
```

```
                        MINUTES:=59;
                        HOURS:=HOURS-1;
        UNTIL (HOURS=0) AND (MINUTES=0) AND (SECONDS=0);
        WRITELN('TIME UP!');
END.
```

Consider the Pascal program's appearance. First, it has a definite structure. The indentations are not required, but because they reflect the structure of the program, they are strongly suggested. Next, like COBOL, Pascal uses sentences whose meanings are immediately apparent. Unlike COBOL, however, Pascal has relatively few predefined statements, and the sentences formed tend to be shorter. In terms of length, Pascal programs are not quite so unwieldy as COBOL but they still remain readable.

Pascal also has an attribute known as *recursiveness.* (To varying degrees, so do Algol, PL/I-80, FORTH, and C.) This means a block within the program may call itself or pass execution back to itself. Long division, that terrible mathematical tool we all struggled with in our elementary education, employs a recursive function; you apply the same concept repeatedly until you get a zero or repeating pattern. Recursiveness is a useful feature for complex procedures that occur regularly within a program. Because of its recursive nature, Pascal is well suited to such tasks.

Programmers like to use Pascal because their conceptions of a program fit directly into the structural constraints of Pascal. In fact, many programmers use a pseudo-Pascal language to describe the flow of program execution.

```
WHILE RESULT NOT ZERO DO
     COMPUTE NEW VALUE
     IF NEW VALUE > OLD
          THEN PERFORM FUNCTION X
     ELSE
          PERFORM FUNCTION Y
     END WHILE
```

The portion of a Pascal program that expresses the same logic may look like this:

```
WHILE RESULT NOT 0 DO
     FIRSTNUM:=SECONDNUM-OFFSET;
     NEWVALUE; <------------------------ passes execution
     IF NEWRESULT > RESULT THEN
          X;
     ELSE
          Y; <--------------------------- x and y represent procedures
END {WHILE}.                              that are performed each time
                                          they are encountered
```

We have discussed the appearance of Pascal programs at length for a number of reasons. Pascal is frequently hailed as the language of the future because of its easily understood structure. Pascal is a good beginner's language because it is straightforward. If you do not try to write Pascal programs off the top of your head, you will easily be able to create working programs. Of course, learning to program any microcomputer requires dedicated effort and time, so seek expert instruction. (Many universities offer free or inexpensive courses in Pascal programming.)

The most popular versions of Pascal for CP/M are Sorcim's Pascal/M, Digital Research's Pascal/MT+, Ithaca Intersystem's Pascal/Z, and JRT's Pascal 3.0.

PL/I

With the introduction of PL/I-80 in mid-1980 by Digital Research, almost every major programming language became available to microcomputer users. PL/I-80 combines the structure of Pascal, the simplicity of Pascal and BASIC, and the ability to perform complex operations with various peripheral devices.

PL/I-80 and its cousin, Intel PL/M, are frequently described as *system development languages,* languages used by computer manufacturers and system integrators to create other software. EBASIC and a good portion of the original CP/M were written in PL/M, as were several other high-level languages.

Digital Research's PL/I compiler uses a subset, called Subset G, of the original language. PL/I programs execute fast and are generally relocatable.

Other Languages

RPG (Report Program Generator) was originally developed by IBM for nonprogrammers. It is less a language than a way of selecting and outputting data from a disk file. The only readily available RPG for microcomputers is marketed by Cromemco; it runs only with the CDOS operating system (see Chapter 12).

LISP (LISt Processing) is an interpretive language that developed out of artificial intelligence research at Stanford University. LISP's primary application is string processing, but it is not particularly well suited for numeric applications. Microsoft offers MuLISP-80 to CP/M users.

APL stands for A Programming Language. Its modest name does not properly reflect the immense power this language possesses. Rather than using words to express a given programming concept, APL uses graphic characters to represent certain commands. The following APL program, which calculates the average of a list of numbers, demonstrates APL's conciseness:

```
average
"Enter the numbers you want averaged"
NUM ← ⎕
SUM ← +/NUM
ANS ← SUM ÷ NUM
"The average of your numbers is ";ANS
```

Note the use of symbols to represent a concept. The third statement specifies a number of computer operations. The number you type is moved to the variable NUM as each number is typed; there is no need to represent each operation with a statement or to repeat a statement's execution within a loop.

EDITORS AND WORD PROCESSORS

One of the most useful application programs you can purchase is a word processor or text editor. The Digital Research editor (ED, described in Chapter 5) provides basic editing functions. You may need to use this editor with CP/M for several reasons:

- To create and edit programs
- To create and edit data files
- To perform emergency maintenance on text files
- To create and edit documents (letters, articles, documentation, and so on)
- To format documents and print them.

Some questions immediately come to mind. The first may be "Why do I need to do all that? I thought the programs I got with CP/M would take care of everything I need." However, that is not really the case. Without an editor, your computer primarily creates and stores information. A typewriter does the same thing, using paper as a storage medium. But just as you would not attempt serious typing without some method of correcting your mistakes, serious computing also requires a way to correct the information you put on disk. A good editor performs this function for you.

Besides ED, Digital Research sells a companion text-formatting program called TEX. ED and TEX do not reflect state-of-the-art editing software, however. Today a number of extremely sophisticated word-processing programs and text editors exist that you should investigate.

The difference between a text editor and a word processor is simple: a text editor allows you to create and modify textual information, but not to change its format on paper; a word processor adds to a text editor the ability to manipulate the appearance of text on paper.

Text editors are normally used for the following purposes:

- To create and edit program source code
- To create and edit data files
- To create and edit SUBMIT files.

Word processors are normally used for creating and editing paper documents. Some word processors, such as the popular WordStar program, display how a document will look before you print it on paper. Thus you can easily correct and modify the document without having to retype it.

Some of the more popular text editors available for CP/M are

Editor	Source
ED	Digital Research
EDIT	Microsoft
VEDIT	Compu View
PMATE	Lifeboat

The most popular word processors for CP/M include

Program	Source
WordStar	MicroPro International
Superwriter	Sorcim
Peachtext (formerly Magic Wand)	Peachtree
Perfect Writer	Perfect Software

This book was written on WordStar. Three features dictated its choice: the capacity to see the text formatted on the screen exactly as it would print out, the capacity to make numerous revisions, and the fact that the publisher could typeset directly from the author's disks.

NUMBER PROCESSORS

Like word processors, number-processing software is extremely popular with CP/M users. Number processing is simply a program that allows you to make instantaneous changes to columns or rows of numbers, with the program automatically updating the results of any formulas or relationships the user has indicated.

The first number-processing program available for microcomputers was VisiCalc, which was originally written for the Apple computer. VisiCalc divided the computer display into rows and columns and allowed the user to place words, numbers, or formulas at any row/column intersection. Changing one number or formula resulted in instantaneous changes to all other row/column intersections that referred to that number or formula.

Number-processing software like SuperCalc is especially useful to managers or businesspeople who perform "spreadsheet" analysis of information. The ability to change an assumption within a particular spreadsheet led to the labeling of number-processing software as "what if?" software.

The most popular number-processing programs for CP/M are

Program	Source
SuperCalc	Sorcim
CalcStar	MicroPro International
Multiplan	Microsoft
Peachcalc	Peachtree
Perfect Calc	Perfect Software

DATABASE PROGRAMS

Data-processing programs, or, as they are sometimes called, database programs, are another type of application program. Database programs are much like file cabinets: with a database program you store information in an organized manner that facilitates retrieval. The data to be stored may be numeric or textual and, in general, can be stored in a format of the user's choosing.

A simple database might store a number of names and addresses. In such a file you would have the following pieces of information:

Name
Street address
City
State
ZIP code

In addition, you might want to include

Title
Company name
Telephone number
Comments

A good database program allows you to retrieve information from a name and address database in any number of ways:

- By ZIP code, state, or city
- By name, title, or company
- By phone number
- In alphabetical order
- By order in which items were entered
- By date on which items were entered.

Most database programs also have ways of creating reports from the information contained in the database. Using our example, the following reports can be created:

- Alphabetical name listing
- Alphabetical company listing
- Phone list, by area code
- Mailing list, by ZIP code
- List of all entries that match a particular position title, city, or state.

Some database programs go even farther, allowing you to link two or more databases together, so that you can relate a name and address entry with, say, an accounts receivable entry. Another feature that is sometimes found in database programs is the ability to perform simple arithmetic on certain pieces of information. For example, if you were keeping an inventory using a database program, you might be able to obtain an inventory report complete with subtotals and a total evaluation of your inventory (calculated from individual entries).

The most popular database programs for CP/M include

Program	Source
dBASE II	Ashton-Tate
InfoStar	MicroPro International
Condor	Condor
Personal Pearl	Pearlsoft

SUMMARY

This chapter expanded your understanding of utilities and introduced you to languages and application programs. In one sense this chapter is one of the most important in this book, since most of your use of CP/M will center around these programs.

We suggest that you consult other sources to learn more about the individual types of programs that were presented in this chapter. Osborne/McGraw-Hill, for example, publishes *Armchair BASIC* (Fox and Fox); *WordStar Made Easy,* Second Edition (Ettlin); *Data Base Management Systems* (Kruglinski); and *The SuperCalc Program Made Easy* (Wood). Other publishers provide similar guides. Your local bookstore can provide you with books on word processing, number processing, data processing, and program languages.

CHAPTER

8 CP/M-80 Assembly Language Utilities

Despite CP/M's simplicity, the programming novice will discover much to learn about it, certainly more than most users require. The information in this chapter has limited application for users who primarily use packaged programs. If you are not developing or modifying programs in assembly language, skip this and the next three chapters and proceed with Chapter 12. (Users of CP/M-PLUS will want to ignore this chapter and proceed to the next, which deals with MAC, RMAC, SID, HEX-COM, LINK, LIB, and XREF, the CP/M-PLUS assembly language tools.) The CP/M-80 user seriously interested in assembly language programming under CP/M may want to explore the tools presented in the next chapter, since most of them are available for sale to CP/M-80 users.

This chapter covers the CP/M-80 assembly language programming aids ASM, DDT, and LOAD. ASM is an assembler. It converts a source code program written in assembly language into an object program in hex format. This product is an intermediate step to a true machine language program that the computer can use. DDT is a debugging program used to locate and correct errors in machine language programs. LOAD performs the final conversion step by creating a machine language program file from the hex format file. (The DUMP program, another useful assembly language programming aid, displays the contents of a file as hexadecimal numbers; see chapter 5.)

Note: This chapter deals only with CP/M-80 assembler utilities. When we refer to CP/M in this chapter, we are referring *only* to CP/M-80 and *not* to CP/M-PLUS.

WHAT ASSEMBLY LANGUAGE IS

Assembly language is two steps removed from the action in the computer. Remember, the computer uses 1's and 0's as the basic elements of data. These bits can be either data or instructions to the computer, depending on the context in which the CPU receives them.

It is inconvenient to think in terms of numbers like 10001010 and 10010010, so we use hexadecimal notation to refer to eight bits at a time. We call these 8-bit groups *bytes* of information. Some hexadecimal representations of bytes are 0C3, 45, and 0D. Remember that the computer itself always uses binary notation (1's and 0's), but we use the hexadecimal representation to help us recognize the patterns.

Since the hexadecimal representations are also awkward, we assign names to the machine instructions and data they represent. The names are the components of the computer language known as *assembly language.* We call the names that represent instructions *mnemonics.* A mnemonic is the assembly language representation of one CPU machine instruction. Other names are used to represent other elements of a program; these names are all described in the sections on ASM in this chapter and MAC/RMAC in the next.

Generally, any machine language program for the 8080 CPU will run correctly on an 8085 CPU or a Z80 CPU. Since CP/M-80 and CP/M-PLUS were written for the 8080, they also run on the 8085 and Z80. This book uses only the 8080 instruction mnemonics designated by Intel when referring to CP/M assembly language, as they represent the assembly language instructions available to all users of CP/M.

The assembly language mnemonics for the 8085 CPU are nearly identical to those of the 8080. Those of the Z80 CPU are completely different, however, even though the same machine language instructions are often intended. CP/M-PLUS users can use an extension of their assembler (MAC, covered in the next chapter) to generate Z80 instructions. ASM and DDT understand only 8080 mnemonics, assembly language, and machine language.

This chapter assumes you understand assembly language programming. If you do not but want to learn, see the bibliography in Appendix G for an appropriate book on the subject.

ASM

Assemble a Program

The CP/M assembler, ASM, converts an assembly language source program into object code that is executable by the computer. ASM generates 8080 object code. The ASM assembler also provides a listing showing each line from the source program together with the corresponding object code it creates, if desired.

Assembly language source code is generated by typing it into a disk file with an editor. CP/M's ED or a more sophisticated editor such as WordStar, PMATE, or VEDIT may be used.

ASM Command Line

Once you have obtained or created the source file, you invoke ASM as follows:

```
A>ASM filename.opt<cr>
```

The file name must be a valid CP/M file with the ASM file type for CP/M. The "opt" in the CP/M command line refers to a series of three options you may specify, not to an OPT file type. The three letters following the period represent

- The drive that contains the source (original) file (FILENAME.ASM).
- The drive that should receive the hex (assembled program) file (FILENAME .HEX).
- The drive that should receive the print (listing of the program, with error messages) file (FILENAME.PRN).

You can use the standard CP/M drive specifiers A through P as option letters, subject to the existence of those drives on your computer. Also, the option letters X and Z have special meanings; they do not mean drives X and Z:

X
: Used as the PRN file option to display the listing on the console instead of storing it in a file.

Z
: Used for either the HEX or PRN file option to skip generation of that file.

If you type

```
A>ASM BSM.AAZ<cr>
```

you are telling the assembler to assemble a file named BSM.ASM, found on drive A, into a hex (object program) file named BSM.HEX, also on drive A, and to skip generation of the print file. The assembled program file always has the HEX file type; the print file always has the PRN file type. If all files are to be placed on the currently logged drive, you need not specify anything after the file name, that is, no options or period. After assembling the program BSM.ASM in such an assembly, you have the following files:

BSM.ASM	Original (source) file
BSM.HEX	Assembled program file
BSM.PRN	Listing file.

Files Used by ASM

What are the ASM, HEX, and PRN files, and what do they do? The ASM file contains the assembly language source program and is created by you with ED or another text editor. The HEX file is used to create an executable program. Created by the assembler, it contains the hexadecimal representations of the instructions in the ASM file. The format for the HEX file in CP/M is known as *Intel Hex Format*. Intel first used the format for storing the hexadecimal characters on paper tape devices, and the disk format is equivalent. Here is an example of a short HEX file:

```
:020100003E00BF
:0000000000
```

Not particularly enlightening, is it? Here is the 8080 assembly language program that created that information:

```
ORG   0100h        ;program starts at address 0100 hex
MVI   A,0          ;move a 00 hex into Register A
END                ;end of program
```

The PRN file is useful in the process of debugging a program (ridding it of errors). The listing in the PRN file is also an important part of the program documentation. PRN combines both the program we originally typed and what the assembler created:

```
0100            ORG   0100h        ;program starts at address 0100 hex
0100  3E 00     MVI   A,0          ;move a 00 hex into Register A
0102            END                ;end of program
```

This type of listing is particularly helpful when you use many labels and symbols.

SOURCE PROGRAM FORMAT

The assembler expects the source file to be in a very specific form. The source file is a sequence of ASCII-coded (text) statements or lines. Each line ends with a CARRIAGE RETURN and LINE FEED.

Assembly Language Statements

Each assembly language statement is composed of between one and five fields. A *field* is a group of characters, and the fields are separated from one another by spaces or tab characters. Tab characters create a more readable source program because the fields are aligned at the tab stops. Tab stops are set at every eight columns, 1, 9, 17, 25, 33, and so on. The general format of the assembly language statement is

line#   label   mnemonic   operand(s)   ;comment

Line Numbers (line #)

The line number is an integer decimal number at the beginning of an 8080 source code line. Some editors insert these line numbers automatically but ED does not. ASM ignores the line number.

Labels

A label is an identifier used to represent an address or value. For ASM it may be from 1 to 16 characters long. The first character must be a letter; the others can be letters or numbers. Lowercase letters are treated as if they were uppercase. A colon may follow a label when it is used in the label field for ASM. ASM ignores the $ character. The label is optional for all statements except those using it in the operand field, such as the EQU and SET directives. Generally, a particular label should appear in the label field of only one statement, but it can appear in the operand field of many statements.

There are certain reserved words that must not be used in the label field because they have predetermined meanings to ASM. The reserved words are

- All the 8080 instruction mnemonics: ADD, ADI, ADC, ACI, ANA, ANI, CALL, CZ, CNZ, CP, CM, CC, CNC, CPE, CPO, CMA, CMC, CMP, CPI, DAA, DAD, DCR, DCX, DI, EI, HLT, IN, INR, INX, JMP, JZ, JNZ, JP, JM, JC, JNC, JPE, JPO, LDA, LDAX, LHLD, LXI, MOV, MVI, NOP, ORA, ORI, OUT, PCHL, POP, PUSH, RAL, RAR, RLC, RRC, RET, RZ, RNZ, RP, RM, RC, RNC, RPE, RPO, RST, SPHL, SHLD, STA, STAX, STC, SUB, SUI, SBB, SBI, XCHG, XTHL, XRA, XRI.
- All the ASM directive names: AND, DB, DW, DS, END, ENDIF, EQU, IF, MOD, NOT, OR, ORG, SHL, SHR, XOR.
- All the 8080 register names: A, B, C, D, E, H, L, M, PC, SP.

Mnemonics

The mnemonic field is the only field that is not optional; it must be included in every statement. This field contains an 8080 instruction mnemonic or the name of an assembler directive. Most of the assembly language programming books listed in Appendix G contain a list of the 8080 instruction mnemonics. Since mnemonics are the heart of assembly language, it is wise to familiarize yourself with the entire set before attempting to write assembly language code.

Operands

Many assembly language instructions require one or more operands, and some require none at all. Assembler directives generally require one or more operands. An operand can be a constant, a label, or an expression. Labels were explained above; constants and expressions, and the rules for forming them, are described in the following sections.

Constants

A numeric constant is a fixed number in one of four number bases. The four number bases are binary, octal, decimal, and hexadecimal.

A binary constant is a sequence of the digits 0 and 1 followed by the letter B to signify that the number is binary.

An octal constant is a sequence of the digits 0 through 7 followed by the letter Q or O to signify that the number is octal.

A decimal constant is a sequence of the digits 0 through 9 optionally followed by the letter D to signify that the number is decimal. If no letter suffix follows the constant, ASM assumes it is a decimal number.

A hexadecimal constant is a sequence of the digits 0 through 9 and letters A through F followed by the letter H to signify that the number is hexadecimal. A hexadecimal constant must begin with a number; this requirement can be satisfied by always preceding these constants with the digit 0.

You can insert the dollar sign within a numeric constant to be used with ASM to make it easier to read. ASM ignores such dollar signs. The following three constants are equal:

11010101B = 1101$0101B = 11$010$101B

A string constant is a sequence of characters that is enclosed between apostrophes ('). A string constant is limited to 64 characters for ASM. Only printable characters are allowed within such strings. Lowercase letters are not converted to uppercase. You can include an apostrophe within a string by typing two apostrophes in a row. ASM computes the value of a string by adding a high-order bit of 0 to the seven-bit ASCII code for each character.

Expressions

You can use expressions in place of operands for many instructions. An expression is a combination of constants, labels, arithmetic operators, logical operators, and parentheses. During assembly, each expression is evaluated and reduced to a single value.

Arithmetic Operators

The assembler can perform simple arithmetic when it evaluates an expression to determine its value. You can use the following arithmetic operators to join labels and constants in expressions:

Operation	Effect
A+B	B added to A.
A−B	B subtracted from A.
+B	Same as B.
−B	B subtracted from zero.
A*B	A multiplied by B (unsigned).
A/B	Quotient of A divided by B (unsigned).
A MOD B	Remainder of A divided by B.
A SHL B	A shifted left B-bit positions; shifted-out high-order bits are discarded; and vacated low-order bits are replaced with zeroes.
A SHR B	A shifted right B-bit positions; shifted-out low-order bits are discarded; and vacated high-order bits are replaced with zeroes.

The assembler performs the operation on 16-bit unsigned values and produces 16-bit unsigned results, modulo 2 to the sixteenth power.

Logical Operators

The assembler can perform Boolean (logical) operations as well as arithmetic operations. The chart shows the operators that can be used.

Operator	Function
NOT B	Complement of B
A AND B	Logical AND of A and B
A OR B	Logical OR of A and B
A XOR B	Logical EXCLUSIVE OR of A and B

Logical operations are performed bit by bit on 16-bit unsigned values and result in a 16-bit unsigned value.

Other Operators

Another frequently used operator is the dollar sign, which, when used as the operand, creates a value equal to the current value of the location counter.

Precedence of Operators

When the assembler evaluates an expression containing several operators, it does not simply proceed from left to right, applying each operator in sequence. Instead it applies certain operators before others. This hierarchy is called the *precedence of the operators*. Operators shown on the first line are always used first if they exist in an expression. Those on the last line are always used last. Within a line the operators have equal precedence and are used from left to right as they are encountered in an expression. The precedence (from highest to lowest) is as follows:

Order of Operation

$

The operation in the innermost parentheses

* / MOD SHL SHR

− +

NOT

AND

OR XOR

You use sets of parentheses in an expression to override this hierarchy or to make the expression easier to read.

Comments

The comment field begins with a semicolon. The field is optional and is ignored by the assembler. However, you should always include comments because they are essential program documentation.

ASSEMBLER DIRECTIVES

You can include a number of "special" instructions to the assembler that are not part of the 8080 assembly language set. These assembler directives control the assembly process and affect the resulting machine code. You place assembler directive statements in the source program in roughly the same form as assembly language statements. The directive name goes in the mnemonic field of the statement.

DB, DW, and DS Assembler Directives

Use the directives DB, DW, and DS to initialize storage areas in memory.

Directive	Function
DB	Define Byte—initializes an area byte by byte.
DW	Define Word—initializes an area two bytes at a time.
DS	Define Storage—reserves an area of a specified size.

Operand expressions in the DB statements are evaluated and stored as 8-bit values in successive memory locations. Expressions in the DW statement are evaluated and stored as 16-bit values in successive pairs of memory locations; within a pair, the low-order byte is stored first, followed by the high-order byte. The expression in the DS directive is evaluated, and then the number of memory locations given by the resulting 16-bit value is reserved. These reserved locations are not filled.

A label is optional in these storage directives. If one is used, ASM assigns the label the value of the address of the first byte defined or reserved by the directive. Any number of expressions, each separated by commas, can be used with the DB and DW storage directives. Only one expression can be used with the DS directive.

ORG, END, EQU, and SET Assembler Directives

The following location directives are available with ASM:

ORG

This directive gives the assembler the memory address to use for the sequence of statements that follow it. The form of the ORG statement is

label ORG expression ;comment

The value of the expression is used by the assembler as the memory address of the next program instruction or define directive; this address is fixed for 8080 code. Comments are optional. You can use more than one ORG in a program.

END

The END directive tells the assembler that it has reached the end of the source statements. The form of the directive is

label END expression ;comment

The END directive is optional; if present it should be the last statement in the source program.

The optional label is assigned the value of the assembler's location counter at that point in the program. The optional expression is evaluated and used as the program starting address in the Intel Hex Format file. If the expression is omitted, a starting address of 0000 is used. The comment field is optional.

EQU

The EQU (equate) directive assigns values or expressions to a label. The format is

label EQU expression ;comments

The expression may be any valid number, address, constant, or expression. The label and expression are required in an equate statement. You may use other labels (if previously defined) within the expression.

SET

A variant of the EQU directive. Unlike EQU, SET allows you to reassign the value to a label. The format of the SET directive is the same as for EQU.

IF and ENDIF Assembler Directives

These directives define a section of assembly language code that will be assembled only if the condition listed in the IF statement is true. The form of these directives is

```
label*    IF        expression ;comment*
                        .
                        .
                    subsequent statements
                        .
                        .
label*    ENDIF                ;comment*
```

The assembler evaluates the expression in the IF statement. If the value of the expression is zero, the assembler ignores the statements between the IF and ENDIF. If the value of the expression is not zero, the statements are assembled.

Using IF statements is called *conditional assembly;* the assembly takes place only if certain conditions are met.

The IF statement may be used in assembly language programming in a number of ways. Here is one of the most frequent:

```
HAVE$TERMINAL   EQU   OFFFFh              ;value = true
NO$TERMINAL     EQU   NOT HAVE$TERMINAL   ;value = false
;
                IF    HAVE$TERMINAL
                      . <---------------- assembly language statements
                      .                   to be used when there is a
                      .                   terminal
                ENDIF
                IF    NO$TERMINAL
                      . <---------------- assembly language statements
                      .                   to be used if there is a
                      .                   no terminal
                ENDIF
```

In the example shown, you can change the program to reflect the presence of a terminal by changing only the HAVE$TERMINAL equate. Note that HAVE$-TERMINAL (a label) is assigned a value that is all 1's; NO$TERMINAL (another

---

*Labels and comments are optional

label) is assigned the complement value of HAVE$TERMINAL. The operator NOT changes each 1 to a 0.

ASSEMBLER PROGRESS MESSAGES

The assembler displays messages when it starts and when it finishes. After you enter the ASM command line, you see a message like

CP/M ASSEMBLER — VER 2.0

This may be followed by error messages if there were any errors.

When ASM has finished its job, it displays a three-line message:

xxxx
yyyH USE FACTOR
END OF ASSEMBLY

In this message, xxxx is the hexadecimal address of the first free (unused) location following the assembly language program. yyyH is a rather perplexing indication of the portion of the symbol table area that has been used; the assembler has a finite amount of room in which to store the values of labels. yyy is a hexadecimal number between 000 and 0FF. This number divided by 0FF hex is the fraction of the symbol table used. If yyy is 080, for example, then about half (80/0FF hex = 128/255 decimal) of the symbol table has been used. The END OF ASSEMBLY message means that ASM is finished; it does not necessarily mean that the assembly language program was created successfully.

ASSEMBLER ERROR MESSAGES

The assembler displays two kinds of error messages. The first kind is terminal error messages indicating that conditions prevented the assembler from completing its job. Problems with disks or files typically cause terminal error messages. The second kind of error message arises when ASM cannot properly assemble a source code statement but can continue the assembly despite the error.

Terminal Error Messages

NO SOURCE FILE PRESENT or NO FILE
The assembler could not find the ASM-type file with the source code.

NO DIRECTORY SPACE or DIRECTORY FULL
CP/M has no more room to keep track of file names; erase a few files from your disk.

SOURCE FILE NAME ERROR
You cannot use * and ? in a file name to be assembled.

SOURCE FILE READ ERROR or DISK READ ERROR
The file containing your source file could not be understood or is damaged.

OUTPUT FILE WRITE ERROR or CANNOT CLOSE or CANNOT CLOSE FILES
Check for a write-protected disk or a disk-full condition.

SYMBOL TABLE OVERFLOW
Your program has too many labels and symbols for the assembler to keep track of.

PARAMETER ERROR
The options following the file name in the command line are incorrect.

Source Program Error Messages

If no messages appear during program assembly, the assembler is proceeding and has encountered nothing. This is much different from saying the program is correct! If ASM encounters something it does not understand, it displays a line in the following format:

```
a bbbb cccc     label     mnemonic     operand     ;comment
```

The a is a letter representing the type of error. The bbbb is the hexadecimal address of the statement at which the error was encountered, and the cccc is the hexadecimal representation of the machine language created by the assembler. When an error occurs, some or all of the machine code is set to zeroes because the assembler did not know what to put there.

ASM displays the following error codes:

D (Data Error)
The value of the expression does not fit into the data area you indicated; it may be too long.

E (Expression Error)
You formed the expression improperly, or its value cannot be computed at assembly time because it is too complex.

L (Label Error)
You used the label incorrectly. This error normally occurs when you use the same label in the label field of more than one statement in a program.

N (Feature Not Implemented)
Digital Research's assemblers MAC and RMAC (described in Chapter 9) accept directives that ASM cannot handle. When ASM encounters something that only MAC or RMAC can recognize, the N error message is given.

O (Overflow Error)
Your expression is so complicated that the assembler cannot handle it in its present form. Separate the expression into smaller pieces or simplify it by reducing the number of operators.

P (Phase Error)
The label changes value during assembly. If you must reassign a value, use the SET directive. A duplicate label can also produce this message.

R (Register Error)
You specified a register that is not compatible with the mnemonic given. For instance, POP B is a valid assembly language statement, but POP A is not. POP A would trigger the R error message.

S (Syntax Error)
This is a catchall error that can result from using an invalid mnemonic or having a typographical error in the source file.

U (Undefined Symbol)
You used a label in an expression without assigning a value to it. For example,

```
U 0102 06 00          MVI          B,ONE
```

appears if ONE is not defined in the program.

V (Value Error)
The operand (expression) encountered is not correct. This usually occurs when you forget to type a comma or certain letter the assembler is expecting.

DDT

Debug a Program

The Dynamic Debugging Tool (DDT) is used to test and debug machine language programs. (CP/M-PLUS comes with SID, the Symbolic Instruction Debugger, described in Chapter 9.) You use DDT to

- Load an assembled program into memory.
- Make simple changes to a machine language program.
- Help locate errors in machine language programs.
- Correct or update your software.
- Install special driver routines (programs that drive a peripheral, like a printer).
- Change disk parameters with CP/M-80 version 2.2.
- Examine and modify the contents of memory.
- Enter assembly language code one line at a time.
- Disassemble a section of a program (turn machine language back into assembly language instructions).
- Examine and modify the contents of the internal registers of the CPU.
- Set breakpoints — locations at which to stop the program and check what has happened so far.
- Trace the execution of a program; follow what is happening to memory and the internal registers of the CPU.

Invoking DDT

DDT is invoked by using one of these two command forms:

DDT
: Loads the Dynamic Debugging Tool program into the memory of your computer, where it waits for further instructions.

DDT d:filename.typ
: Loads DDT and also the designated file into memory for examination, modification, or extension. The file type must be COM or HEX. DDT then waits for further instructions.

When DDT is resident in your computer's memory, it displays a hyphen as its prompt. The hyphen indicates that DDT is waiting for a command.

DDT Commands

Once DDT has been loaded into memory (with the optional file name, if specified, being placed into memory as well), DDT is ready to accept commands. A summary of the available commands is shown in Table 8-1.

Most of these commands require additional information in order to be used. Often this information is a memory address or a hexadecimal value. Valid addresses are in the range 0000-FFFF hexadecimal.

As

The Assemble command enters assembly language instructions beginning at address s. There should be no space between the A and the address you specify. After you press CARRIAGE RETURN, DDT displays the memory address and waits for you to type a valid 8080 mnemonic or operand. The mnemonic and operand should be separated by one space, and each instruction is terminated by a CARRIAGE RETURN. After each instruction is entered, the next available address is displayed, and you may continue entering assembly language instructions in the fashion just described. To end the entry of assembly language instructions, simply type a period followed by a CARRIAGE RETURN instead of a valid instruction. Entry can also be terminated by merely pressing the CARRIAGE RETURN key as the first character on a new line.

If DDT does not understand your instruction, it presents a question mark and repeats the memory address to be filled.

An example using the A command:

```
-A0100<cr>
0100 MOV A,C<cr>
0101 .<cr>
-
```

TABLE 8-1. DDT Commands and Functions

Function	Letter Typed
Assemble instruction	A
Display memory	D
Fill memory	F
Execute program	G
Hexadecimal arithmetic	H
Set up FCB	I
List instructions	L
Move memory	M
Read disk file	R
Set memory to value	S
Trace program	T
Execute partially	U
Examine/modify registers	X

D
Ds
Ds,f

The Display command displays the contents of memory in hex and ASCII. As many as 16 locations appear on each line. D followed by a CARRIAGE RETURN (on most systems) causes the next 12 lines from the last address to be displayed. Some systems, notably those with screens less than 80 characters wide, may display fewer characters, but otherwise the command does not function differently. A period is used to substitute for any non-displayable character in the ASCII display portion.

```
-D<cr>
0100  3A 07 00 FE C8 DA AC 03 21 00 00 39 22 25 07 31 :.......!..9"%.1
0110  00 C8 3E 11 D3 FD 21 27 07 7D D3 FD 7C D3 FD CD ..>...!'.}..|...
0120  3B 02 11 13 04 CD 28 02 CD 3B 02 11 55 04 CD 28 ;.....(..;..U..(
0130  02 1E 07 0E 02 CD 05 00 0E 01 CD 05 00 FE 1B CA ................
0140  A1 03 FE 0D C2 28 01 11 91 04 CD 28 02 3E 4D 32 .....(.....(.>M2
0150  2A 07 21 1D 07 36 0B 7E D6 0D D3 FF 3E 07 32 1E *.!..6. ....>.2.
0160  07 21 2A 07 35 3E 01 32 2B 07 11 AE F9 CD AB 02 .!*.5>.2+.......
0170  3E 04 32 20 07 CD 65 02 21 27 07 36 21 CD 2E 02 >.2 ..e.!'.6!...
0180  FA D6 02 CD C5 02 C2 6A 01 21 1E 07 35 C2 61 01 ........j.!..5.a
0190  3E 02 32 24 07 CD 65 02 3A 2A 07 C6 07 32 2A 07 >.2$..e.:*...2*.
01A0  36 07 21 2A 07 35 3E 02 32 21 07 CD 65 02 21 27 6.!*.5..2!..e.!'
01B0  07 36 32 CD 2E 02 FA E9 02 3E 01 32 2B 07 11 AE .62......>.2+...
-
```

Each successive display memory command displays the next 192 bytes of memory. The starting address for the first use of D depends upon the file, if any, loaded with DDT. Common starting values are 0100 hex and 0000 hex.

D used with a starting address, s, allows you to specify the starting address. If you start a display command with an address that is not a multiple of 16 (does not end with a zero), the first line of the display will not have 16 locations represented. If we typed D501, the first line of our displayed memory would show only 15 bytes, for example. Any subsequent letter D typed without an address will resume execution where the previous display left off.

```
-D501<cr>
0501   52 4F 52 20 20 20 44 52 3E 42 24 52 45 41 44     ROR   DR=B$READ
0510   20 45 52 52 4F 52 20 20 20 20 44 52 3D 42 24 56  ERROR      DR=B$V
0520   45 52 49 46 59 20 45 52 52 4F 52 20 20 42 4C 4F ERIFY ERROR  BLO
0530   43 4B 3D 2D 2D 24 20 20 54 52 4B 3D 2D 2D 20 20 CK=--$  TRK=--
0540   53 43 54 52 3D 2D 2D 24 20 20 53 54 53 57 44 3D SCTR=--$  STSWD=
0550   2D 2D 2D 2D 2D 2D 2D 2D 20 20 24 AE 05 C1 05 D5 --------  $.....
0560   05 E5 05 F5 05 08 06 1A 06 9B 05 2F 06 3F 06 58 .........../.?.X
0570   06 9B 05 9B 05 9B 05 9B 05 9B 05 71 06 83 06 95 ...........q....
0580   06 A7 06 BE 06 D4 06 EB 06 FF 06 9B 05 9B 05 9B ................
0590   05 9B 05 9B 05 9B 05 9B 05 9B 05 4E 4F 20 45 52 ...........NO ER
05A0   52 4F 52 20 4D 53 47 20 46 4F 55 4E 44 24 44 52 ROR MSG FOUND$DR
05B0   49 56 45 20 4E 4F 54 20 4F 50 45 52 41 42 4C 45 IVE NOT OPERABLE
-
```

The third form of this command allows you to specify both a beginning and ending address. If either of these addresses does not end with a zero, your display will not have exactly 16 bytes in the beginning or ending lines. Any subsequent letter D typed without an address will resume execution where the previous display left off.

Fs,f,b

The Fill command fills memory from the starting address, s, through the finishing address, f, with the single constant byte value, b. A common use of this instruction is to put the null character (00 hex) into a section of memory before doing any new work in that area. The following command places the value A0 hex in every memory location from 0100 hex to 01F0 hex inclusive:

```
-F0100,01F0,A0<cr>
-
```

You can use the fill memory command as a crude test to isolate blatant memory errors. Try filling memory with 00, 55, AA, and FF with successive commands. After each command, use the display memory command to make sure that memory actually received the characters you sent it. If you fill memory with 55 hex and see a byte with 54 in it, you most likely have a memory problem—take your machine to your vendor for repairs. **Note:** Be careful not to fill memory locations used by CP/M or DDT (generally the first 256 memory locations and the last 6K-10K memory locations).

G Gs,b1,b2
Gs G,b1
Gs,b1 G,b1,b2

The Go command begins execution at the starting address, s, with one or two optional breakpoint addresses, b1 and b2. If a starting address is not specified, then DDT begins executing the instructions in memory from the current address in the CPU's program counter.

You seldom use the G command when debugging a program without specifying at least one breakpoint address as the ending point. Without a breakpoint address you have no control over execution from that point on unless you have placed the correct RST (restart) instruction for DDT somewhere in the executed code.

Ha,b

The Hexadecimal math command computes and displays the sum of and difference between the two hexadecimal numbers you specify. The numbers are first converted to 16-bit values (if you type less than four hexadecimal digits) before the calculations are made. The first number shown will be the sum, the second the difference between the two numbers.

Ifilename

The Input command prepares a file control block and buffer for use with the R command. The first file name following the I command is placed into the default file control block (normally at 005C hex). If more than one file name is specified (each separated by a space), the second one is placed in the second portion of the file control block (normally 006C hex). The length of the command following the I is placed at 0080 hex; the command and then a terminating binary zero character come next.

The I command always sets up the file control block for accessing by using the currently logged disk drive. You cannot include a drive specifier such as B: with the I command; an error message is issued if you do. You could, however, modify the file control block by using the S command to change the byte at memory location 005C from 00 to the value that corresponds to the desired drive. Thus, drive A will be 01, drive B will be 02, and so on through drive P.

Because the I command also fills in the command buffer at 0080 hex exactly as if the user had done it, the I command can be used to simulate what would happen if a user had typed in a command at the CP/M prompt level and to trace execution of the program with DDT.

L
Ls
Ls,f

The List command lists the next 11 lines of disassembled machine code from the current address if a starting address, s, is not specified. If a finishing address, f, is specified, the listing will be from the starting address to the finishing address, as follows:

```
-L<cr>
0151 MOV D,A
0152 MVI E,00
0154 PUSH D
0155 LXI H,0200
0158 MOV A,B
0159 ORA C
015A JZ 0165
015D DCX B
015E MOV A,M
015F STAX D
0160 INX D
-
```

When DDT does not know how to display a hexadecimal value encountered in 8080 assembly language, the message ??=## is displayed; ## is the hexadecimal byte found by DDT.

Each successive use of L disassembles the next 11 instructions if a starting address is not given. Operands that are numeric values are always displayed as hexadecimal numbers; labels and symbols are not displayed. (Digital Research's SID [Symbolic Debugger] displays labels if they are known; see Chapter 9.)

Ms,f,d

The Move command moves a block of memory from the starting address, s, through the finishing address, f, to the memory block starting at the destination address, d. If d lies between s and f, then part of the block is overwritten before it is moved.

The move command does not relocate a program; a program usually contains references to other locations within the program. The move command does a *literal move;* each byte in the original block is moved exactly as is to the new location. If a program is moved away from its normal location, it most likely will not work at its new location.

If a question mark appears after you type the M command, at least one of the numbers you specified is not a valid hexadecimal address. Also, if the last memory location to be moved is a lower address than the starting memory location, nothing is moved by DDT.

R
Ro

The Read command, which must be preceded by the I command, reads a file from disk into memory with an optional offset address, o. If the offset, or *bias,* as Digital Research refers to it, is omitted, an offset of zero is assumed. The offset is added to the normal load location, and the file is loaded at the resulting address.

Any address that would exceed FFFF hex wraps around to 0000 hex. Thus a file that would load at 8000 hex with an offset of zero would load at 0100 with an offset of 8100 (R8100<cr>).

You should not load a file that will load into any part of memory used by CP/M. The forbidden areas are 0000 to 0100 hex and the CP/M area below FFFF hex. The address of the start of this area can be found by entering the command L5,7<cr>; the address shown after the JMP mnemonic is the lowest address used by CP/M and DDT.

If you enter a file type of COM with the I command, then loading begins at 0100 plus the offset. If you enter any other file type, including HEX, the R command assumes the file will be in Intel hex format and it will add the offset to the addresses contained in the hex format file to determine load addresses.

Ss

The Set command displays memory contents, starting at s, with the option to change the contents.

As you can see from the following example, DDT displays a memory location and the current contents of that location, and then waits for you to enter a byte (or word) value. You can simply press CARRIAGE RETURN to leave the setting as is.

```
-S0100<cr>
0100 C3 3D<cr> <------------- C3 becomes 3D
0101 28 4F<cr> <------------- 28 becomes 41
0102 38 <cr> <--------------- Leave as is
0103 C3 .<cr> <-------------- Terminate input
-
```

A question mark appears if DDT cannot understand your input (for example, if you type an invalid hexadecimal digit or address).

T
Tn

The Trace command traces the program execution for n instructions or for one step if n is not specified. Trace displays the CPU registers as they exist immediately prior to the next program instruction's execution. Pressing any key terminates tracing and returns control to DDT.

A program being traced runs about 500 times slower than normal because DDT instructions simulate each program instruction. The trace command enables interrupts. This can be a major problem if your program requires that interrupts be disabled.

The trace display looks like this:

```
C0Z0M0E0I0 A=00 B=0FB6 D=0000 H=0000 S=0100 P=013D LXI SP,0200
```

where C0 means the carry flag is set at zero
Z0 means the zero flag is set at zero
M0 means the minus flag value is zero
E0 means the even-parity flag is zero
I0 means the intermediate carry flag is zero
A=00 means the A register contents are 00
B=0FB6 means the BC register contents are 0FB6
D=0000 means the DE register contents are 0000
H=0000 means the HL register contents are 0000
S=0100 means the stack pointer is at 0100
P=013D means the program counter is at 013D
LXI SP,0200 is the next instruction to execute.

U
Un

The Untrace command is identical to the T command, but the CPU state is displayed only before the first instruction is executed, rather than before each step. It is similar to setting a breakpoint in a G command and preceding this with an X command. Using U is faster than using T but slower than using G. However, using U is preferable to using G without breakpoints, because you can interrupt execution by pressing any key.

X
Xr
Xf

The eXamine command displays the CPU registers and flags if r (a register) and f (a flag) are not specified. If r or f is specified, then its respective value or state is displayed and can be changed. If only the X command is given, the format of the display is the same as with the T and U commands. Registers and flags that can be specified are as follows:

Registers and Flags	Meaning
XC	Carry flag
XZ	Zero flag
XM	Minus flag
XE	Even-parity flag
XI	Interdigit carry flag
XA	Accumulator
XB	Register pair BC
XD	Register pair DE
XH	Register pair HL
XS	Stack pointer register
XP	Program counter register

LOAD

Create an Executable Program

The LOAD command has only one function: it takes a file of type HEX and converts it into an executable file of the COM file type.

A HEX-type file is created by ASM and contains Intel hex format machine code ready to be tested using DDT or converted into an executable file. LOAD creates a COM file, which begins at 0100 hex and which contains executable machine code.

First assemble your file using ASM. Next use LOAD to create a COM-type file:

```
A>LOAD B:POX<cr>
FIRST ADDRESS     0100
LAST ADDRESS      0234
BYTES READ        0135
RECORDS WRITTEN     02
A>
```

If your HEX file is large, the disk drive may be active for a fairly long time as LOAD performs its function. The messages printed out are informational only and tell you the size of the new COM-type file.

Several error messages may be presented by LOAD if your file is in the incorrect format or if a problem occurs in making the conversion:

CANNOT OPEN SOURCE, LOAD ADDRESS xxxx
: This message is displayed if LOAD cannot find the file name you specify or if no file name is specified.

INVERTED LOAD ADDRESS

The program origin is less than 0100 hex, or the program contains at least one statement with an address less than the address of the previous instruction (that is, the hex format records are not in ascending order by address). Check the ORG statements in your assembly language file.

INVALID HEX DIGIT or CHECKSUM ERROR

These messages appear when the information within the HEX-type file is incorrect. This problem normally will not occur if you immediately load the output of an assembly, but it may occur if you use Intel hex format to pass information between computers and then edit the file.

DISK READ or DISK WRITE or NO MORE DIRECTORY SPACE or CANNOT CLOSE FILE

Each of these errors is printed when LOAD encounters problems in trying to read from or write to the disk. Check whether the disk or directory is full or whether the disk is set to read-only status.

SUMMARY

CP/M-80 users should now be familiar with Digital Research's basic assembly language tools, ASM, DDT, and LOAD. These tools provide the simplest form of assembly language utilities in CP/M-80. Again, if you are seriously interested in assembly language programming under CP/M, you may want to explore the tools discussed in the next chapter, most of which are available for sale to CP/M-80 users. You may also be interested in reading the following books on assembly language programming published by Osborne/McGraw-Hill: *The Programmer's CP/M Handbook* by Andy Johnson-Laird, and *Z80 Assembly Language Programming* and *8080/8085 Assembly Language Programming* by Lance Leventhal.

CHAPTER

9 CP/M-PLUS Assembly Language Utilities

The CP/M-PLUS assembly language programs are similar to those for CP/M-80. Indeed, most of the assembly language software supplied with CP/M-PLUS was first made available as optional software for CP/M-80. But as you can see from Table 9-1, CP/M-PLUS not only supplies different assembly language programs; it also supplies far more of them. In this chapter we will examine CP/M-PLUS's extensive set of assembly language programs: MAC/RMAC, SID, HEXCOM, LIB, LINK, XREF, and GENCOM.

MAC

Macro Assembler (CP/M-PLUS, optional for CP/M-80)

RMAC

Relocating Macro Assembler (CP/M-PLUS, optional for CP/M-80)

MAC and its brother RMAC are the assemblers that come with CP/M-PLUS. They, like ASM (provided with CP/M-80), generally work with 8080 assembly language instructions. But unlike ASM, MAC and RMAC add two major capabilities:

- They allow most of the Z80 mnemonics (with the addition of the Z80.LIB file to your assembly language program).
- They allow special groups of instructions, called *macros,* to be used within your programs.

We will primarily deal with the added features of MAC in this chapter. You should already be familiar with assembly language as well as the ASM assembler and its features (discussed in Chapter 8), to which we will relate many of MAC's features. Note that MAC and RMAC are basically the same assembler, with the primary

TABLE 9-1. Assembler Tools Supplied With CP/M-80 and CP/M-PLUS

Program	CP/M-80	CP/M-PLUS
Assembler	ASM.COM	MAC.COM RMAC.COM
Debugger	DDT.COM	SID.COM
Format Converters	LOAD.COM	HEXCOM.COM GENCOM.COM
Other		LINK.COM LIB.COM XREF.COM

difference being that MAC generates code at fixed memory locations, while RMAC generates relocatable program code.

Assembling a Program

MAC and RMAC behave differently from ASM at the CP/M command level. Instead of the ASM command line, MAC and RMAC use the following:

```
A>MAC filename $options<cr>
A>RMAC filename $options<cr>
```

The file name should be a valid CP/M file with the ASM file type.

The specification of options in MAC is different from that of ASM. If you type a period followed by three letters after the file name, MAC thinks this is the file type for that source code program file. Options are specified after a space and dollar sign. The options in MAC are as follows:

Option	Function
A~	Specifies source code input location
H*	Specifies hex file output location
L*	Specifies where to search for LIB files
+L	Lists contents of all LIB files encountered
−L	Suppresses listing contents of all LIB files
+M	Lists all macro lines during substitution
−M	Does not list macro lines during substitution
*M	Lists only hex generated by macro expansion
P*	Specifies print file output location
+Q	Includes local symbols in the symbol table
−Q	Does not include local symbols in the symbol table
+R	Adds 100h to all operands of all ORG statements
S*	Specifies symbol file output location
+S	Writes the symbol table following the print file on the print file's destination
−S	Suppresses the symbol table display
+1	Produces a listing on first pass
−1	Suppresses listing on pass 1

Each option must be separated from the others by a space. All are optional; any that are not specified will be assumed to default to the current logged disk drive or normal setting.

The ~ and * following some of the options stand for a second letter, as follows:

Option	Function
~	Can be any valid disk drive specifier (A-P).
*	Can be any valid disk drive specifier (A-P) or can be X to specify the console device, Y to specify the printer device, or Z to suppress output.

The options may be entered in any order following the dollar sign. Thus, the following is a valid MAC command line:

```
A>MAC FILE-19.MAC $FI HB PY SB<cr>
```

This line assembles the contents of FILE-19.MAC found on drive A (the default) in Intel hex format (the FI) on drive B (the HB), prints the listing (PY), and saves the symbol table file on drive B (SB). When this option is finished, the following files will exist:

Sample	Type
FILE-19.MAC	Source file
B:FILE-19.HEX	Assembled program file
B:FILE-19.SYM	Symbol table listing file

The listing file, FILE-19.LST, will not exist because we sent the listing to the printer device.

Files Used by MAC

Here is a summary of the different files used by the CP/M assemblers:

CP/M-80	CP/M-PLUS	Input/Output Files
ASM.COM	MAC.COM RMAC.COM	Assembler(s)
filename.ASM	filename.ASM	Source code
filename.HEX	filename.HEX	Hex format program code (MAC)
	filename.REL	Hex format program code (RMAC)
filename.PRN	filename.PRN	Program listing
	filename.SYM	Symbol table listing

In addition to the HEX and PRN files created by ASM, MAC creates one additional file, the symbol table file, with the SYM file type.

Note that RMAC outputs its program code into a file with the type of REL (for Relocatable). You must use a linker (LINK.COM, described later in the chapter) to convert this code into meaningful, executable program form.

Source Program Format

Like ASM, MAC expects the source file to be in a specific form. The source file is a sequence of ASCII-coded (text) statements or lines. Each line ends with a CARRIAGE RETURN and LINE FEED.

Also like ASM, a source code line consists of a line number, label (optional), mmenomic, operand (if any), and comments (optional). Comments may be started with either a ; or a * character.

Numeric constants in MAC are formed just as they are in ASM:

- An appendix of B stands for binary (001010B)
- An appendix of O or Q stands for octal (056Q)
- An appendix of D (or no appendix) stands for decimal (45D)
- An appendix of H stands for hexadecimal (45H).

The $ symbol may be used to separate long numbers for readability (000$0101), and is also used to represent the current memory location when it is used as an operand by itself.

The following expressions are allowed in MAC and RMAC:

Expression	Meaning
+x	Same as x
−x	Two's complement of x
x+y	y added to x (unsigned)
x−y	y subtracted from x (unsigned)
x*y	x multiplied by y (unsigned)
x/y	Quotient of x divided by y (unsigned)
x MOD y	Remainder of x divided by y (unsigned)
HIGH x	Same as x SHR 8
LOW x	Same as x AND 00FFh
NOT x	One's complement of x
x AND y	Logical ANDing of x and y
x OR y	Logical ORing of x and y
x XOR y	Logical XORing of x and y
x SHL y	x shifted left y bits
x SHR y	x shifted right y bits
x LT y	FFFFh if x < y, else 0000h
x EQ y	FFFFh if x = y, else 0000h
x GE y	FFFFh if x >= y, else 0000h
x LE y	FFFFh if x <= y, else 0000h
x NE y	FFFFh if x ≠ y, else 0000h
x GT y	FFFFh if x > y, else 0000h

Assembler Directives

MAC includes the following directives in addition to those previously discussed for ASM in Chapter 8:

MACLIB

The MACLIB directive allows an assembly language program to wholly contain another assembly language program without having the actual text of the included program present. The form of the directive is

```
MACLIB    filename
```

The type of the file being read by MACLIB must be LIB:

```
MACLIB    CPMEQUS    ;Insert CPMEQUS.LIB here
```

A file that is included during assembly cannot contain a MACLIB directive; no nested MACLIBs are allowed.

TITLE

The listing file prints a title at the top of each page as defined by the TITLE directive:

```
TITLE    'string'
```

PAGE

The PAGE directive can force page breaks in the listing file. When a PAGE directive is encountered, printing resumes at the top of the next page.

An operand included with PAGE sets the number of lines on the page. For example,

```
PAGE    48
```

sets the page length to 48 lines.

$-PRINT

This directive blocks the creation of the print file for all subsequent assembly.

$+PRINT

This directive restores the creation of the print file for all subsequent assembly.

$+MACRO

This directive starts listing lines produced by macro assembly.

$-MACRO

This directive stops listing lines produced by macro assembly.

$*MACRO

This directive begins listing only the object code produced by a macro; no source code is listed.

REPT

The REPT directive is used to repeat a section of text a specified number of times. The operand for REPT must be a number, which indicates the number of times to repeat the assembly code text. For example,

```
REPT 12
```

will repeat the following assembly language text 12 times. All text up to the matching ENDM statement is repeated.

```
REPT    6
DB      0,0,0,0,0,0,0,0
ENDM
```

will result in

```
DB      0,0,0,0,0,0,0,0
DB      0,0,0,0,0,0,0,0
DB      0,0,0,0,0,0,0,0
DB      0,0,0,0,0,0,0,0
DB      0,0,0,0,0,0,0,0
DB      0,0,0,0,0,0,0,0
```

MACRO

A macro directive is a labeled "definition" that can be used to clone repeated assembly language code like the REPT directive, except that the programmer can include portions of the assembly language code in the processed text being substituted for. The format of a MACRO directive line is as follows:

```
label MACRO names
```

where "label" is a valid assembly language label used to identify the macro, and "names" are one or more identifiers used for the substitution process. Perhaps the easiest way to explain macros is to show a simple one.

The macro:

```
DOIT        MACRO       ?NUM, ?DE
            PUSH        B
            PUSH        D
            PUSH        H
            LXI         D,?DE
            MVI         C,?NUM
            CALL        BDOS
            POP         H
            POP         D
            POP         B
            ENDM
```

Code that uses the macro:

```
PSTRING     DOIT        9,STRING
            RET
```

In this example, MAC uses the macro template first shown when it encounters the "label" used for the macro later in the source code. The operands following the label (9 and STRING in the example) serve as values for the "names" following the MACRO directive (?NUM and ?DE). Thus, the resulting code at PSTRING becomes

```
PSTRING     PUSH    B
            PUSH    D
            PUSH    H
            LXI     D,STRING
            MVI     C,9
            CALL    BDOS
            POP     H
            POP     D
            POP     B
            RET
```

Extremely complicated macros are possible, since the MACRO directive may be used within a MACRO directive, as can the REPT, IRP, and IRPC directives.

IRP

The IRP directive combines the MACRO and REPT directives. The form of the IRP directive is

label IRP dummy,<items>

The "label" is optional. "Dummy" is an identifier that is replaced by one of the "items" for each repetition of the IRP. The ENDM statement is used to close the IRP directive. Again, a simple example serves to explain IRP:

```
        IRP     ?REPLACE,<B,D,H>
        PUSH    ?REPLACE
        ENDM
```

This results in the following code:

```
        PUSH B
        PUSH D
        PUSH H
```

There are three items to substitute and so the IRP is repeated three times. All text between the IRP and ENDM statements is repeated, with the first item used for replacement on the first pass, the second item used for replacement on the second pass, and so on. The item list contains items, separated by commas, that are used in the replacement process and that determine the number of times the IRP code is repeated. If an item has a space or special characters, it should be enclosed in angle brackets by itself. For example,

```
        IRP     ?REPLACE,<B,<D,>,H>
```

has items that are

```
        B
        D,
        H
```

IRPC

The IRPC directive is similar to IRP, except that it replaces only single characters. The number of characters in the item list dictates the number of times the IRPC text is repeated, with the next character in the item list being used for replacement. Our example for IRP could have therefore been coded like this:

```
IRPC        ?REPLACE,BDH
PUSH        ?REPLACE
ENDM
```

Since there are three characters in the item list (note that no angle brackets are used), IRPC repeats three times. A single character from the list, in sequential order, is used during each repeat; thus the results are the same as in the IRP example:

```
PUSH        B
PUSH        D
PUSH        H
```

EXITM

The EXITM directive immediately stops the expansion of a macro definition, with assembly continuing with the statement that follows the use of the macro. EXITM may be used with IRP, IRPC, REPT, and MACRO directives. EXITM is normally used as an error-checking device and almost always in conjunction with an IF directive (otherwise the macro definition would never get a chance to complete itself).

ENDM

The ENDM directive is used to identify the end of a MACRO, IRP, IRPC, or REPT section of code.

LOCAL

The LOCAL directive is used only within a macro definition (MACRO, IRP, IRPC, and REPT) to generate unique, local labels (four-digit numbers beginning with 0001) replacing the label used in the macro. The format of the instruction is

```
LOCAL names
```

where "names" can be any number of label names that are to be replaced with unique numbered identifiers.

ELSE

Both MAC and RMAC allow the use of the ELSE construct in assembly language code. MAC, RMAC, and ASM all allow IF and ENDIF within assembly language code, providing the means to test whether the following code should be interpreted:

```
IF expression
   code
ENDIF
```

"Code" is interpreted by the assembler if the expression is non-zero (TRUE). The ELSE directive expands that basic structure to

```
IF expression
   code1
ELSE
   code2
ENDIF
```

"Code1" is interpreted if the expression is non-zero, while "code2" is interpreted if the expression is evaluated to zero (FALSE).

RMAC adds several more directives to those of ASM and MAC:

DSEG, ASEG, CSEG, COMMON, NAME, EXTRN, PUBLIC

We will not elaborate on these directives here, as their use is complex and out of the realistic range of this book.

Assembler Progress Messages

Like ASM, MAC displays a message when it starts assembly:

CP/M MACRO ASSEMBLER VER 1.1

During assembly, the following appears:

END OF PASS 1
END OF PASS 2

These messages indicate MAC's progress in assembly. Upon completion, the following message appears:

END OF ASSEMBLY. NUMBER OF ERRORS: 0

This message is self-explanatory, but again, it does not indicate that an assembly language program was *successfully* assembled, only that no coding errors were detected during assembly. MAC may be stopped by pressing any key while it is assembling.

Assembler Error Messages

MAC displays two kinds of error messages. The first is a terminal error message indicating that conditions prevented the assembler from completing its job. Terminal error messages are typically caused by problems with disks or files and are very similar to those listed for ASM in Chapter 8. The second kind of error message arises in program assembly when MAC or RMAC cannot properly assemble a source code statement but can continue the assembly despite the error. If no messages appear, then the assembler is proceeding and has encountered nothing it cannot understand (this is much, much different from saying the program is correct!). If MAC or RMAC encounters something it does not understand, it displays a line in the following format:

a bbbb cccc label mnemonic operand ;comment

The a is a letter representing the type of error. The bbbb is the hexadecimal address of the statement at which the error was encountered, and the cccc is the hexadecimal representation of the machine language created by the assembler. When an error occurs, some or all of the machine code is set to zeroes because the assembler did not know what to put there.

The following are the error codes MAC displays:

B (Balance Error)
A normally balanced pair of statements does not balance; there is an extra ELSE, ENDM, or ENDIF, or one out of place.

C (Close Error)
One expression is not properly set off from another. Use parentheses and spaces to delimit expressions.

D (Data Error)
The value of the expression does not fit into the data area you indicated; it may be too long.

E (Expression Error)
You formed the expression improperly, or its value is too complex to be computed at assembly time.

I (Invalid Character)
A non-printable character occurs in the source code.

L (Label Error)
You used the label incorrectly. This normally occurs when you use the same label in the label field of more than one statement in a program.

M (Macro Error)
The macro expansion facility has no more room; it is possible that you have a recursive macro.

N (Not Implemented)
Feature not implemented or recognized.

O (Overflow Error)
Your expression is so complicated that the assembler cannot handle it in its present form. Divide the expression into smaller pieces or simplify it by reducing the number of operators.

P (Phase Error)
The label changes value during assembly. If you must reassign a value, use the SET directive. A duplicate label can also cause this error.

R (Register Error)
You specified a register that is not compatible with the mnemonic given. For instance, POP B is a valid assembly language statement, but POP A is not. POP A will trigger the R error message.

S (Syntax Error)
This catchall error can be caused by an invalid mnemonic or a typographical

error in the source file. Generally, a required field is missing, or double quotes have been used in place of single quotes in a DB constant.

U (Undefined Symbol)
You used a label in an expression without assigning a value to it. For example,

```
U 0102 06 00          MVI       B,ONE
```

appears if ONE is not defined in the program.

V (Value Error)
The operand (expression) encountered is not correct. This usually occurs with a typing error, such as a missing comma or letter the assembler is expecting.

LINK

Linking Loader (CP/M-PLUS, optional for CP/M-80)

The LINK command allows you to take the relocatable code output of MAC or RMAC and produce a COM-type file from it. In addition, you may use LINK to create a single COM-type file from several relocatable (REL-type) code files.

LINK d:filename.typ[options]
This format loads LINK and then converts a specified file of relocatable object code to one of executable program code. The name of the COM-type file will be the same as the REL-type file; only the file types will be different.

LINK d:filename.typ[options]=filename.typ[options]
This is the same as the above command except that the first file name and type are used for the creation of the COM-type file, while the second name and type are used for the source (REL-type) file.

LINK d:filename.typ[options], d:filename.typ[options] ...
This is the same as the first LINK command shown, except that subsequent file names (separated by commas) will be appended to LINK's output before the COM-type executable file is created. If external references are used within the source files, they are resolved during the appending process.

LINK Options

[A]
Additional memory. Reduces the buffer space used by LINK and writes temporary data to the disk in order to add memory to a file.

[B] (Banked CP/M-PLUS only)
BIOS link. Aligns data segments used on memory page boundaries, puts the length of the code segment in the header, and defaults the resulting file to the SPR type instead of COM.

[Dn]
Data origin. Sets the memory address (n in the example, specified in hex) for the common and data areas to be used.

[Gn]
Go. Sets starting address at the label n.

[Ln]
Load origin. Sets the default program load address to the hexadecimal number indicated (n). The default is 0100h.

[Mn]
Memory size. Sets the free-memory requirements necessary for MP/M modules to the hexadecimal number indicated (n).

[NL]
No Listing. Specifies that no listing of the symbol table should be output to the console.

[NR]
No Symbol Table File. Specifies that no symbol table file is to be used.

[OC]
Output in a COM-type file format. This is a default setting.

[OP]
Output in a PRL-type (page relocatable) file format.

[OR]
Output in an RSP-type (resident system process) file format.

[OS]
Output in an SPR-type (system page relocatable) file format.

[Pn]
Program origin. Sets the default program origin address to the hexadecimal number indicated (n).

[Q]
Lists local symbols with a leading question mark.

[S]
Searches preceding file as a library file.

[$Cx]
Specifies destination for console messages: x can be X for console, Y for printer, Z for no output. The default is X.

[$Id]
Specifies location of intermediate files. The default is the current drive.

[$Ld]
Specifies location of library files. The default is the current drive.

[$Od]
Specifies destination of object file. The default is the current drive; may be any drive A-P, or Z to indicate no output file.

[$Sx]
Specifies destination of symbol file. The default is the same drive as the first file mentioned in the LINK command. May be Y for printer, Z for no output, or any disk drive letter A-P.

Here is an example of LINK:

```
A>LINK B:THOMPROG[$SY Q],THOMLIB[S]<cr>
```

This code creates a new executable program file, THOMPROG.COM, out of THOMPROG.REL and the system library file THOMLIB.REL. In addition, the $SY option sends the resulting symbol table to the printer, while the Q option specifies that local symbols are to be listed

LIB

Library File Handler (CP/M-PLUS, optional for CP/M-80)

The LIB command is a utility that allows the user to create or modify library files. A library file is simply a collection of object code modules created by RMAC or any other Digital Research or Microsoft REL-format compatible program. Library files can be used by LINK to connect new object code with the code contained in a library.

Library files are best utilized when a section of program code is repeated in a number of separately compiled programs. Many software programmers develop a set of "standard" program modules they use over and over—input/output routines, common math routines, and so on. Once these are compiled and placed into an object code library file using LIB, the programmer need not duplicate that code in subsequent programs. Instead, the programmer places external routine and variable references to the library file within the new program and later uses LINK to connect the library file to the new program code.

The REL format is common to many programming languages and utilities. The object code created by all of the Microsoft compilers uses this format, as do many of the compilers offered by other independent software companies.

LIB has three basic formats:

LIB filename.typ[options]
This invokes the LIB utility, which then performs the option specified on the indicated file name.

LIB newname.typ[options]=oldname.typ[modifier]
This format of the LIB command invokes LIB, then creates a new library file from the old one, using the options and modifier indicated.

LIB newname.typ[options]=oldname1.typ[modifier],oldname2.typ[modifier]
This last form of the LIB command allows the user to combine library files into a single, new library file. A comma separates each source library file from the previous one.

LIB Options

[I]
Creates an indexed library file of the IRL (as opposed to the standard REL). LINK searches faster on indexed library files than it does on non-indexed files, thereby reducing the time it takes to create a completed object code file.

[M]
Displays the module names within the library.

[P]
Displays the module names and public variables within the new library file.

[D]
Dumps the contents of the object modules in ASCII form.

LIB Modifiers

<MODULE=>
Specifying a module name followed by an equals sign causes the named module to be deleted during the creation of the new library file.

<MODULE=filename.REL>
This replaces the named module with the file indicated during the creation of the new library file. May be abbreviated to <filename> if the file name is the same as the module name.

<MODULE, MODULE, ...>
This uses only the named modules in the creation of the new library file. If a large number of grouped modules are to be selected, the form module1-module2 can also be used, which selects all modules from module1 to module2 inclusive.

Now look at the following example of LIB. This code creates an indexed library file URTY.IRL from the existing library file URTY.REL.

```
A>LIB URTY[I]<cr>
```

This next example creates the library file RAREY.REL from the file URTY.REL, and the modules M1-M20 and Z7 from URATION.REL:

```
A>LIB RAREY=URTY,URATION(M1-M20, Z7)<cr>
```

HEXCOM

Generate a COM File From a HEX File (CP/M-PLUS)

The HEXCOM command takes an existing HEX-type file and generates a COM-type file. (HEX-type files can be created using ASM or MAC.) This command is similar to CP/M-80's LOAD command. Only one form of this command exists.

HEXCOM filename

This format generates a new file with the type of COM from an existing named file with the type of HEX (note that no file type is specified on the command line—HEX is assumed).

The following example creates a command file named HALOWEEN.COM from the instructions in file HALOWEEN.HEX:

```
A>HEXCOM HALOWEEN<cr>
```

GENCOM

Generate a COM File From an RSX File (CP/M-PLUS)

GENCOM is similar to HEXCOM in that it creates a COM-type file, although GENCOM does so only from RSX-type files. The commands differ because RSX files (resident system extension files) contain additional information that requires different loading and execution than the code contained in a HEX-type file. GENCOM places a special "loader" header at the start of the COM file so that CP/M-PLUS can load the program correctly. RSX files can also be appended to an existing COM-type file by means of GENCOM.

GENCOM filename.COM filename.RSX [options]

This format of GENCOM appends the named RSX-type file to the existing COM-type file, creating a new COM-type file with the same name as the original COM-type file.

GENCOM filename.RSX [options]

This format creates a file name of type COM from the named RSX-type file.

Note: All forms of the GENCOM command may have up to 15 named RSX-type files, each separated by a space, in the order you wish them appended. For example,

GENCOM filename1.RSX filename2.RSX filename3.RSX

GENCOM Options

[LOADER]

Sets a flag (memory location) that tells CP/M-PLUS to keep the program loader active.

[NULL]

Indicates that only RSX files are specified and that a dummy COM-type program must be created by GENCOM. The name of the COM-type file is taken from the first RSX file specified.

[SCB=(offset,value)]

Sets the System Control Block from the program as indicated by the offset and value in the option line. Offset and value must be specified in hexadecimal format.

The following example creates a new COM-type file of name PROGRAM from PROGRAM.COM and the appended files RSX1.RSX and RSX2.RSX:

```
A>GENCOM PROGRAM RSX1 RSX2<cr>
```

The next example is similar, but it creates a dummy COM-type file named RSX1.COM to which RSX1.RSX and RSX2.RSX are appended:

```
A>GENCOM RSX1 RSX2 [NULL]<cr>
```

XREF

Create a Cross-Reference File (CP/M-PLUS, optional for CP/M-80)

The XREF command creates a cross-reference summary of the variable usage within a program produced by MAC or RMAC. XREF uses the PRN and SYM files produced by MAC/RMAC to create the cross-reference.

One format of the XREF command exists:

XREF filename $option

Creates the file filename.XRF from the source files filename.SYM and filename.PRN. All file names must be the same. The only option allowed is $P, which directs the output of the cross-referencing to the printer.

The following example prints the cross-reference listing from the files URRY.SYM and URRY.PRN:

```
A>XREF URRY $P<cr>
```

SID

Symbolic Instruction Debugger (CP/M-PLUS, optional for CP/M-80)

The Symbolic Instruction Debugger (SID) is used to test and debug machine language programs. CP/M-80 comes with DDT (see Chapter 8), while CP/M-PLUS comes with SID. Like DDT, you use SID to

- Load an assembled program into memory.
- Make simple changes to a machine language program.
- Help locate errors in machine language programs.
- Correct or update your software.
- Install special driver routines (programs that drive a peripheral, such as a printer).
- Change disk parameters.
- Examine and modify the contents of memory.
- Enter assembly language code one line at a time.
- Disassemble a section of a program (turn machine language back into assembly language instructions).
- Examine and modify the contents of the internal registers of the CPU.

- Set breakpoints at which to stop the program and check what has happened so far.
- Trace the execution of a program; follow what is happening to memory and the internal registers of the CPU.

SID differs from DDT in two main ways:

- SID allows the "symbolic" debugging of programs; in other words, it can use a symbol table to keep track of the names you gave various program subroutines and memory locations in MAC or RMAC.
- SID has two utility files, HIST.UTL and TRACE.UTL, that allow you to create histograms (frequency-distribution graphs) and to do program tracing.

SID
: This loads the Symbolic Instruction Debugger program into the memory of your computer, where it waits for further instructions.

SID d:filename.typ
: This format loads SID into memory and also loads the designated file into memory for examination, modification, or extension. The file type is normally COM or HEX.

SID d:filename1.typ d:filename2.typ
: This loads SID and the file filename1.typ into memory, then loads the symbol table file, filename2.typ (created with MAC or RMAC), into memory for use.

SID d:filename.UTL
: This loads SID and the named SID utility file into memory for use. HIST. UTL creates a histogram of the frequency of selected program segments in the program being tested. HIST.UTL, when loaded, prompts you to enter the starting and ending hexadecimal addresses of the area of memory you want to analyze. TRACE.UTL adds another feature to the tracing capabilities of SID: when loaded into memory, TRACE.UTL allows SID to show you the (as many as) 256 instructions that were executed before the current breakpoint.

When SID is resident in your computer's memory, it displays a pound sign prompt (#). The pound sign indicates that SID is waiting for a command.

Note: If you intend to work extensively with a Z80-based system, you may wish to purchase ZSID from Digital Research. ZSID operates identically to SID but works with the entire Z80 instruction set; SID works only with the 8080 instruction set.

SID Commands

Once SID has been loaded into memory (along with the optional file name, if specified), it is ready to accept commands. A summary of the available commands is shown in Table 9-2.

Most of these commands, like those of DDT, require additional information in order to be used. Often this additional information is a memory address or a hexadecimal value. Valid addresses are in the range 0000-FFFF hexadecimal.

TABLE 9-2. SID Commands and Functions

Function	Letter Typed
Assemble instructions	A
Call address	C
Display memory	D
Examine/execute program	E
Fill memory	F
Execute program	G
Hexadecimal arithmetic	H
Set up FCB	I
List instructions	L
Move memory	M
Set passpoint	P
Read disk file	R
Set memory to value	S
Trace program	T
Execute partially	U
Write memory to disk file	W
Examine/modify registers	X

Unlike DDT, SID has these capabilities:

- A decimal number can be input by prefixing the number with a pound sign (#35 is decimal 35, not hexadecimal 35).
- ASCII characters can be typed between apostrophes ('). Up to two characters may be in an ASCII string ('ST' is a valid string in SID).
- SID accepts symbolic references if the symbol file has been loaded for the HEX or COM file being debugged. The following forms are used within SID:

.symbol	represents the address of the symbol
@symbol	represents the 16-bit value at .symbol
=symbol	represents the 8-bit value at .symbol.

In the following instruction summary, we will deal primarily with the differences between SID and DDT.

As

The Assembly command enters assembly language instructions beginning at address s. After a CARRIAGE RETURN is pressed, SID displays the memory address and waits for you to type a valid 8080 mnemonic, operand, or symbol (if a symbol table is loaded into memory).

```
#A0100<cr>
0100 MOV A,C<cr>
0101 .<cr>
#
```

A.symbol
A@symbol

These are the same as the As format but they use the symbol table to determine the starting address.

```
#A.PRINT<cr>
0109 RET<cr>
010A .<cr>
#
```

—A

This format discards the assembler/disassembler portions of SID and the symbol table information. Subsequent A and L instructions will be ignored.

Cs
C.symbol
C@symbol

The Call command performs a direct call to the location specified by address s or by use of the symbol table, without disturbing the CPU state of the program under test. Normally used with SID utilities.

D	**D,f**	**DWs,f**
Ds	**DW**	**DW,f**
Ds,f	**DWs**	

Display shows a dump of memory contents similar to that of the DUMP command. The numbers specify the starting address, s, or the finishing address, f. If the DW forms are used, the display is in 16-bit word format instead of byte format. You may use symbols for memory locations if the symbol table has been activated.

E

The Execution command loads a program and/or symbol table for examination and execution. Three forms are allowed:

Efilename.typ
  Loads program file for execution.

Efilename.typ, filename.sym
  Loads program file and symbol table for execution.

E* filename.sym
  Loads symbol table for use.

SID retains control when the program and/or symbol table is loaded.

Fs,f,b

The Fill command fills memory from the starting address, s, through the finishing address, f, with the single, constant byte value, b. You may use symbol entries if they are known.

The following command places the value A0 hex in every memory location from the location of "symbol" to the address indicated by the 16-bit contents of "other":

```
#F.symbol,@other,A0<cr>
#
```

G
Gs
Gs,b1
Gs,b1,b2
G,b1
G,b1,b2

The Go command begins execution at the starting address, s, with one or two optional breakpoint addresses, b1 and b2. If a starting address is not specified, then SID begins executing the instructions in memory from the current address in the CPU's program counter.

When debugging a program, you seldom use the G command without specifying at least one breakpoint address to stop at. Without a breakpoint address, execution will continue beyond the desired limit unless you have placed the correct RST (restart) instruction for SID somewhere in the executed code.

The breakpoint(s) you specify with the G command is not set "permanently"; you need to respecify it each time you use the G command. To set "permanent" breakpoints, refer to the P command.

Breakpoints display in the form

*nnnn

where nnnn is the location encountered that caused the break.

Ha,b

The Hexadecimal math command computes and displays the sum of and difference between the two hexadecimal numbers you specify. The numbers are converted to 16-bit values (if you type less than four hexadecimal digits) before the calculations are made. The first number shown will be the sum, the second the difference between the two numbers.

Hn

This format displays the number in several forms:

nnnn #ddddd 'c' .ssss

where nnnn is the hexadecimal number entered, #ddddd is the decimal equivalent, 'c' is the ASCII equivalent, and .ssss is the symbol table entry, if any.

H

This format displays the hex values for each symbol table element.

Ifilename

The Input command prepares a file control block and buffer for use with the R command. The first file name following the I command is placed into the default file control block (normally at 005C hex). If more than one file name is specified (separated with a space), the second one is placed in the second portion of the file control block (normally 006C hex). The length of the command following the I is placed at 0080 hex, followed by the command and then a terminating binary zero character.

The I command always sets up the file control block for accessing the currently logged disk drive. You cannot include a drive specifier such as B: with the I command; an error message is issued if you do. You could, however, modify the file control block with the S command to change the byte at memory location 005C from 00 to the value corresponding to the desired drive. Thus, drive A will be 01, drive B will be 02, and so on through drive P.

Because the I command also fills in the command buffer at 0080 hex exactly as if the user had done it, the I command can be used to simulate what would happen if a user had typed in a command at the CP/M prompt level and traced execution of the program with SID.

L
Ls
Ls,f
L,f

The List command lists the next 11 lines of disassembled machine code, with symbols (if they are known), from the current address if the starting address, s, is not specified. If a finishing address, f, is specified, the listing will be from the starting address to the finishing address. If a starting address has not been listed, the default address is 0100 hex.

```
#L<cr>
0151 MOV D,A
0152 MVI E,00
0154 PUSH D
0155 LXI H,.THERE
0158 MOV A,B
0159 ORA C
015A JZ .SYMBOL
015D DCX B
015E MOV A,M
015F STAX D
0160 INX D
#
```

When SID does not know how to display a hexadecimal value encountered in 8080 assembly language, the message ??=## is displayed; ## is the hexadecimal byte found by SID.

Each successive use of L disassembles the next 11 instructions.

–L

If a minus sign precedes the L instruction, the symbol table entries are not used in the disassembly.

Ms,f,d

The Move command moves a block of memory spanning from the starting address, s, through the finishing address, f, to the memory block starting at the destination address, d. If d lies between s and f, then part of the block is overwritten before it is moved.

The Move command does not relocate a program; a program usually contains references to other locations within the program. However, the Move command does a *literal* move; each byte in the original block is moved exactly as is to the new location. If a program is moved away from its normal location, it most likely will not work at its new location.

If a question mark appears after you type the M command, at least one of the numbers you specified is not a valid hexadecimal address. Also, if the last memory location to be moved is at a lower address than the starting memory location, nothing is moved by SID.

Pb
Pp,n

The Passpoint command sets the pass pointer to the passpoint address, p, with a count, n (01-FF hex), if specified. If n is not specified, a count of 1 is assumed. Otherwise, the count is decremented on each pass through the passpoint until a count of 1 is reached. Each time p is reached thereafter, the state of the CPU will be displayed in the same format as that of the T command. Unlike the breakpoints given with the G command, the passpoints set with the P command are "permanent" until you disable them.

P

Displays active passpoints.

–P

Disables all active passpoints.

–Pp

Disables the passpoint specified.

R
Ro

The Read command reads a file from disk into memory, after first encountering the I command, with an optional offset address, o. If the offset, or *bias* as Digital Research refers to it, is omitted, an offset of zero is assumed. The offset is added to the normal load location, and the file is loaded at the resulting address.

Any address exceeding FFFF hex wraps around to 0000 hex. Thus a file that loads at 8000 hex with an offset of zero will load at 0100 if it is loaded with an offset of 8100 (R8100<cr>). You may not load a file so that it resides in the portion of memory between 0000 and 0100 hex or so that it overlays SID. In addition, you may not load a file that will load into any part of memory used by CP/M-PLUS. The forbidden areas are 0000 to 0100 hex and the CP/M-PLUS area below FFFF hex. The address of the start of this area can be found by entering the command L5,7<cr>; the address shown after the JMP mnemonic is the lowest address used by CP/M and SID.

If you enter a file type of COM with the I command, then loading begins at 0100 plus the offset. If you enter any other file type, including HEX, the R command assumes the file will be in Intel hex format, and it adds the offset to the addresses contained in the hex format file to determine the load addresses.

The following example shows how to load and read HEX and SYM files:

```
#I PROGRAM.HEX PROGRAM.SYM<cr>
#R<cr>
```

Ss
SWs

The Set command displays the memory contents, starting at s, with the option to change (set) the contents, in bytes. Data values of 16 bits are used with the SWs form.

SID displays a memory location and the current contents of that location, then waits for you to enter a byte (or word) value or only a CARRIAGE RETURN to leave the setting as is.

```
#S0100<cr>
0100 C3 3D<cr>  ← C3 becomes 3D
0101 28 4F<cr>  ← 28 becomes 4F
0102 38 <cr>    ← Leave as is
0103 C3 .<cr>   ← Terminate input
#
```

A question mark appears when SID cannot understand your input (for example, if you type an invalid hexadecimal digit or address).

T **Tn,u**
Tn **TW**

The Trace command traces the program execution for n instructions or for one step if n is not specified. Trace displays the CPU registers as they exist immediately prior to the execution of the next program instruction. Pressing any key terminates tracing and returns control to SID. The SID trace display is similar to that of DDT.

If u is included, a call to the SID utility specified by the second number is performed after the trace is completed.

If the TW form is used, only local execution is performed—no calls are allowed.

—T **—Tn,u**
—Tn **—TW**

Same as the previous forms, but the minus signs disable the use of symbolic references.

U
Un
UW

The Untrace command is identical to the T command. However, the Untrace command displays the CPU state only before the first instruction is executed, rather than before each step. It is similar to setting a breakpoint in a G command and preceding this with an X command. Using U is faster than using T but slower than using G. However, it is preferable to using G without breakpoints because you can interrupt execution by pressing any key.

If the UW form is used, only local execution is performed — no calls are allowed.

−U
−Un
−UW

Same as the previous forms, but the passpoint trace should be disabled (see the P command).

Wfilename.typ,s,f

The Write command writes the contents of memory spanning from the starting address, s, through the finishing address, f, to the disk file specified. The addresses, s and f, are optional.

X
Xr
Xf

The eXamine command displays the CPU registers and flags if r (a register) and f (a flag) are not specified. If r or f is specified, then its respective value or state is displayed and can be changed. If only the X command is given, the format of the display is the same as that of the T and U commands. Registers and flags that can be specified are as follows:

Registers and Flags	Function
XC	Carry flag
XZ	Zero flag
XM	Minus flag
XE	Even-parity flag
XI	Interdigit carry flag
XA	Accumulator
XB	Register pair BC
XD	Register pair DE
XH	Register pair HL
XS	Stack pointer register
XP	Program counter register

SID Utilities

When a SID utility is loaded into memory, it displays a special symbol table of three entries:

.INITIAL
Memory location to reinitialize the utility.

.COLLECT
Memory location to start the utility's collection of data.

.DISPLAY
Memory location to display current data collected by the utility.

To restart the utility, type .INITIAL in response to a SID prompt. To start collecting data, type .COLLECT in response to a SID prompt. To display collected data, type .DISPLAY in response to a SID prompt.

SUMMARY

We have now examined all the Digital Research-supplied programs and commands for both CP/M-80 and CP/M-PLUS. In the following two chapters we will examine some technical information about CP/M that is more general in nature and not related to a specific program.

CHAPTER

10 The Technical Aspects of CP/M

This chapter is certainly not for everyone. Some users may benefit from reading this description of CP/M's internal structure—it does explain a few idiosyncracies of CP/M-80 and CP/M-PLUS. Other readers will find this material less interesting, since it covers the more technical aspects of CP/M.

The first seven chapters of this book presented information you *must* know to use CP/M. Chapters 8 and 9 began a discussion of the assembly languages used by CP/M-80 and CP/M-PLUS. This chapter presents information the assembly language programmer must know to program effectively in the CP/M environment. If you found Chapters 8 and 9 difficult, then skip this chapter. If you are extremely curious about assembly language or find computers fascinating, by all means read on.

THE STRUCTURE OF CP/M-80

When you cold start CP/M in your computer, CP/M-80 normally gets loaded into the topmost free memory block. CP/M-80 itself takes approximately 6 Kbytes of memory space, but the machine-dependent portion may take anywhere from another 1K to 8K of memory. Thus, in a normal CP/M-80 system the top 7K-14K of memory are occupied by the instructions we have been referring to as CP/M-80 (CP/M-PLUS will be dealt with later in this chapter). The structure of all CP/M-80 machines is shown in Figure 10-1.

In addition to the chunk of memory CP/M-80 occupies at the top of memory, the first 256 bytes of memory (called the *base page*) in your computer system are reserved for use by CP/M-80. Your programs and data may occupy the area in memory between 0100 hex and the bottom of CP/M-80. A 32K CP/M-80 system does not contain 32K of memory for your programs and data; instead it allows about 24K of memory to be used as you please.

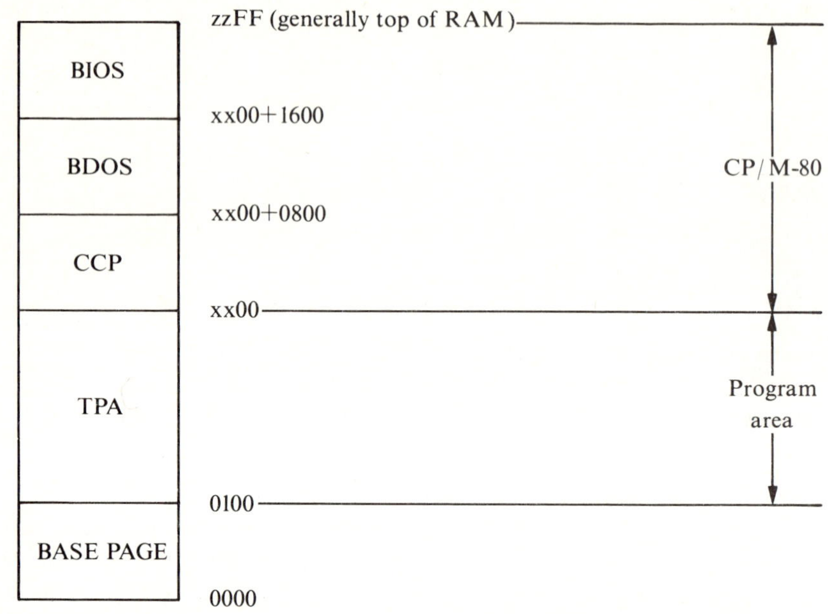

Note: All addresses are in hexadecimal. The xx and zz are dummy arguments representing addresses that change depending upon memory size.

FIGURE 10-1. Memory layout of a CP/M-80 system

When CP/M-80 is first started, the base page is filled in with some special information. We will detail this information later in the chapter, but for now a summary of the information that is stored in the base page is shown in Figure 10-2.

Now that you know the basic overall structure of CP/M-80, let us take a look at the pieces one by one.

CCP

The Console Command Processor

The CCP module interprets the CP/M-80 commands you type. This portion of CP/M is generally only relevant when you see an A> (or the prompt for another drive) on your terminal. The CCP recognizes only a few commands and a handful of control characters (see Chapter 4).

The command you type when you see the A> is first stored at location 0080-00FF hex, and then the CCP, if it doesn't recognize the command, checks the disk directory

Memory Location	Function
0000-0002	Jump to BIOS warm start routine
0003	IOBYTE
0004	Current drive number, current user number
0005-0007	Jump to BDOS entry vector
0008-0037	Reserved for machine interrupts
0038-003A	RST7, used by DDT
003B-003F	Reserved for machine interrupts
0040-004F	Reserved for "scratch" use by BIOS
0050	Drive command was loaded from (CP/M 3, MP/M 2)
0051	Address of password for first default FCB (CP/M 3, MP/M 2)
0053	Length of password for first FCB (CP/M 3, MP/M 2)
0054	Address of password for second default FCB (CP/M 3, MP/M 2)
0056	Length of password for second FCB (CP/M 3, MP/M 2)
0057-005B	Reserved
005C-006B	First default file control block (FCB) (CP/M 3, MP/M 2)
006C-007F	Second default file control block (FCB) (CP/M 3, MP/M 2)
0080-00FF	Default disk buffer/command buffer

Note: CP/M 1.4, CP/M 2.2, and MP/M 1 all use only one file control block beginning at 005C hex, with the area from 007D-007F hex reserved for the random record position in CP/M 2.2 and MP/M 1. Digital Research has changed the base page in CP/M-PLUS to add special functions like file protection and multi-user capabilities.

FIGURE 10-2. Base page layout

for a file with the type COM whose name matches the first eight characters (or the characters up to the first space in the command line). The "matched" file is loaded into memory beginning at 0100 hex and execution is passed to 0100 hex when the file is completely loaded (Digital Research calls such a file a *transient command*).

The command buffer extends from 0080 hex to 00FF hex, meaning that the longest command CP/M-80 can recognize is 128 characters in length.

Since the default disk buffer is not used to load the program, the command that the CCP executed still begins at 0080 hex and may be used by the program for subsequent processing. This is how long command lines, like MBASIC FILENAME /F:3, are executed. In this example, the CCP would first load the contents of MBASIC.COM into memory and then pass execution to 0100 hex. The MBASIC program then looks at the command line beginning at 0080 hex, detects that additional information was typed, and attempts to continue executing your original command.

There is another trick that the layout of the CCP allows advanced programmers to use: that of automatically starting a program. Some special locations within the CCP must first be learned:

```
CCP start + 07 hex  ———————————►  length of the command
CCP start + 08 hex  ———————————►  first byte of command
               .
               .
               .
CCP start + 87 hex  ———————————►  last byte available for command
CCP start + 88 hex  ———————————►  low-order byte of pointer
CCP start + 89 hex  ———————————►  high-order byte of pointer
```

Simply place your command in the area beginning at the memory location of the CCP plus eight bytes; the command may be up to 80 hex (128 decimal) characters in length. The command string must end with a 00 character (a null) for the automatic starting to work properly.

The two "pointer" bytes must contain the location of the first byte of the command (low-order byte first, high-order second, as is normal in 8080 programming conventions). The reason this pointer is necessary is that the CCP uses it to keep track of how much of the command has been processed. If you do not reset the pointer, the CCP may assume it has already processed part of your command.

A short assembly language program that uses the autostart concept is shown in Figure 10-3. You can append this program to another assembly language program in order to automatically transfer execution from one program to another.

There are more elegant methods of programming this action—especially if you have a Z80-based computer—but the programming in the above example is deliberately awkward so that the steps of the process are not masked by programming tricks. You could even recode it into BASIC if you wanted; it would be slow and cumbersome, but if done properly, it will still perform the same function: directly executing any valid CP/M-80 command at the end of any program.

BDOS

The Basic Disk Operating System

All disk drive activity and most console activity passes through this section of CP/M-80. The BDOS is not accessible through direct commands at the console, however. Instead, the CCP or a transient program places the number of the desired function in the microprocessor's internal C register and then executes a CALL instruction to location 0005 hex.

Some BDOS functions also require that extra information be placed in other internal registers of the microprocessor. For example, if you wanted to make a particular character appear on the console display, you would put the character in internal register E.

```
;------------------------------------------------------------
;
;  AUTOSTRT.ASM      version 1.0          10/12/81
;
;  copyright 1981 by Thom Hogan
;
;  May be used for non-commercial purposes without
;    permission.
;
;------------------------------------------------------------
;
BDOS        EQU       0005H            ;CP/M BDOS entry point
;
            ORG       0100H
;
START:      LHLD      0001H            ;Get address of BIOS+3
            MVI       L,00H            ;Subtract 3 to get BIOS
            MOV       A,H              ;Get it where we can use it
            SUI       16H              ;Subtract offset to CCP
            MOV       H,A              ;Put it back in HL
            SHLD      CCP              ;Save CCP location for later use
;
;------------------------------------------------------------
;
;  DO ANY PROCESSING YOU WISH HERE.
;    OSBORNE COMPUTER CORPORATION USES THIS AREA
;    TO AUTOMATICALLY PLACE THE LOGO AND PROGRAM
;    NAME THAT IS BEING LOADED ON THE SCREEN.
;
;------------------------------------------------------------
;
MIDDLE:     LXI       D,FILENAME       ;Point to COMMAND
            LXI       B,10             ;Set to length of COMMAND + 1
            LHLD      CCP              ;Get CCP location
            MVI       L,07             ;Location of length
            CALL      MOVE             ;Move command string
            LHLD      CCP              ;Get back CCP location
            MVI       L,88H            ;Location of LSB pointer
            MVI       A,08H            ;Get default LSB start
            MOV       M,A              ;Put it in place
            INX       H                ;Location of MSB pointer
            MOV       A,H              ;Get default MSB start
            MOV       M,A              ;Put it in place
            LHLD      CCP              ;Get back CCP location
            PCHL                       ;And go to it!
;
MOVE:       LDAX      D                ;Get byte to move
            MOV       M,A              ;Move it
            INX       H                ;Increment destination
            INX       D                ;Increment source
            DCX       B                ;Decrement count
            MOV       A,B              ;Get counter into A
            ORA       C                ;Check if done
            JNZ       MOVE             ;Not done
            RET                        ;Done
;
CCP:        DS        2
FILENAME:   DB        00,'XXXXXXXXX',00
;                     /          |     \
;     COMMAND LENGTH        COMMAND     TRAILING ZERO AT END
;
            END
```

FIGURE 10-3. Typical autostart routine

Other BDOS functions return information to the calling program (or portion of CP/M-80). If you ask BDOS to get a character from the console, the character will be returned to your program in the A register.

Also, CP/M-80 always copies the contents of the H register in the A register if nothing is to be specifically returned in the A register. Some manufacturers, specifically Microsoft, make use of such information to reduce movement of information between the H and A registers.

Table 10-1 is a summary of the BDOS functions available in CP/M-80.

To use any BDOS function, a program simply loads the function number into register C, loads other registers as required, and calls the BDOS via memory location 0005 hex. The BDOS performs the function and returns control to the calling program. A fuller description of programming considerations with the CP/M BDOS is detailed in Chapter 11.

TABLE 10-1. BDOS Function Definitions for CP/M-80 Version 2.2

Function		Entry Parameters	Exit Parameters	Explanation
No.	**Name**			
00	SYSTEM RESET	None	None	Terminates the calling program and returns control to the CCP via a warm start sequence. Calling this function has the same effect as a jump to location 0000 hex of Page Zero.
01	CONSOLE INPUT	None	A = ASCII character	Reads the next character from the logical console to register A. Graphic characters, along with CARRIAGE RETURN, LINE FEED, and BACKSPACE, are echoed on the console. Tab characters are expanded in columns of 8 characters. CONTROL-S, CONTROL-Q, and CONTROL-P are normally intercepted. All other non-graphic characters are returned in register A but not echoed on the console. Control of the program will not resume until a character has been typed.

SOURCE: *CP/M 2 Interface Guide*, copyright © 1979, Digital Research, Pacific Grove, Calif.

TABLE 10-1. BDOS Function Definitions for CP/M-80 Version 2.2 (*continued*)

Function		Entry Parameters	Exit Parameters	Explanation
No.	**Name**			
02	CONSOLE OUTPUT	E = ASCII character	None	Sends the ASCII character in register E to the logical console device.
03	READER INPUT	None	A = ASCII character	Reads the next character from the reader device into register A. Control does not return until a character has been read.
04	PUNCH OUTPUT	E = ASCII character	None	Sends the ASCII character in register E to the punch device.
05	LIST OUTPUT	E = ASCII character	None	Sends the ASCII character in register E to the list device.
06	DIRECT CONSOLE IN DIRECT CONSOLE OUT	E = FF hex E = ASCII character	A = ASCII character None	If register E contains an FF hex, the console device is checked to see if a character is ready. If there is no character, 00 hex is returned in register A. Otherwise, the character is returned. Any other character will be echoed on the console.
07	GET IOBYTE	None	A = IOBYTE	Places a copy of the value found at location 0003 hex into register A.
08	SET IOBYTE	E = IOBYTE	None	Places a copy of register A into location 0003 hex.
09	PRINT STRING	DE = String address	None	Sends to the printer device the string whose address is found in register pair DE. The string must end with a dollar sign, $.
0A	READ CONSOLE BUFFER	DE = Buffer address	Data in buffer	Performs the same function as the CCP in that it takes characters typed and stores them into the buffer

SOURCE: *CP/M 2 Interface Guide*, copyright ©1979, Digital Research, Pacific Grove, Calif.

TABLE 10-1. BDOS Function Definitions for CP/M-80 Version 2.2 (*continued*)

Function No.	Function Name	Entry Parameters	Exit Parameters	Explanation
0A (cont.)				that begins with the address found in register pair DE. The first byte must be the maximum length of the commands. The second byte will contain the actual length. It will be returned by the BDOS. All standard CCP editing commands are recognized during entry.
0B	GET CONSOLE STATUS	None	A = Status	Checks to see if a character has been typed. A 00 hex is returned if no character is present, or a FF hex is returned if a character has been typed.
0C	RETURN VERSION NUMBER	None	HL = Version	Register H is set to 00 hex if CP/M is being used, 01 hex if MP/M is being used. Register L is set to 00 hex if the version is earlier than 2.0, 20 hex if version 2.0, 21 hex if version 2.1, and so on.
0D	RESET DISK SYSTEM	None	All drives set to R/W	Resets the entire system during operation. Should be used if disks are changed at any time.
0E	SELECT DISK	E = Disk number	None	Designates the drive named in register E as the default drive for subsequent BDOS file operations.
0F	OPEN FILE	DE = FCB address	A = Found/not found code	Activates the FCB for a file that exists in the disk directory. A value of 00 hex to 03 hex in register A indicates the open was successful. A FF hex indicates the file could not be opened.

SOURCE: *CP/M 2 Interface Guide*, copyright ©1979, Digital Research, Pacific Grove, Calif.

TABLE 10-1. BDOS Function Definitions for CP/M-80 Version 2.2 (*continued*)

Function No.	Function Name	Entry Parameters	Exit Parameters	Explanation
10	CLOSE FILE	DE = FCB address	A = Found/not found code	Closes a previously opened file. This function must be performed if any records were written to the file while it was open.
11	SEARCH FOR FIRST	DE = FCB address	A = Found/not found code	Performs the same as the open file function except that the disk buffer is filled with the directory entry of the matched file.
12	SEARCH FOR NEXT	DE = FCB address	A = Found/not found code	Performs the same as function 11, but continues on from the last matched entry.
13	DELETE FILE	DE = FCB address	A = Found/not found code	Changes the first byte in the directory entry for the file to F5 hex. This signifies to the system that the blocks previously allocated are now available for other files.
14	READ SEQUENTIAL	DE = FCB address	A = Error code	Reads the next 128-byte record from a file into memory beginning at the current DMA address.
15	WRITE SEQUENTIAL	DE = FCB address	A = Error code	Writes the next 128-byte record from memory to disk beginning at the current DMA address.
16	MAKE FILE	DE = FCB address	A = DIR code	Creates a new directory entry for a file under the current user number. You must check that a file with the same name does not already exist on the disk, since CP/M-80 does no checking when performing this function. Newly created files are already opened when this function is complete.

SOURCE: *CP/M 2 Interface Guide*, copyright ©1979, Digital Research, Pacific Grove, Calif.

TABLE 10-1. BDOS Function Definitions for CP/M-80 Version 2.2 (*continued*)

Function		Entry Parameters	Exit Parameters	Explanation
No.	**Name**			
17	RENAME FILE	DE = FCB address	A = DIR code	Changes the name of the file referenced by the first 16 bytes of the FCB block to the name given in the second 16 bytes.
18	RETURN LOGIN VECTOR	None	HL = Disk login	Returns the bit map for all possible drives in register pair HL. Bit 0 is the status of drive A; bit 15 is the status of drive P. A logic 1 means the drive is active, a logic 0 means inactive.
19	RETURN CURRENT DISK	None	A = Current disk	Returns the number of the current default drive (00 hex to 10 hex).
1A	SET DMA ADDRESS	DE = DMA	None	Sets the DMA address for all disk operations to the address found in register pair DE.
1B	GET ALLOC ADDRESS	None	HL = Allocation address	Returns the address of the allocation vector for the currently selected drive in register pair HL.
1C	WRITE-PROTECT DISK	None	None	Provides temporary write-protection for the currently selected drive. A drive RESET operation must be performed so the disk can be written to.
1D	GET R/O VECTOR	None	HL = Disk R/O	Returns a bit vector for all possible drives in the system. The format and meaning of the bits are the same as that returned by function 18.
1E	SET FILE ATTRIBUTES	DE = FCB address	A = DIR code	Sets to either R/O or R/W the attributes of a file whose FCB address is found in register pair DE.

SOURCE: *CP/M 2 Interface Guide*, copyright © 1979, Digital Research, Pacific Grove, Calif.

TABLE 10-1. BDOS Function Definitions for CP/M-80 Version 2.2 (*continued*)

Function		Entry Parameters	Exit Parameters	Explanation
No.	**Name**			
1F	GET DISK PARMS	None	HL = DPB address	Returns in register pair HL the address of the BIOS-resident Disk Parameter Block for the current default drive.
20	GET USER CODE SET USER CODE	E = FF hex E = User code	A = Current user None	Used to change or interrogate the current user number. The value in register E must be between 00 hex and 0F hex.
21	READ RANDOM	DE = FCB address	A = Error code	Reads the next random record pointed to by the FCB.
22	WRITE RANDOM	DE = FCB address	A = Error code	Writes the next random record pointed to by the FCB.
23	COMPUTE FILE SIZE	DE = FCB address	RRF (Random Record Field) set	Determines the size of a file based on the address of the last actual record found in a randomly written file. The DMA address is set to that record's address.
24	SET RANDOM RECORD	DE = FCB address	RRF set	Returns the next random record after the last sequential READ has been performed.
25	RESET DRIVE	DE = Reset drive bits	A = Error code	Restores the specified drives to a RESET condition. The format of the word used corresponds to the same layout as that used in function 18.
28	WRITE RANDOM (ZERO)	DE = FCB address	A = Error code	Performs the same as function 22, but the buffer specified by register pair DE is set to all zeroes before the WRITE is performed. Useful for identifying unused records in a randomly written file.

SOURCE: *CP/M 2 Interface Guide*, copyright ©1979, Digital Research, Pacific Grove, Calif.

BIOS

The Basic Input/Output System

BIOS stands for Basic Input / Output System. Like the BDOS, the BIOS provides a number of routines that may be used by other software. The BIOS is provided by the manufacturer, dealer, or software vendor from whom you purchased CP / M-80, not Digital Research.

A great deal of confusion about CP / M-80 originates with the BIOS. Many people purchase CP / M-80 and discover that the BIOS section is not configured properly for their particular machine. Configuring a CP / M-80 BIOS is fairly straightforward for software developers and computer dealers but can be frustrating for the computer novice. If you do not know assembly language, or if you do not have a working computer system, or if you are a newcomer to microcomputers, then do not try to write a BIOS section for CP / M-80.

The BIOS performs crucial functions for CP / M-80. It tells CP / M-80 how to access the various devices that constitute your computer system, and most important, how to make the head of the disk drive move from place to place. Any problems in the BIOS section can cause CP / M-80 to function improperly or not at all.

The BIOS for CP / M-80 version 2.2 begins at the memory location 1600 hex bytes after the location of the CCP and starts with a series of jump instructions called, appropriately enough, the *jump table*. These instructions must be arranged in the proper order, and none may be left out for the BIOS to work properly. Figure 10-4 shows a typical jump table as found in a typical CP / M-80 machine.

Each of the "jumps" in Figure 10-4 point to a routine in your BIOS. Below is an example of a BIOS routine for output to a printer (which the BIOS finds with JMP LISTOUT):

```
;------------------------------------------------
; LIST OUTPUT ROUTINE
;------------------------------------------------
;
; This routine provides output to the Vector Graphic
; Bitstreamer II I/O board addressed at port 02 hex.
; All CP/M-80 list output will be directed to this
; routine.
;
; Assumptions:
;          o  Bitstreamer is initialized by cold start.
;          o  Character to be printed is in C.
;          o  Bitstreamer is addressed at port 02 hex.
;
LISTST:         EQU        03h        ;Status port
LISTDAT:        EQU        02h        ;Data port
;
LISTOUT:
                IN         LISTST     ;Get current status
                ANI        1          ;Check if ready
                JNZ        LISTOUT    ;Not ready
;
; Printer is ready if routine gets this far.  Print it!
;
LISTON:
                MOV        A,C        ;CP/M-80 has char in C
                OUT        LISTDAT    ;Send it
                RET                   ;Done, return
```

```
;-----------------------------------------------
;
;  BIOS FOR TYPICAL CP/M-80 SYSTEM
;
;-----------------------------------------------
;
; The following JMPs must be left in the order in
;    which they are presented.
;
; The following ORG statement applies to CP/M-80
;    version 2.2
;
ORG         CCP+1600h         ;Start of BIOS
;
            JMP         COLDSTART       ;Restart CP/M from scratch
            JMP         WARMSTART       ;Restart CP/M
            JMP         CONSTATUS       ;Console device status
            JMP         CONINPUT        ;Console device input
            JMP         CONOUTPUT       ;Console device output
            JMP         LISTOUT         ;List device output
            JMP         PUNCH           ;Punch device output
            JMP         READER          ;Reader device input
            JMP         HOME            ;Reset disk head to home
            JMP         SETDISK         ;Select disk to use
            JMP         SETTRACK        ;Select track to use
            JMP         SETSECTOR       ;Select sector to use
            JMP         SETDMA          ;Select DMA address to use
            JMP         READDISK        ;Read current sector
            JMP         WRITEDISK       ;Write current sector
;
; The following two jumps do not apply to CP/M-80
;    version 1.4, but are necessary for version 2.2.
;
            JMP         LISTSTATUS      ;list device status
            JMP         SECTORTRAN      ;sector translation
;
; End of standard CP/M-80 jump table, but you may
;    extend the table to add other functions
;
```

FIGURE 10-4. Jump table for CP/M-80 system

Each routine in your BIOS concludes with a RET (return from subroutine) instruction. Our sample routine consists of only six instructions; the rest of the routine lines are comments used to explain the operation of the routine.

As in the BDOS routines, there are certain assumptions made by CP/M-80 as to the entry and exit values of each BIOS routine. Table 10-2 shows a listing of the needed BIOS routines along with entry and exit parameters.

How to Modify the BIOS

Most CP/M-80 suppliers provide a sample BIOS with the original disk. Digital Research provides both a skeletal BIOS (just the bones and a number of comments; the routines do not include specific instructions) and a completed one for the system it uses. Many microcomputer manufacturers remove these two sample BIOSs and include their own. Some "hide" the BIOS from the user and supply only the routines that may need changing (the printer, punch, and reader routines).

TABLE 10-2. CP/M-80 Version 2.2 BIOS Routine Definitions

Label in Jump Table	Entry Parameters	Exit Parameters	Explanation
COLDSTART	None	C = Default drive	Initializes any system hardware that was not setup with the Cold Start Loader and initializes the base page.
WARMSTART	None	None	Resets the Page Zero, jumps and loads the CCP. After the CCP has been loaded, the routine must transfer control over to the CCP.
CONSTATUS	None	A = Status	Reads the status of the currently assigned console device. Returns a 00 hex if no character is ready and a FF hex if a character is present.
CONINPUT	None	A = Character	Reads the next character from the currently assigned console device into register A. Routine waits until a character is present.
CONOUTPUT	C = Character	None	Sends the character in register C out to the currently assigned console device.
LISTOUT	C = Character	None	Sends the character in register C out to the currently assigned printer device.
PUNCH	C = Character	None	Sends the character in register C out to the currently assigned punch device.
READER	None	A = Character	Reads the next character from the currently assigned reader device into register A. Routine waits until a character is present.
HOME	None	None	Moves the disk head of the currently selected drive to the track 00 position.

SOURCE: *CP/M2 Alteration Guide*, Copyright © 1979, Digital Research, Pacific Grove, Calif.

TABLE 10-2. CP/M-80 Version 2.2 BIOS Routine Definitions (*continued*)

Label in Jump Table	Entry Parameters	Exit Parameters	Explanation
SETDISK	C = Drive	HL = DPH	Selects the drive specified by the value in register C. Register pair HL contains the address of the Disk Parameter Header of the drive.
SETTRACK	BC = Track	None	Selects the next track number for a subsequent disk access.
SETSECTOR	BC = Sector	None	Selects the next sector number for a subsequent disk access.
SETDMA	BC = DMA	None	Sets the DMA address for the subsequent READ or WRITE operation.
READDISK	None	A = Status	Reads the next sector off the disk once the disk, track, sector, and DMA address have been selected.
WRITEDISK	None	A = Status	Writes the next sector onto the disk once the disk, track, sector, and DMA address have been selected.
LISTSTATUS	None	A = Status	Returns the status of the currently assigned list device.
SECTORTRAN	DE = Table address	HL = Physical sector number	Translates the logical sequential sector wanted to the actual physical sector on the disk.

SOURCE: *CP/M2 Alteration Guide*, Copyright © 1979, Digital Research, Pacific Grove, Calif.

To create a new or modified BIOS, perform the following steps:

1. On a freshly initialized/formatted disk, copy the sample BIOS, an editor program, ASM.COM, DDT.COM, and any SYSGEN/MOVCPM utilities. Use SYSGEN to copy an unmodified CP/M-80 system onto the disk. You want to use a new disk for creating your new BIOS so that you do not accidentally destroy a working system.
2. Print a copy of the sample BIOS (if you can; you may be changing the BIOS to include routines for a printer). Study the copy carefully. Become familiar with

its structure, the individual routines required, and the comments included in the sample.

3. Invoke your editor and edit the sample BIOS. Begin by inserting a comment to indicate the date, your name, the reason you are changing the BIOS, and any other identification that will help you and others trace problems that may occur later.
4. Minor additions or changes should not prove too difficult, assuming you understand assembly language and the device you wish to manipulate. An example of a simple modification follows. Here's what you might find in the sample BIOS:

```
SIGNON:
          DB      14h,0Dh,0Ah         ;Clear screen, move down
          DB      'CP/M-80 version 2.2',0Dh,0Ah,'$'
MOVEIT:
          LXI     H,SIGNON            ;Point to signon message
KEEPON:
          MOV     A,M                 ;Get a byte
          CPI     '$'                 ;Check for end of message
          RZ                          ;End of message
          MOV     C,A                 ;Not end, get ready
          CALL    CONOUT              ;  to send it to console
          INX     H                   ;Increment memory location
          JMP     KEEPON              ;Do it again
```

This routine displays the CP/M-80 sign-on message and initializes the terminal screen with the 14 hex character that starts the message. But what if the terminal you own requires a 04 hex to be initialized (clear the screen)? Let's change the BIOS to reflect the new terminal and to personalize the message that is displayed.

```
SIGNON:
          DB      04h,0Dh,0Ah         ;Clear screen, move down
          DB      'Thom Hogan's Vectrola 1.1',0Dh,0Ah
          DB      '-------------------------',0Dh,0Ah,0Ah
          DB      'CP/M-80 2.2 -- 10/17/80 last update',0Dh,0Ah
          DB      'no printer installed',0Dh,0Ah,0Ah,0Ah,'$'
MOVEIT:
          LXI     H,SIGNON            ;Point to signon message
KEEPON:
          MOV     A,M                 ;Get a byte
          CPI     '$'                 ;Check for end of message
          RZ                          ;End of message
          MOV     C,A                 ;Not end, get ready
          CALL    CONOUT              ;  to send it to console
          INX     H                   ;Increment memory location
          JMP     KEEPON              ;Do it again
```

After the screen has been cleared, the sample BIOS signs on like this:

```
CP/M-80 version 2.2
A>
```

The new version instead displays the following:

```
Thom Hogan's Vectrola 1.1
-------------------------

CP/M-80 2.2 -- 10/17/80 last update
no printer installed


A>
```

In this example we have not changed anything important. Notice that the DB '$' line remains so that our routine knows where the end of the message is.

There are three basic types of changes to make to BIOS:

- Inserting new material
- Deleting old material
- Changing existing material.

When you insert information into BIOS, previously entered information remains unchanged. Thus, you can easily retrace your steps and restore the BIOS to its original form. We suggest that you identify where you have inserted new material so that it is easier to locate later. A line of hyphens (----------) can separate individual routines. A line of equal signs (======) can delineate instructions added later. A section of the BIOS might look like this:

```
;-----------------------------------------------------------
;
;  MODEM ROUTINES -- substitute for PUNCH/READER
;
MODEM           EQU     TRUE            ;Yes, we have a modem today
DCH             EQU     FALSE           ;No, it isn't a DC Hayes
;
                IF      NOT DCH         ;If standard modem:
MODEMCTL        EQU     03h             ;Modem control port
MODEMSBIT       EQU     80h             ;Modem send control bit
MODEMRBIT       EQU     40h             ;Modem receive control bit
MODEMDATA       EQU     02h             ;Modem data port
                ENDIF
;
;===========================================================
; 10/17/81 -- Gee, we finally got a D.C. Hayes Modem board
;             for our birthday.  Here are the EQUs that we
;             think will operate our new modem.   When we've
;             had a chance to check these out, we'll go
;             back and change the DCH EQU to TRUE.
;
                IF      DCH
MODEMCTL        EQU     82h             ;DC Hayes control port
MODEMSBIT       EQU     2               ;Modem send control bit
MODEMRBIT       EQU     1               ;Modem receive control bit
MODEMDATA       EQU     80h             ;Modem data port
MODEMCTL2       EQU     81h             ;Second control port needed
                ENDIF
;===========================================================
;
                LXI     H,0
                DAD     SP
                SHLD    STACK
                etc.
```

The routines for the Hayes Microcomputer Products modem are not yet fully implemented, but you can see how we clearly identified the newly inserted section of program code.

When you delete a section from an existing BIOS, do not erase it; make it a comment instead. Insert semicolons in front of each line you wish to make inoperative, and add a note to explain the deletion.

```
RCVSOH:
                MVI     B,1             ;Timeout = 1 second
                CALL    RECV            ;Get sector
                JC      RCVSTOT         ;Got timeout
                MOV     D,A             ;D = block number
                MVI     B,1             ;Timeout = 1 second
                CALL    RECV            ;Get CMA'd sect number
```

```
;
; THE NEXT JUMP CANCELLED 10/1/80 TO DISABLE TIMEOUT
;
;               JC          RCVSTOT         ;Got timeout
;               CMA                         ;Calculate complement
;               CMP                         ;Good sector number?
;               JZ          RCVDATA         ;Yes, got data
;
; END OF DELETED SECTION OF CODE
;
; Note: this routine is from MODEM527.ASM by Ward
;       Christiansen -- a public domain program available
;       from the CP/M User's Group
```

By making the deleted section a comment, you can easily restore the file to its original form; just remove the semicolons.

Changing an area of the BIOS is more difficult; it is not so easy to document changes. To trace changes, make the original line a comment and insert the new line below it. With many changes, however, the results are difficult to read, so be sure you always have a copy of the original BIOS; name it BIOSOLD.ASM, BIOS001.ASM, or something similar to indicate that it is not the current version. Each time you edit the BIOS, save a copy of the previous version and date all versions.

5. Before leaving the editor, return to the beginning of the BIOS file and examine the ORG (origin) directive and any labels named BIOS, BIAS, or OFFSET. Instructions to the assembler on where to start assembling the BIOS differ among programs. Usually the BIOS is either origined absolutely (by a statement like ORG 0EF00h) or is calculated by the following methods suggested by Digital Research:

```
CCP:            EQU         2900H           ;For 16K CP/M-80 version 1.4
BIOS:           EQU         1500H+CCP       ;Location of BIOS
                ORG         BIOS
```

or

```
CCP:            EQU         3400H           ;For 20K CP/M-80 version 2.2
BIOS:           EQU         1600H+CCP       ;Location of BIOS
                ORG         BIOS
```

Check the CP/M-80 size indicated. If it matches the CP/M-80 size you are using, go to the next step. (Size means 48K CP/M-80, 56K CP/M-80, and so on.) If it does not match or if you cannot tell whether it matches, do not proceed.

Unfortunately, there is no absolute rule about the relationship of the BIOS section with the base section (CCP) of CP/M-80. Knowing the starting location of CP/M-80 does not necessarily mean you can calculate the beginning location of the BIOS section. Digital Research has tried to standardize this, but several distributors and computer manufacturers continue to change the pattern. However, you can always use DDT to locate the BIOS by examining the jump instruction at locations 0000 hex through 0002 hex. Remember, this instruction jumps to the *second* entry of the BIOS jump table, so you must subtract 3 from the address you find to locate the correct start of the BIOS.

For those of you with a standard CP/M-80 version 2.2, Table 10-3 shows the relationship of CP/M-80 size, location of CCP, and location of the BIOS.

TABLE 10-3. Relationship between CP/M-80 Version 2.2 Size, CCP Location, and BIOS Location

Size	CCP	BIOS
20K	3400h	4A00h
24K	4400h	5A00h
28K	5400h	6A00h
32K	6400h	7A00h
36K	7400h	8A00h
40K	8400h	9A00h
44K	9400h	AA00h
48K	A400h	BA00h
52K	B400h	CA00h
56K	C400h	DA00h
60K	D400h	EA00h
64K	E400h	FA00h

6. Assemble the new BIOS. If the BIOS assembles without any error messages, proceed to the next step. Always correct your errors before proceeding.
7. To test a new BIOS do the following:
   - Create a new CP/M-80 image using MOVCPM * *.
   - SAVE the new CP/M-80 image by using SAVE 34 CPMxx.COM, where xx is the size of the CP/M-80 system, such as 32K. **Note:** In some versions of CP/M-80 the MOVCPM message following the SAVE command will tell you to use a number other than 34; you should follow such advice.

   Use DDT to load the CP/M-80 image into memory. If your version of MOVCPM operates correctly, the following addresses apply:

```
BOOT      900h
CCP       980h      (Sometimes 0A00h if long BOOT)
BDOS     1180h      (Sometimes 1200h if long BOOT)
BIOS     1F80h      (CP/M 2.2)
         1E80h      (CP/M 1.4)
```

   Use DDT to load the assembled BIOS into the correct area of memory. The proper method is

```
-IBIOS.HEX<cr>
-R#<cr>
```

   where # is an offset that loads your BIOS at the proper point in the CP/M-80 image and not at its eventual location.

   The offset is calculated by adding a number to the eventual location of BIOS (its permanent address) so that it loads at 1F80 hex (version 2.2) or 1E80 hex (version 1.4). To calculate this number, first subtract the loading address (1F80 hex or 1E80 hex) from the eventual address.

For a version 2.2 system of 56K, for example:

DA00h − 1F80h = B580h

Therefore you type

```
-IBIOS.HEX<cr>
-R-B580
```

It is a good idea to fill memory beginning at 1F80 hex or 1E80 hex with zeroes before loading in the BIOS; this helps you tell whether or not the BIOS is correctly loaded.

Exit from DDT with a CONTROL-C and save the new CP/M-80 system with a SAVE 34 CPMxxOK.COM, in which xx is the size of the system you are creating.

If you have CP/M-80 version 2.2, you may use SYSGEN to save the new system on disk by typing

```
A>SYSGEN CPMxxOK.COM<cr>
```

Older versions of CP/M-80 require that you reload the system image before using SYSGEN as follows:

```
A>DDT CPMxxOK.COM<cr>
^C
A>SYSGEN<cr>
```

THE IOBYTE

The IOBYTE is a reserved byte of memory that indicates the current assignment of physical devices to logical devices. Its concept predates CP/M-80 by several years. Gary Kildall used it in some sample implementations of CP/M-80, and it is documented in most of the Digital Research manuals. Other software creators writing BIOS modules have elaborated upon the IOBYTE concept, but have not changed its basic function.

In CP/M-80, you have four logical devices:

CON:	Console device
LST:	List device
RDR:	Reader device
PUN:	Punch device.

When you have two different printers, terminals, or paper tape readers, the IOBYTE indicates which device is to be used.

The IOBYTE is normally located at 0003 hex. The physical arrangement of the IOBYTE fields is shown in Figure 10-5.

Table 10-4 shows how CP/M-80 interprets the two bits assigned to each device. The device names should look familiar; they are the physical devices that PIP and STAT address. An IOBYTE value of 00100100 (or 24 hex) means the physical devices are currently assigned to logical functions as follows:

The TTY: device is performing the CONSOLE function
The PTR: device is performing the READER function

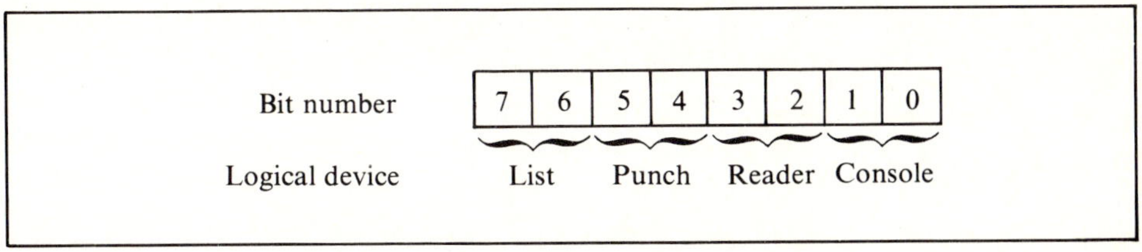

FIGURE 10-5. Arrangement of the IOBYTE

The UP1: device is performing the PUNCH function
The TTY: device is performing the LIST function.

A BIOS routine that you or your computer vendor wrote examines the IOBYTE to see where to send or receive information. The console status, console input, console output, reader, punch, and list jumps in the BIOS jump table should all point to special routines to see which device to use. These routines proceed as follows:

1. Get the IOBYTE
2. Determine which device to use
3. Go to the routine for that device.

DISK OPERATIONS

Some explanation of how CP/M-80 stores information on a disk is appropriate for this chapter. Unfortunately, this explanation cannot include all versions of CP/M since each different type of disk drive usually requires a slightly different set of parameters. To avoid confusion, we will focus on single-density CP/M-80 version 2.2 and attempt to indicate how other versions may differ.

You already know that information is stored on disks in "sectors" that divide "tracks" of information into blocks of information, each sector storing 128 bytes of information. Standard 8-inch, single-sided, single-density disks have 26 sectors on

TABLE 10-4. IOBYTE Values

Logical Device	Physical Device			
	00	**01**	**10**	**11**
Console (CON:)	TTY:	CRT:	BAT:	UC1:
Reader (RDR:)	TTY:	PTR:	UR1:	UR2:
Punch (PUN:)	TTY:	PTP:	UP1:	UP2:
List (LST:)	TTY:	CRT:	LPT:	UL1:

each of 77 tracks. Table 10-5 shows some common disk formats and indicates how they differ from the industry standard.

On most implementations of CP/M-80 the first two tracks are reserved as "system tracks"; this is where CP/M-80 is stored by SYSGEN, and sometimes this area also contains special utilities used by your particular computer. The third track on most floppy disk systems is reserved for the directory. The remaining tracks are used to store data.

CP/M-80 assigns files to "groups" of sectors. A group is composed of a fixed number of sectors, usually 8 or 16. CP/M-80 stores blocks of data 128 bytes at a time; so even if a file holds only 1 byte of information, it uses the entire group it has been assigned to, for example, 8 sectors times 128 bytes, or 1024 bytes. While this kind of organization can waste space, it is efficient: the directory need only keep track of groups rather than individual sectors.

If you have a hard disk or a double-density floppy disk on your system, it is likely that it has more than 8 sectors per group, resulting in 2028-, 4056-, and even 8112-byte groups.

Each directory entry is composed of 32-byte blocks as follows:

Byte 1 indicates whether the file is active or erased
Bytes 2 through 9 are the file name
Bytes 10 through 12 are the file type
Byte 13 is the extent number
Bytes 14 and 15 are reserved for CP/M's use
Byte 16 is the extent size in sectors
Bytes 17 through 32 store the groups assigned to the file.

TABLE 10-5. Comparison Between Common Disk Formats

Format	Number of	
	Sectors	**Tracks**
8-inch Single-Density	26	77
8-inch Double-Density	26	77
8-inch Double-Sided, Double-Density	26	144
North Star Single-Density	20	35
North Star Double-Density	40	35
Micropolis MOD II	32	77
Intertec Superbrain	40	35
Apple (256-byte sectors)	16	35
Altos Double-Density	48	77
Pickles & Trout TRS-80	64	77
Osborne 1 (256-byte sectors)	10	40

CP/M-80 uses a concept called *extents*. An extent is really a group of groups, again usually 8 or 16 in number. Each directory entry for a given file is allocated one extent. If a file is larger than 8 (or 16) groups, a second directory entry—and extent—is created for the file. The maximum size of a file is limited by the maximum number of extents allowed by your version of CP/M-80 multiplied by 128 times the number of sectors per group.

This is not as complex as it seems: a file consists of some number of extents, each extent of which consists of some number of groups, each group of which consists of some number of sectors. To illustrate this concept, here are four directory entries as they would appear in both hexadecimal and ASCII format:

```
00 41 53 4D 20 20 20 20 20 43 4F 4D 00 00 00 40 .ASM     COM...@
1B 1C 1D 1E 00 00 00 00 00 00 00 00 00 00 00 00 ................

00 5A 53 4D 20 20 20 20 20 43 4F 4D 00 00 00 3B .ZSM     COM...;
1F 20 21 22 00 00 00 00 00 00 00 00 00 00 00 00 . !"............

00 4D 38 30 20 20 20 20 20 43 4F 4D 00 00 00 80 .M80     COM....
23 24 25 26 27 28 29 2A 00 00 00 00 00 00 00 00 #$%&'()*........

00 4D 38 30 20 20 20 20 20 43 4F 4D 01 00 00 09 .M80     COM....
2B 00 00 00 00 00 00 00 00 00 00 00 00 00 00 00 +...............
```

This directory comes from an assembly language disk the author uses on his Vector Graphic computer system. This particular implementation of CP/M-80 allows only 8 groups per extent. Thus the file M80.COM occupies 9 groups (23 hex through 2B hex). Note that the second extent is marked with a 01 hex immediately following the name of the file, while the first extent has a 00 hex immediately following the name.

Disk Parameter Tables

The Disk Parameter Header (DPH) is a special area of BIOS memory reserved for important information that CP/M-80 needs to know in order to use the disk drives you own. Each disk drive has a corresponding 16-byte parameter header that contains information about the drive and provides space which the BDOS writes temporary information. Table 10-6 shows the information contained within the header.

The Disk Parameter Headers for each drive appear in order, one immediately following the other. The SELDSK routine in the BIOS should return the base address of the header for the drive selected. If a drive does not exist, SELDSK returns a 0000 hex.

Translation Vectors are referred to by the DPH but may be located elsewhere in BIOS. These are simply a listing of the sectors in the order in which they are to be read. A valid sector translate table might look like this:

```
DISKXLATE:
                DB          01,07,13,19,25
                DB          05,11,17,23,03
                DB          09,15,21,02,08
                DB          14,20,26,06,12
                DB          18,24,04,10,16
                DB          22
```

This table shows a skew factor of six (the disk drive reads a sector, then reads the

TABLE 10-6. Parameter Header Information

Byte	Title	Description
1-2	XLT	Translation Vector: the address of the sector translation table that contains the skew factor for the drive. A value of 0000 hex indicates no translation takes place. Drives using the same skew factors may share the same translate tables.
3-8	None	Two bytes of scratchpad RAM for BDOS to use.
9-10	DIRBUF	Directory Buffer: the address of a 128-byte RAM area to be used for the drive's directory operations. All drives share the same directory buffer.
11-12	DPB	Disk Parameter Block: the address of the Disk Parameter Block. Drives with identical characteristics may share the same Disk Parameter Block.
13-14	CSV	Check for Changed Disks: the address of a scratchpad area used to check for changed disks. The address must be different for each drive.
15-16	ALV	Disk Allocation Vector: the address of a scratchpad area used to keep information about the disk drive's storage allocation. The address must be different for each drive.

sector that comes six later, and so forth). With judicious experimenting and testing, changing the translate table is one way of adding disk speed.

The *Disk Parameter Block* tells CP/M-80 the layout of a drive:

Bytes	Name	Description
1-2	ST	Sectors per track
3	BS	Block shift
4	BM	Block Mask
5	EM	Extent mask
6-7	MAB	Maximum allocation block number
8-9	NDE	Number of directory entries
10-11	DGA	Directory group allocation
12-13	CDE	Check directory entry
14-15	TBD	Number of tracks skipped at beginning of disk.

THE INTERNAL STRUCTURE OF CP/M-80

Now you know the basics of CP/M-80's internal workings. If you want to find out more, consult the annotated bibliography in Appendix G; it includes a number of excellent books on the technical aspects of CP/M-80.

DIFFERENCES BETWEEN CP/M-80 AND CP/M-PLUS

CP/M-80 and CP/M-PLUS are designed to work with the same CPUs; there are only a few structural differences between CP/M-80 and CP/M-PLUS that are important to users. Most important, CP/M-PLUS can address (use) more memory than CP/M-80, which is limited to a maximum of 64K bytes. CP/M-PLUS also extends some of CP/M-80's functions and includes additional CCP, BDOS, and BIOS functions.

Two versions of CP/M-PLUS are available, banked and nonbanked. The nonbanked version, shown in Figure 10-6, works within a standard 64K memory range, like CP/M-80, and is very similar to CP/M-80 in layout.

Note that the CCP for CPM-PLUS is treated almost like a program: it resides beginning at 0100 hex and is erased when another program is brought into memory. This is not true of CP/M-80's CCP.

Banked versions of CP/M-PLUS involve multiple 64K banks of memory (not all of the 64K is taken up in every bank, however). Different implementations exist,

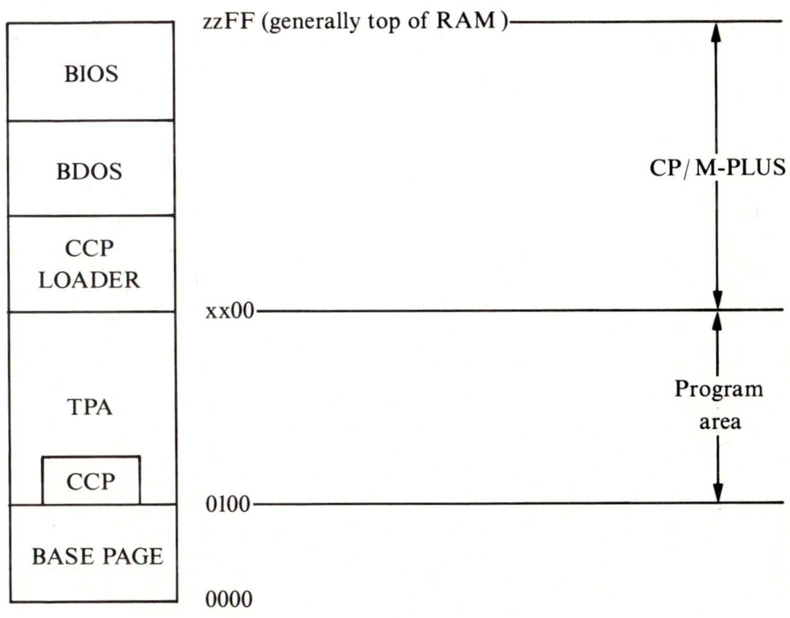

Note: All addresses are in hexadecimal. The xx and zz are dummy arguments representing addresses that change depending upon memory size.

FIGURE 10-6. Memory layout of nonbanked CP/M-PLUS system

primarily differing in the way hardware performs the actual switching between banks, but a simple banked version of CP/M-PLUS may look like that shown in Figure 10-7.

The net result of the CP/M-PLUS banked version is that the TPA is generally increased over CP/M-80's TPA (usually by about 4K-6K; it still may not be over 64K in CP/M PLUS), and large buffers are available to store the most recently used information from the disk. CP/M-PLUS itself, in the banked version, is a little larger and does a few more things than the nonbanked version (notably the line-editing commands).

Banked versions of CP/M-PLUS are desirable when performance (for instance, the speed at which disk I/O is done) is important, or when you must absolutely have the largest possible TPA.

The BIOS for a CP/M-PLUS system is identical to a CP/M-80 BIOS, with the addition of as many as 16 additional routines. Figure 10-8 shows what the new jump table looks like.

Table 10-7 explains all but USERF, RESERV1, and RESERV2 of the CP/M-PLUS BIOS functions. USERF is dependent on the system implementation, while RESERV1 and RESERV2 are reserved by Digital Research for future use.

Table 10-8 shows the BDOS functions available in CP/M-PLUS.

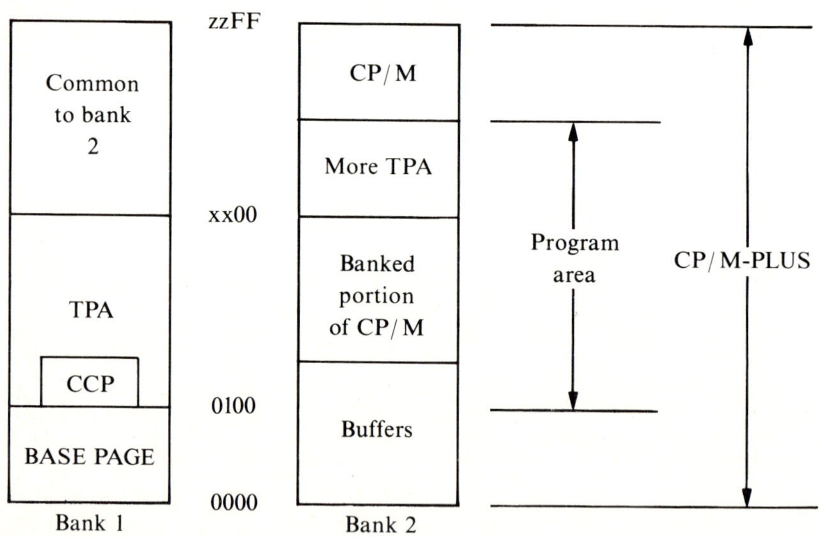

Note: All addresses are in hexadecimal. The xx and zz are dummy arguments representing addresses that change depending upon memory size.

FIGURE 10-7. Memory layout of banked CP/M-PLUS system

```
;--------------------------------------------------
;
;  BIOS FOR TYPICAL CP/M-PLUS SYSTEM
;
;--------------------------------------------------
;
;  The following jump vectors are the same as in
;    CP/M-80 version 2.2
;
         JMP   COLDBOOT
         JMP   WRMBOOT
         JMP   CONSTAT
         JMP   CONIN
         JMP   CONOUT
         JMP   LIST
         JMP   AUXOUT
         JMP   AUXIN
         JMP   HOME
         JMP   SELDISK
         JMP   SETTRACK
         JMP   SETSECTOR
         JMP   SETDMA
         JMP   READ
         JMP   WRITE
         JMP   LISTSTAT
         JMP   SECTRAN
;
;  The following are the new jump vectors that
;    must be added to a CP/M-PLUS system
;
         JMP   CONOST
         JMP   AUXIST
         JMP   AUXOST
         JMP   DEVTBL
         JMP   DEVINI
         JMP   DRVTBL
         JMP   MULTIO
         JMP   FLUSH
         JMP   MOVE
         JMP   TIME
         JMP   SELMEM
         JMP   SETBNK
         JMP   XMOVE
         JMP   USERF
         JMP   RESERV1
         JMP   RESERV2
;
; End of standard CP/M-PLUS jump table, but you may
;    extend the table to add other functions
;
```

FIGURE 10-8. Jump table for CP/M-PLUS system

TABLE 10-7. BIOS Routine Definitions for CP/M-PLUS

Label in Jump Table	Entry Parameters	Exit Parameters	Explanation
COLDBOOT	None	None	Initializes any system hardware that was not setup with the boot ROMs, the Cold Start Loader, or the LDRBIOS; initializes Page Zero jumps and loads the CCP.

SOURCE: *CP/M-PLUS System Guide,* Copyright © 1982, Digital Research, Pacific Grove, Calif.

TABLE 10-7. BIOS Routine Definitions for CP/M-PLUS (*continued*)

Label in Jump Table	Entry Parameters	Exit Parameters	Explanation
WRMBOOT	None	None	Resets Page Zero jumps and loads the CCP. After the CCP has been loaded, the routine must transfer control to the CCP.
CONSTAT	None	A = Status	Reads the status of the currently assigned console device. Returns a 00 hex if no character is ready and an FF hex if a character is present.
CONIN	None	A = Character	Reads the next character from the currently assigned console device into register A. Routine waits until a character is present.
CONOUT	C = Character	None	Sends the character in register C out to the currently assigned console device.
LIST	C = Character	None	Sends the character in register C out to the currently assigned printer device.
AUXOUT	C = Character	None	Sends the character in register C out to the currently assigned AUXOUT device.
AUXIN	None	A = Character	Reads the next character from the currently assigned AUXIN device into register A. Routine waits until a character is present.
HOME	None	None	Returns the disk head of the currently selected drive to the track 00 position.
SELDISK	C = Drive	HL = DPH	Selects the drive specified by the value in register C. Register pair HL must contain the address of the Disk Parameter Header of the drive on return.
SETTRACK	BC = Track	None	Selects the next track number for a subsequent disk access.

SOURCE: *CP/M-PLUS System Guide,* Copyright © 1982, Digital Research, Pacific Grove, Calif.

TABLE 10-7. BIOS Routine Definitions for CP/M-PLUS (*continued*)

Label in Jump Table	Entry Parameters	Exit Parameters	Explanation
SETSECTOR	BC = Sector	None	Selects the next sector number for a subsequent disk access.
SETDMA	BC = DMA	None	Sets the DMA address for the subsequent READ or WRITE operation.
READ	None	A = Status	Reads the next sector off the disk once the disk, track, sector, and DMA address have been selected.
WRITE	None	A = Status	Writes the next sector onto the disk once the disk, track, sector, and DMA address have been selected.
LISTSTAT	None	A = Status	Returns the status of the currently assigned list device.
SECTRAN	DE = Table address	HL = Physical sector number	Translates the logical sequential sector wanted to the actual physical sector on the disk.
CONOST	None	A = Status	Reads the status of the console. Returns FF hex if the console can display another character. Allows for full polled handshaking.
AUXIST	None	A = Status	Checks the input status of the auxiliary port.
AUXOST	None	A = Status	Checks the output status of the auxiliary port.
DEVTBL	None	HL = CHRTBL address	Returns the address of the character I/O table. CHRTBL replaces the IOBYTE in CP/M-PLUS.
DEVINI	C = Device number	None	Initializes the baud rate of the device specified in register C to the corresponding entry point in CHRTBL.

SOURCE: *CP/M-PLUS System Guide*, Copyright © 1982, Digital Research, Pacific Grove, Calif.

TABLE 10-7. BIOS Routine Definitions for CP/M-PLUS (*continued*)

Label in Jump Table	Entry Parameters	Exit Parameters	Explanation
DRVTBL	None	HL = DPH address	Returns the address of the disk drive tables to determine system configuration.
MULTIO	C = Multisector count	None	Sets the sector count for disk READ and WRITE operations. CP/M-PLUS can read and write anywhere from 1 to 128 sectors at a time.
FLUSH	None	A = Status	Used to flush dirty buffers from memory when blocking and deblocking is performed by the BIOS.
MOVE	HL = Destination address DE = Source address BC = Count	HL + BC DE + BC	Used to perform memory-to-memory block moves, similiar to the Z80 LDIR instruction.
TIME	C = Time get/set flag	None	Used by BDOS to indicate to the BIOS whether the time and date fields of the SCB have just been set or are about to be read. If the time is being set, the BIOS needs to update its clock.
SELMEM	A = Memory bank	None	Only used in banked systems. Used to select a particular memory bank for further execution or buffer references.
SETBNK	A = Memory bank	None	Only used in banked systems. Used to select a particular memory bank for further READ/WRITE operations.
XMOVE	B = Destination bank C = Source Bank	None	Only used in banked systems. Used in memory-type DMA operations over the entire memory range.

SOURCE: *CP/M-PLUS System Guide*, Copyright © 1982, Digital Research, Pacific Grove, Calif.

TABLE 10-8. BDOS Function Definitions for CP/M-PLUS

Function		Entry Parameters	Exit Parameters	Explanation
Number	Name			
00	SYSTEM RESET	None	None	Terminates the calling program and returns control to the CCP via a warm start sequence. Calling this function has the same effect as a jump to location 0000 hex of Page Zero. The disk subsystem is not reset by this function in CP/M-PLUS.
01	CONSOLE INPUT	None	A = ASCII character	Reads the next character from the logical console to register A. Graphic characters, along with CARRIAGE RETURN, LINE FEED, and BACKSPACE are echoed on the console. Tab characters are expanded in columns of 8 characters. CONTROL-S, CONTROL-Q, and CONTROL-P are normally intercepted. All other non-graphic characters are returned in register A but not echoed on the console. Control of the program will not resume until a character has been typed.
02	CONSOLE OUTPUT	E = ASCII character	None	Sends the ASCII character in register E to the logical console device.
03	AUXILIARY INPUT	None	A = ASCII character	Reads the next character from the logical auxiliary input device into register A. Control does not return until a character has been read.

SOURCE: *CP/M-PLUS Programmer's Guide*, Copyright © 1982, Digital Research, Pacific Grove, Calif.

TABLE 10-8. BDOS Function Definitions for CP/M-PLUS (*continued*)

Function		Entry Parameters	Exit Parameters	Explanation
Number	**Name**			
04	AUXILIARY OUTPUT	E = ASCII character	None	Sends the ASCII character in register E to the logical auxiliary output device.
05	LIST OUTPUT	E = ASCII character	None	Sends the ASCII character in register E to the logical list device.
06	DIRECT CONSOLE I/O	E = FF hex E = FE hex E = FD hex E = ASCII character	A = Input/status A = Status A = Input A = Output	Used to do direct I/O to and from the logical console. This function bypasses all normal control character functions. Programs should now use the function rather than do direct I/O through the BIOS.
07	AUXILIARY INPUT STATUS	None	A = Status	Returns the status (FF hex if character waiting, 00 hex if not) of the logical auxiliary input device.
08	AUXILIARY OUTPUT STATUS	None	A = Status	Returns the status (FF hex if character can be sent, 00 hex if not) of the logical auxiliary output device.
09	PRINT STRING	DE = String address	None	Sends to the logical console device the string whose address is found in register pair DE. The string must end with a dollar sign, $.
0A	READ CONSOLE BUFFER	DE = Buffer address	Data in buffer	Performs the same function as the CCP in that it takes characters typed and stores them in the buffer that begins with the address found in register pair DE. The first byte must be the maximum length of the command.

SOURCE: *CP/M-PLUS Programmer's Guide*, Copyright © 1982, Digital Research, Pacific Grove, Calif.

TABLE 10-8. BDOS Function Definitions for CP/M-PLUS (*continued*)

Function		Entry Parameters	Exit Parameters	Explanation
Number	**Name**			
0A (cont.)				The second byte will contain the actual length. It will be rcturned by the BDOS. All standard CCP editing commands are recognized during entry.
0B	GET CONSOLE STATUS	None	A = Status	Checks to see if a character has been typed. A 00 hex is returned if no character is present, or an FF hex is returned is a character has been typed.
0C	RETURN VERSION NUMBER	None	HL = Version	Register H is set to 00 hex if CP/M is being used, 01 hex if MP/M is being used. Register L is set to 00 hex if the version is earlier than 3.0, 30 hex if version 3.0, 31 hex if version 3.1 and so on.
0D	RESET DISK SYSTEM	None	All drives set to R/W	Used to reset the entire system during operation. Should be used if disks are changed during the running of a program.
0E	SELECT DISK	E = Drive number	A = Error flag H = Physical error	Designates the drive named in register E as the default drive for subsequent BDOS file operations.
0F	OPEN FILE	DE = FCB address	A = Directory code H = Physical or extended error	Activates the FCB for a file that exists in the disk directory under the current user number or user zero.

SOURCE: *CP/M-PLUS Programmer's Guide,* Copyright ©1982, Digital Research, Pacific Grove, Calif.

TABLE 10-8. BDOS Function Definitions for CP/M-PLUS (*continued*)

Function		Entry Parameters	Exit Parameters	Explanation
Number	Name			
10	CLOSE FILE	DE = FCB address	A = Directory code H = Physical error	Closes a previously opened file. This function must be performed if any records were written to the file while it was open.
11	SEARCH FOR FIRST	DE = FCB address	A = Directory code H = Physical error	Performs the same as the open file function except that the disk buffer is filled with the directory entry of the matched file. This function also initializes function 12.
12	SEARCH FOR NEXT	DE = FCB address	A = Directory code H = Physical error	Performs the same as function 11, but continues on from the last matched entry.
13	DELETE FILE	DE = FCB address	A = Directory code H = Extended or physical error	Performs the first byte in the directory entry for the file or XFCB to F5 hex. This signifies to the system that the blocks previously allocated are now available for other files.
14	READ SEQUENTIAL	DE = FCB address	A = Error code H = Physical error	Reads the next 128-byte record(s) from a file into memory beginning at the current DMA address.
15	WRITE SEQUENTIAL	DE = FCB address	A = Error code H = Physical error	Writes the next 128-byte record(s) from memory to disk beginning at the current DMA address.

SOURCE: *CP/M-PLUS Programmer's Guide*, Copyright © 1982, Digital Research, Pacific Grove, Calif.

TABLE 10-8. BDOS Function Definitions for CP/M-PLUS (*continued*)

Function		Entry Parameters	Exit Parameters	Explanation
Number	Name			
16	MAKE FILE	DE = FCB address	A = DIR code H = Extended or physical error	Creates a new directory entry for a file under the current user number. An XFCB is also created if a password is assigned to the file.
17	RENAME FILE	DE = FCB address	A = DIR code H = Extended or physical error	Changes the name of the file referenced by the first 16 bytes of the FCB block to the name given in the second 16 bytes.
18	RETURN LOGIN VECTOR	None	HL = Disk login	Returns the bit map for all possible drives in register pair HL. Bit 0 is the status of drive A; bit 15 is the status of drive P. A logic 1 means the drive is active; a logic 0 means inactive.
19	RETURN CURRENT DISK	None	A = Current disk	Returns the number of the current default drive (00 hex to 10 hex).
1A	SET DMA ADDRESS	DE = DMA	None	Sets the DMA address for all disk operations to the address found in register pair DE.
1B	GET ALLOC ADDRESS	None	HL = Allocation address	Returns the address of the Allocation Vector for the currently selected drive in register pair HL.
1C	WRITE-PROTECT DISK	None	None	Provides temporary write-protection for the currently selected drive. A drive RESET operation must be performed so the disk can be written to.
1D	GET R/O VECTOR	None	HL = Disk R/O	Returns a bit vector for all possible drives in the

SOURCE: *CP/M-PLUS Programmer's Guide*, Copyright ©1982, Digital Research, Pacific Grove, Calif.

TABLE 10-8. BDOS Function Definitions for CP/M-PLUS (*continued*)

Function		Entry Parameters	Exit Parameters	Explanation
Number	**Name**			
1D (cont.)				system. The format and meaning of the bits is the same as that returned by function 18.
1E	SET FILE ATTRIBUTES	DE = FCB address	A = DIR code H = Extended or physical error	Sets the attributes of a file whose FCB address is found in register pair DE. The attributes that can be set or reset are read-only, system, and archive.
1F	GET DISK PARMS	None	HL = DPB address	Returns in register pair HL the address of the BIOS-resident Disk Parameter Block for the current default drive.
20	GET USER CODE SET USER CODE	E = FF hex E = User code	A = Current user None	Used to change or interrogate the current user number. The value in register E must be between 00 hex and 0F hex. If the value in register E is not FF hex or in the set range, then the current user number is set to 0E hex.
21	READ RANDOM	DE = FCB address	A = Error code H = Physical error	Reads the next random record pointed to by the FCB.
22	WRITE RANDOM	DE = FCB address	A = Error code H = Physical error	Writes the next random record pointed to by the FCB.
23	COMPUTE FILE SIZE	DE = FCB address	RRF set A = Error code H =	Determines the size of a file based on the address of the last actual record found in a randomly

SOURCE: *CP/M-PLUS Programmer's Guide,* Copyright © 1982, Digital Research, Pacific Grove, Calif.

TABLE 10-8. BDOS Function Definitions for CP/M-PLUS (*continued*)

Function		Entry Parameters	Exit Parameters	Explanation
Number	Name			
23 (cont.)			Extended or physical error	written file. The DMA address is set to that record's address.
24	SET RANDOM RECORD	DE = FCB address	RRF set	Returns the next random record after the last sequential READ has been performed.
25	RESET DRIVE	DE = Reset drive bits	A = 00	Restores the specified drives to a RESET condition. The format of the word used corresponds to the same layout as that used in function 18.
28	WRITE RANDOM (ZERO)	DE = FCB address	A = Error code H = Extended or physical error	Performs the same as function 22, but the buffer specified by register pair DE is set to all zeroes before the WRITE is performed. Useful for identifying unused records in a randomly written file.
2C	SET MULTI-SECTOR COUNT	E = Number of sectors	A = Return code	Enables a program to READ and WRITE from 1 to 128 records during read and write operations.
2D	SET BDOS ERROR MODE	E = BDOS error mode	None	Used to determine how errors are handled by a program. Modes are default, Return Error, and Return and Display.
2E	GET DISK FREE SPACE	E = Drive	First 3 bytes of current DMA buffer A = Error flag H = Physical error	Used to determine how many free sectors are available on the specified drive.

SOURCE: *CP/M-PLUS Programmer's Guide,* Copyright © 1982, Digital Research, Pacific Grove, Calif.

TABLE 10-8. BDOS Function Definitions for CP/M-PLUS (*continued*)

Function		Entry Parameters	Exit Parameters	Explanation
Number	Name			
2F	CHAIN TO PROGRAM	E = Chain flag	None	Allows a program to chain from one program to another without an operator being needed.
30	FLUSH BUFFERS	E = Purge flag	A = Error flag H = Physical error	Used to flush any WRITE-pending records from the internal buffers.
31	GET/SET SYSTEM CONTROL BLOCK	DE = SCB PB address	A = Returned byte HL = Returned word	Allows access to the System Control Block parameters.
32	DIRECT BIOS CALLS	DE = BIOS PB address	BIOS RETURN	Used to make direct BIOS calls through the BDOS.
3B	LOAD OVERLAY	DE = FCB address	A = Error code H = Physical error	Used only with programs with an RSX header. Allows absolute and relocatable modules to be loaded.
3C	CALL RESIDENT SYSTEM EXTENSION	DE = RSX PB address	A = Error code H = Physical error	Used only with programs with an RSX header. Allows you to use Resident System Extensions.
62	FREE BLOCKS	None	A = Error flag H = Physical error	Used to return to free space all temporarily allocated data blocks on all logged-in drives.
63	TRUNCATE FILE	DE = FCB address	A = Directory code H = Extended or physical error	Sets the last record of a file to the random record number contained in the FCB.

SOURCE: *CP/M-PLUS Programmer's Guide*, Copyright ©1982, Digital Research, Pacific Grove, Calif.

TABLE 10-8. BDOS Function Definitions for CP/M-PLUS (*continued*)

Function		Entry Parameters	Exit Parameters	Explanation
Number	Name			
64	SET DIRECTORY LABEL	DE = FCB address	A = Directory code H = Physical or extended error	Creates a directory label or updates the current label for the specified drive.
65	RETURN DIRECTORY LABEL DATA	E = Drive	A = Directory Label Data Byte H = Physical error	Returns the data byte of the directory label for the specified drive.
66	READ FILE DATE STAMPS AND PASSWORD MODE	DE = FCB address	A = Directory code H = Physical error	Returns the date and time stamp information and password mode for the specified file given in the FCB.
67	WRITE FILE XFCB	DE = FCB address	A = Directory code H = Physical error	Creates a new XFCB or updates the existing XFCB for the specified file.
68	SET DATE AND TIME	DE = DAT address	None	Sets the system internal date and time.
69	GET DATE AND TIME	DE = DAT address	DAT set A = seconds	Obtains the system internal date and time.
6A	SET DEFAULT PASSWORD	DE = Password address	None	Used to specify a password for a file before the file is accessed.
6B	RETURN SERIAL NUMBER	DE = Serial number field	Serial number field set	Returns the system's CP/M-PLUS serial number.

SOURCE: *CP/M-PLUS Programmer's Guide*, Copyright © 1982, Digital Research, Pacific Grove, Calif.

TABLE 10-8. BDOS Function Definitions for CP/M-PLUS (*continued*)

Function		Entry Parameters	Exit Parameters	Explanation
Number	Name			
6C	GET PROGRAM RETURN CODE SET PROGRAM RETURN CODE	DE = FFFF DE = Code	HL = Program return code None	Allows a program in batch mode to pass to the next program an error code or special value.
6D	GET CONSOLE MODE SET CONSOLE MODE	DE = FFFF DE = Mode	HL = Console mode None	Used to determine the action of the BDOS console I/O functions.
6E	GET OUTPUT DELIMITER SET OUTPUT DELIMITER	DE = FFFF E = Delimiter	A = Output delimiter None	Used to set or get the current Print String delimiter
6F	PRINT BLOCK	DE = CCB address	None	Sends the string located by the CCB to the logical console
70	LIST BLOCK	DE = CCB address	None	Sends the string located by the CCB to the logical list device.
98	PARSE FILENAME	DE = PFCB address	Parsed FCB HL = Return code	Used to parse an ASCII file specification and prepare an FCB.

SOURCE: *CP/M-PLUS Programmer's Guide,* Copyright ©1982, Digital Research, Pacific Grove, Calif.

SYSTEM CONTROL BLOCK

Many of the internal portions of CP/M-PLUS and CP/M-80 are different, primarily because CP/M-PLUS can extend across banks of memory. One primary component that is unique to CP/M-PLUS is the *System Control Block,* or SCB as it is often referred to. The SCB is a 100-byte data structure that resides within the BDOS and contains important information needed by the BDOS and the CCP. It is from data within the SCB that many of the additional CP/M-PLUS features are controlled. The following is a list of the data kept by the SCB:

- BDOS version number
- Console width
- Console page length

- Drive search chain
- Common memory address
- Current disk
- Current user number
- Console column position
- Redirection flags for CON, AUX, LST date stamp active
- DMA address.

The SCB thus serves as a clearinghouse for information about CP/M-PLUS's current status. And while not in the scope of this book, adding functions to CP/M using RSX files involves the information in the SCB.

Except for the SCB, CP/M-PLUS is extremely similar to CP/M-80 in both structure and use. Digital Research provides three manuals with CP/M-PLUS, the *CP/M 3 User's Guide*, the *CP/M 3 Programmer's Guide*, and the *CP/M 3 System Guide*. These manuals are invaluable in learning more about the differences between CP/M-PLUS and CP/M-80.

CHAPTER

11 Assembly Language Programming With CP/M

This chapter combines many of the things you learned in the previous three chapters with a logical programming style for CP/M. We will create and assemble a small CP/M assembly language program, with an emphasis on program "portability" (the capability of the program to be used on many different systems without changes).

We will just touch on some basic programming practices here. If you desire more information about programming with CP/M, you should consult *The Programmer's CP/M Handbook*, by Andy Johnson-Laird (see Bibliography, Appendix G).

USING BDOS

What probably trips up most beginning CP/M programmers is the use of CP/M BDOS functions to make program code not dependent upon finding CP/M at any given fixed memory location. The exact location of CP/M in memory depends upon which version of CP/M you are using, how much memory the computer has, and whether any changes have been made to CP/M. That's a lot of variables, and what is true for the system today may not be true for it tomorrow (you may add more memory, for instance). Therefore, instead of referring to a fixed location within BDOS to get CP/M to perform a function, we use what is known as a BDOS *call.*

We will demonstrate the proper way of using BDOS by writing a short program to display a string on the console. As noted in Chapter 10, the print string function number is 09 hex. The DE register pair must contain the address of the string, and the string must be terminated by a $ in order for the function to work properly. To display a string,

1. Your program must place the string somewhere in memory, terminated by a $.
2. The program places an 09 hex in the C register.
3. The program places the starting address of the string in register pair DE.
4. The program calls BDOS via BDOS entry vector at 0005 hex.
5. BDOS performs the "print string" function and returns execution to your program.

Note step number 4; this is the clue to writing programs that will work on any CP/M system. All versions of CP/M use memory location 0005 to store a 3-byte instruction (ostensibly JMP BDOS). If you call this known, unchanging memory location, proper operation is guaranteed.

Here is one way to perform these steps in assembly language:

```
;-----------------------------------------------
; PRINT A STRING EXAMPLE
; Uses BDOS entry vector at 0005 hex.
;-----------------------------------------------
;
BDOS        EQU      0005H      ;The BDOS entry vector
STRING      EQU      09H        ;The PRINT STRING function #
;
            ORG      0100H      ;Start in the TPA please
DOIT:       MVI      C,STRING   ;Prepare the function call
            LXI      D,LABEL    ;Point to the string
            CALL     BDOS       ;Do it!
;
GETOUT:     JMP      0000H      ;Restart CP/M (not part of
                                ;  the example, but necessary
                                ;  to make this a "runnable"
                                ;  example.)
;
LABEL:      DB       'DOCTOR, MY PROBLEM IS$'
;
            END
```

This is a complete CP/M program that should run if you type it in and assemble it as explained in Chapters 8 and 9.

Most experienced assembly language programmers use equates to assign names to the values for each function and for the location of BDOS, as in the previous example. This practice makes the program much easier to understand. A novice programmer might create the same assembly language program like this:

```
ORG      100H
MVI      C,9
LXI      D,$+10
CALL     5
JMP      0
DB       'DOCTOR,'
DB       'MY PROBLEM IS'
DB       '$'
END
```

While this is functionally accurate, it is unnecessarily vague.

In addition, it is wise to begin building a set of standard routines for your assembly language programming, all of which should utilize BDOS functions when possible. For example, an experienced programmer might code the same program like this:

```
;-----------------------------------------
; PROGRAM TO PRINT OUT A STRING          |
;-----------------------------------------
;
WARM        EQU      0000H      ;CP/M restart
BDOS        EQU      0005H      ;BDOS entry
STRING      EQU      09H        ;Print string function
;
BEGIN:      LXI      D,LABEL
            CALL     PRINT
            JMP      WARM
;
; PRINT STRING FUNCTION:
; Expects string address in DE register.
; String MUST be terminated with a $.
;
; Uses DE, C registers
;
PRINT:      MVI      C,STRING
            JMP      BDOS
;
LABEL:      'This is the string to print$.'
            END
```

The advantage of using standard routines is that it avoids some unnecessary, repeated steps when the program must print out strings several times. It also helps isolate your custom programming from programming that should be standardized and always work the same way (BDOS calls). We did introduce one trick here: the PRINT routine "jumps" to BDOS instead of calling it. By noting that the routine is repetitive in this instance, we save an extra byte (a RET instruction) and a bit of execution time, since BDOS will provide the RET instructions.

A STANDARDIZED WAY OF CODING ASSEMBLY LANGUAGE IN CP/M

As mentioned earlier, good CP/M programmers tend to gather the sets of routines and equates that they use over and over. Creating these files is easy to do in CP/M, since it need be done only once, no matter how many CP/M assembly language programs you create.

One such file is shown in Figure 11-1, a commented file called EQUATES.ASM that defines all of the standard CP/M equates you may commonly use.

Many computers use different characters and sequences of characters to perform cursor handling and other functions. Therefore, we will use a file containing these

```
;------------------------------------------------------------
;   SOME COMMON DEFINITIONS
;------------------------------------------------------------
;
FALSE       EQU   00H                 ;Standard false value
TRUE        EQU   NOT FALSE           ;Standard true value
;
;   One of the following should be set to TRUE, others FALSE:
;
CPM80       EQU   TRUE                ;CP/M-80 present if TRUE
MPM80       EQU   FALSE               ;MP/M-80 present if TRUE
CPMPLUS     EQU   FALSE               ;CP/M-PLUS present if TRUE
;
WARM        EQU   0000H               ;Warm start in BIOS
IOBYTE      EQU   0003H               ;I/O device block
CDISK       EQU   0004H               ;Current disk drive
BDOS        EQU   0005H               ;CP/M function access
CPMFCB      EQU   005CH               ;Standard file control block
CPMBUFF     EQU   0080H               ;Standard file buffer
TPA         EQU   0100H               ;Transient program area
;
;------------------------------------------------------------
;   COMMON CHARACTER EQUATES
;------------------------------------------------------------
;
CR          EQU   0DH                 ;Carriage return
LF          EQU   0AH                 ;Line feed
BS          EQU   08H                 ;Destructive backspace
TAB         EQU   09H                 ;Tab over 8 spaces
BELL        EQU   07H                 ;Sound bell
ESCAPE      EQU   1BH                 ;Escape character
BLANK       EQU   20H                 ;Space character
;
;------------------------------------------------------------
;   CP/M FUNCTION EQUATES
;------------------------------------------------------------
;
RESET       EQU   0                   ;System reset
INCON       EQU   1                   ;Console input
OUTCON      EQU   2                   ;Console output
INREAD      EQU   3                   ;Reader input
OUTPUN      EQU   4                   ;Punch output
OUTLST      EQU   5                   ;List output
DIRECT      EQU   6                   ;Direct console I/O
GETIOB      EQU   7                   ;Get current IOBYTE
SETIOB      EQU   8                   ;Set current IOBYTE
STRING      EQU   9                   ;Print string
CBREAD      EQU   10                  ;Read console buffer
GETSTAT     EQU   11                  ;Get console status
VERSION     EQU   12                  ;Get CP/M version number
SETDISK     EQU   13                  ;Reset disk system
SELDISK     EQU   14                  ;Select disk to use
OPEN        EQU   15                  ;Open file
CLOSE       EQU   16                  ;Close file
SRCHONE     EQU   17                  ;Search for first record
SRCHNXT     EQU   18                  ;Search for next record
```

FIGURE 11-1. EQUATES.ASM

```
DELETE    EQU  19          ;Delete file
SEQREAD   EQU  20          ;Sequential file read
SEQRITE   EQU  21          ;Sequential file write
CREATE    EQU  22          ;Make file
RENAME    EQU  23          ;Rename file
LOGIN     EQU  24          ;Return login vector
CURDISK   EQU  25          ;Return current disk used
SETDMA    EQU  26          ;Set DMA address
GETADDR   EQU  27          ;Get address allocation
PROTECT   EQU  28          ;Write protect disk
GETRO     EQU  29          ;Get receive only vector
SETFILE   EQU  30          ;Set file attributes
GETPARM   EQU  31          ;Get address disk parameters
SETUSER   EQU  32          ;Set/Get user code
RANREAD   EQU  33          ;Read random record
RANRITE   EQU  34          ;Write random record
COMPUTE   EQU  35          ;Compute file size
SETRAN    EQU  36          ;Set random record
;
          IF   CPMPLUS OR MPM80
RESETDR   EQU  37          ;Reset drive
ACCDRV    EQU  38          ;Access drive
FREEDRV   EQU  39          ;Free drive
RANZERO   EQU  40          ;Write random with zero fill
TSTRITE   EQU  41          ;Test and write record
LOCKREC   EQU  42          ;Lock record
FREEREC   EQU  43          ;Unlock record
MULTIS    EQU  44          ;Multi-sector I/O
ERRORM    EQU  45          ;Set error mode
DSKSPACE  EQU  46          ;Get disk free space
CHAIN     EQU  47          ;Chain program
FLUSHB    EQU  48          ;Flush buffers
SCBSET    EQU  49          ;Get/Set system control block
DIRBIOS   EQU  50          ;Direct BIOS call
LOVER     EQU  59          ;Load overlay
CALLRSX   EQU  60          ;Call resident system extension
FREEBLK   EQU  98          ;Free blocks
TRUNK     EQU  99          ;Truncate file
DIRLABEL  EQU  100         ;Set directory label
DIRDATA   EQU  101         ;Return directory label data
READSTMP  EQU  102         ;Read date/time stamps
RITEXFCB  EQU  103         ;Write XFCB
SETTIME   EQU  104         ;Set date and time
GETTIME   EQU  105         ;Get date and time
SETPASS   EQU  106         ;Set default password
SERIAL    EQU  107         ;Return serial number
PROGSET   EQU  108         ;Get/Set program return code
CONSET    EQU  109         ;Get/Set console mode
DELIMSET  EQU  110         ;Get/Set output delimiter
PRBLOCK   EQU  111         ;Print block
LSTBLOCK  EQU  112         ;List block
PRSENAME  EQU  152         ;Parse filename
          ENDIF
;
```

FIGURE 11-1. EQUATES.ASM (*continued*)

definitions. Figure 11-2 shows this file, called OSBORNE.ASM because it contains Osborne 1 definitions.

Next we need a standard method of entering and leaving a CP/M program. We will handle this with two assembly language routines, START and STOP. This file, called FRAME.ASM, is shown in Figure 11-3.

```
;----------------------------------------------
; CONTROL CHARACTER AND LOCATION DEFINITIONS
;
; FOR OSBORNE 1
;----------------------------------------------
;
; CURSOR EQUATES:
;
LEFT      EQU  08H            ;Left cursor key
DOWN      EQU  0AH            ;Down
UP        EQU  0BH            ;Up
RIGHT     EQU  0CH            ;Right
XY        EQU  3DH            ;Goto xy lead-in
HOME      EQU  1EH            ;Home cursor
;
; SCREEN CONTROL:
;
SCRCLR    EQU  1AH            ;Clear screen
SCRXY     EQU  53H            ;Screen xy lead-in
CHRINS    EQU  51H            ;Insert character at cursor
CHRDEL    EQU  57H            ;Delete character
LININS    EQU  45H            ;Insert line
LINDEL    EQU  52H            ;Delete line
EOLDEL    EQU  54H            ;Delete to end of line
;
; HIGHLIGHTING:
;
DIM       EQU  29H            ;Begin dim characters
BRIGHT    EQU  28H            ;Begin bright
GRAPH     EQU  67H            ;Begin graphic
NOGRAPH   EQU  47H            ;End graphic
ULINE     EQU  6CH            ;Begin underline
NOULINE   EQU  6DH            ;End underline
;
; ADDRESSES:
;
CURSOR    EQU  0EF5AH         ;Location of cursor
SCREEN    EQU  0F000H         ;Beginning of screen RAM
;
; SIZES:
;
OFFSET    EQU  2020H          ;Offset bias for cursor position
SCRWIDE   EQU  80H            ;Width of line in RAM
SCRHITE   EQU  20H            ;Height of line in RAM
DISWIDE   EQU  34H            ;Width of display
DISHITE   EQU  18H            ;Height of display
;
```

FIGURE 11-2. OSBORNE.ASM

```
;------------------------------------------------------------
; START: PROGRAM ENTRY ROUTINE
;------------------------------------------------------------
;
          ORG   TPA
START:    LHLD  BDOS+1      ;Move BDOS location to HL
          SPHL              ;Set stack pointer to BDOS
          LXI   D,0-128     ;Set stack size to 128
          DAD   D           ;Calculate bottom of stack area
          DCX   H           ;HL = last byte of TPA
          JMP   GO          ;Go to beginning of user program
;
;------------------------------------------------------------
; STOP: PROGRAM EXIT ROUTINE
;------------------------------------------------------------
;
STOP:     JMP   WARM        ;Do a CP/M warm start
```

FIGURE 11-3. FRAME.ASM

Common functions can be grouped into yet another source file. Figure 11-4 shows this file, called ROUTINES.ASM.

We are now ready to begin programming.

We invoke our editor and then read in the following files in this order:

EQUATES.ASM
OSBORNE.ASM
FRAME.ASM
FUNCTIONS.ASM

The busywork for our programming task is done by reading in these four files—all we have to do is type in the statements needed to create a full program. Granted, we may have source code in our final file that is not used, but that does not really matter, since the assembly process will simply ignore it. To create a program that clears the screen and then presents a message on the screen until the user presses a key, we only have to add the following statements to those of our standard files already entered:

```
;==========================================================
; PROGRAM STARTS HERE
;
GO:   CALL CLEAR                  ;Clear the screen
      LXI  D,MESSAGE              ;Point to message
      CALL PRINT                  ;Print it
      CALL CONIN                  ;Get a keyboard response
      JMP  STOP                   ;End of program
;
MESSAGE:   DB   'This is a sample message$'
;
      END
```

```
;--------------------------------------------------------
; ROUTINES.ASM
; COMMON CP/M FUNCTIONS USING THE BDOS
;--------------------------------------------------------
;
STRIP       EQU  TRUE               ;Strip high order bit
;
; CONIN:    console input
;           entry:    nothing
;           exit:     character in A register
;
CONIN:      CALL      CONST
            ORA       A
            JZ        CONIN         ;No character yet
            RET
;
; CONST:    console status
;           entry:    nothing
;           exit:     status in A (FF=no char  00=char)
;
CONST:      PUSH B
            PUSH D
            PUSH H
            MVI  E,TRUE             ;Input please
            MVI  C,DIRECT           ;Use direct console I/O
            CALL BDOS
            POP  H
            POP  D
            POP  B
            RET
;
; CONOUT:   console output
;           entry:    character to display in A
;           exit:     nothing
;
CONOUT:     PUSH B
            PUSH D
            PUSH H
            IF   STRIP
            ANI  7FH                ;Strip high order bit (optional)
ENDIF
            MOV  E,A                ;Get character in C for CP/M
            MVI  C,DIRECT
            CALL BDOS
            POP  H
            POP  D
            POP  B
            RET
;
; XYOUT:    XY position cursor
;           entry:    Y position in H, X in L
;           exit:     nothing
;
XYOUT:      MVI  A,ESCAPE           ;First lead-in character
            CALL CONOUT
            MVI  A,XY               ;Second lead-in character
```

FIGURE 11-4. ROUTINES.ASM

```
             CALL CONOUT
             LXI  D,OFFSET         ;Offset for cursor position
             DAD  D                ;Added to HL
             MOV  A,H              ;Y out
             CALL CONOUT
             MOV  A,L              ;X out
             CALL CONOUT
             RET
;
; CRLF:      display CR/LF pair on screen
;            entry:     nothing
;            exit:      nothing
;
CRLF:        PUSH PSW
             MVI  A,CR
             CALL CONOUT
             MVI  A,LF
             CALL CONOUT
             POP  PSW
             RET
;
; SPACE:     display a space on screen
;            entry:     nothing
;            exit:      nothing
;
SPACE:       PUSH PSW
             MVI  A,BLANK
             CALL CONOUT
             POP  PSW
             RET
;
; CLEAR:     clear display
;            entry:     nothing
;            exit:      nothing
;
CLEAR:       PUSH PSW
             MVI  A,SCRCLR
             CALL CONOUT
             POP  PSW
             RET
;
; PRINT: print string on display
;           entry:     DE = string address (terminated with $)
;           exit:      nothing
;
PRINT:     PUSH B
           PUSH D
           PUSH H
           MVI  C,STRING
           CALL BDOS
           POP  H
           POP  D
           POP  B
           RET
;
```

FIGURE 11-4. ROUTINES.ASM (*continued*)

Not much to type, is it? By using standardized "header" files to do all the dirty work, we have reduced the actual programming task to some simple, easily scanned lines. The result, after assembling the sample file above (the PRN listing), is shown in Figure 11-5.

```
                 ;-------------------------------------------------
                 ;  SOME COMMON DEFINITIONS
                 ;-------------------------------------------------
                 ;
0000 =           FALSE      EQU   00H              ;Standard false value
FFFF =           TRUE       EQU   NOT FALSE        ;Standard true value
                 ;
                 ;  One of the following should be set to TRUE, others FALSE:
                 ;
FFFF =           CPM80      EQU   TRUE             ;CP/M-80 present if TRUE
0000 =           MPM80      EQU   FALSE            ;MP/M-80 present if TRUE
0000 =           CPMPLUS    EQU   FALSE            ;CP/M-PLUS present if TRUE
                 ;
0000 =           WARM       EQU   0000H            ;Warm start in BIOS
0003 =           IOBYTE     EQU   0003H            ;I/O device block
0004 =           CDISK      EQU   0004H            ;Current disk drive
0005 =           BDOS       EQU   0005H            ;CP/M function access
005C =           CPMFCB     EQU   005CH            ;Standard file control block
0080 =           CPMBUFF    EQU   0080H            ;Standard file buffer
0100 =           TPA        EQU   0100H            ;Transient program area
                 ;
                 ;-------------------------------------------------
                 ;  COMMON CHARACTER EQUATES
                 ;-------------------------------------------------
                 ;
000D =           CR         EQU   0DH              ;Carriage return
000A =           LF         EQU   0AH              ;Line feed
0008 =           BS         EQU   08H              ;Destructive backspace
0009 =           TAB        EQU   09H              ;Tab over 8 spaces
0007 =           BELL       EQU   07H              ;Sound bell
001B =           ESCAPE     EQU   1BH              ;Escape character
0020 =           BLANK      EQU   20H              ;Space character
                 ;
                 ;-------------------------------------------------
                 ;  CP/M FUNCTION EQUATES
                 ;-------------------------------------------------
                 ;
0000 =           RESET      EQU   0                ;System reset
0001 =           INCON      EQU   1                ;Console input
0002 =           OUTCON     EQU   2                ;Console output
0003 =           INREAD     EQU   3                ;Reader input
0004 =           OUTPUN     EQU   4                ;Punch output
0005 =           OUTLST     EQU   5                ;List output
0006 =           DIRECT     EQU   6                ;Direct console I/O
0007 =           GETIOB     EQU   7                ;Get current IOBYTE
0008 =           SETIOB     EQU   8                ;Set current IOBYTE
0009 =           STRING     EQU   9                ;Print string
000A =           CBREAD     EQU   10               ;Read console buffer
000B =           GETSTAT    EQU   11               ;Get console status
000C =           VERSION    EQU   12               ;Get CP/M version number
000D =           SETDISK    EQU   13               ;Reset disk system
000E =           SELDISK    EQU   14               ;Select disk to use
000F =           OPEN       EQU   15               ;Open file
0010 =           CLOSE      EQU   16               ;Close file
0011 =           SRCHONE    EQU   17               ;Search for first record
0012 =           SRCHNXT    EQU   18               ;Search for next record
0013 =           DELETE     EQU   19               ;Delete file
0014 =           SEQREAD    EQU   20               ;Sequential file read
0015 =           SEQRITE    EQU   21               ;Sequential file write
0016 =           CREATE     EQU   22               ;Make file
0017 =           RENAME     EQU   23               ;Rename file
```

FIGURE 11-5. Assembled program using standard header files

```
0018 =          LOGIN     EQU  24             ;Return login vector
0019 =          CURDISK   EQU  25             ;Return current disk used
001A =          SETDMA    EQU  26             ;Set DMA address
001B =          GETADDR   EQU  27             ;Get address allocation
001C =          PROTECT   EQU  28             ;Write protect disk
001D =          GETRO     EQU  29             ;Get receive only vector
001E =          SETFILE   EQU  30             ;Set file attributes
001F =          GETPARM   EQU  31             ;Get address disk parameters
0020 =          SETUSER   EQU  32             ;Set/Get user code
0021 =          RANREAD   EQU  33             ;Read random record
0022 =          RANRITE   EQU  34             ;Write random record
0023 =          COMPUTE   EQU  35             ;Compute file size
0024 =          SETRAN    EQU  36             ;Set random record
                ;
                          IF   CPMPLUS OR MPM80
                RESETDR   EQU  37             ;Reset drive
                ACCDRV    EQU  38             ;Access drive
                FREEDRV   EQU  39             ;Free drive
                RANZERO   EQU  40             ;Write random with zero fill
                TSTRITE   EQU  41             ;Test and write record
                LOCKREC   EQU  42             ;Lock record
                FREEREC   EQU  43             ;Unlock record
                MULTIS    EQU  44             ;Multi-sector I/O
                ERRORM    EQU  45             ;Set error mode
                DSKSPACE  EQU  46             ;Get disk free space
                CHAIN     EQU  47             ;Chain program
                FLUSHB    EQU  48             ;Flush buffers
                SCBSET    EQU  49             ;Get/Set system control block
                DIRBIOS   EQU  50             ;Direct BIOS call
                LOVER     EQU  59             ;Load overlay
                CALLRSX   EQU  60             ;Call resident system extension
                FREEBLK   EQU  98             ;Free blocks
                TRUNK     EQU  99             ;Truncate file
                DIRLABEL  EQU  100            ;Set directory label
                DIRDATA   EQU  101            ;Return directory label data
                READSTMP  EQU  102            ;Read date/time stamps
                RITEXFCB  EQU  103            ;Write XFCB
                SETTIME   EQU  104            ;Set date and time
                GETTIME   EQU  105            ;Get date and time
                SETPASS   EQU  106            ;Set default password
                SERIAL    EQU  107            ;Return serial number
                PROGSET   EQU  108            ;Get/Set program return code
                CONSET    EQU  109            ;Get/Set console mode
                DELIMSET  EQU  110            ;Get/Set output delimiter
                PRBLOCK   EQU  111            ;Print block
                LSTBLOCK  EQU  112            ;List block
                PRSENAME  EQU  152            ;Parse filename
                          ENDIF
                ;
                ;------------------------------------------------------
                ; CONTROL CHARACTER AND LOCATION DEFINITIONS
                ;
                ; FOR OSBORNE 1
                ;------------------------------------------------------
                ;
                ; CURSOR EQUATES:
                ;
0008 =          LEFT      EQU  08H            ;Left cursor key
000A =          DOWN      EQU  0AH            ;Down
000B =          UP        EQU  0BH            ;Up
000C =          RIGHT     EQU  0CH            ;Right
003D =          XY        EQU  3DH            ;Goto xy lead-in
001E =          HOME      EQU  1EH            ;Home cursor
                ;
                ; SCREEN CONTROL:
                ;
001A =          SCRCLR    EQU  1AH            ;Clear screen
0053 =          SCRXY     EQU  53H            ;Screen xy lead-in
0051 =          CHRINS    EQU  51H            ;Insert character at cursor
0057 =          CHRDEL    EQU  57H            ;Delete character
0045 =          LININS    EQU  45H            ;Insert line
0052 =          LINDEL    EQU  52H            ;Delete line
0054 =          EOLDEL    EQU  54H            ;Delete to end of line
```

FIGURE 11-5. Assembled program using standard header files (*continued*)

```
                    ;
                    ; HIGHLIGHTING:
                    ;
0029 =              DIM         EQU   29H            ;Begin dim characters
0028 =              BRIGHT      EQU   28H            ;Begin bright
0067 =              GRAPH       EQU   67H            ;Begin graphic
0047 =              NOGRAPH     EQU   47H            ;End graphic
006C =              ULINE       EQU   6CH            ;Begin underline
006D =              NOULINE     EQU   6DH            ;End underline
                    ;
                    ; ADDRESSES:
                    ;
EF5A =              CURSOR      EQU   0EF5AH         ;Location of cursor
F000 =              SCREEN      EQU   0F000H         ;Beginning of screen RAM
                    ;
                    ; SIZES:
                    ;
2020 =              OFFSET      EQU   2020H          ;Offset bias for cursor position
0080 =              SCRWIDE     EQU   80H            ;Width of line in RAM
0020 =              SCRHITE     EQU   20H            ;Height of line in RAM
0034 =              DISWIDE     EQU   34H            ;Width of display
0018 =              DISHITE     EQU   18H            ;Height of display
                    ;
                    ;-------------------------------------------
                    ; START: PROGRAM ENTRY ROUTINE
                    ;-------------------------------------------
                    ;
0100                            ORG   TPA
0100 2A0600         START:      LHLD  BDOS+1      ;Move BDOS location to HL
0103 F9                         SPHL              ;Set stack pointer to BDOS
0104 1180FF                     LXI   D,0-128     ;Set stack size to 128
0107 19                         DAD   D           ;Calculate bottom of stack area
0108 2B                         DCX   H           ;HL = last byte of TPA
0109 C37401                     JMP   GO          ;Go to beginning of user program
                    ;
                    ;-------------------------------------------
                    ; STOP: PROGRAM EXIT ROUTINE
                    ;-------------------------------------------
                    ;
010C C30000         STOP:       JMP   WARM        ;Do a CP/M warm start
                    ;
                    ;-------------------------------------------
                    ; ROUTINES.ASM
                    ; COMMON CP/M FUNCTIONS USING THE BDOS
                    ;-------------------------------------------
                    ;
FFFF =              STRIP       EQU   TRUE           ;Strip high order bit
                    ;
                    ; CONIN:    console input
                    ;           entry:    nothing
                    ;           exit:     character in A register
                    ;
010F CD1701         CONIN:      CALL       CONST
0112 B7                         ORA        A
0113 CA0F01                     JZ         CONIN     ;No character yet
0116 C9                         RET
                    ;
                    ; CONST:    console status
                    ;           entry:    nothing
                    ;           exit:     status in A (FF=no char  00=char)
                    ;
0117 C5             CONST:      PUSH  B
0118 D5                         PUSH  D
0119 E5                         PUSH  H
011A 1EFF                       MVI   E,TRUE         ;Input please
011C 0E06                       MVI   C,DIRECT       ;Use direct console I/O
011E CD0500                     CALL  BDOS
0121 E1                         POP   H
0122 D1                         POP   D
0123 C1                         POP   B
0124 C9                         RET
```

FIGURE 11-5. Assembled program using standard header files (*continued*)

```
                ;
                ; CONOUT: console output
                ;         entry:    character to display in A
                ;         exit:     nothing
                ;
0125 C5         CONOUT:   PUSH B
0126 D5                   PUSH D
0127 E5                   PUSH H
                          IF   STRIP
0128 E67F                 ANI  7FH            ;Strip high order bit (optional)
                ENDIF
012A 5F                   MOV  E,A            ;Get character in C for CP/M
012B 0E06                 MVI  C,DIRECT
012D CD0500               CALL BDOS
0130 E1                   POP  H
0131 D1                   POP  D
0132 C1                   POP  B
0133 C9                   RET
                ;
                ; XYOUT:  XY position cursor
                ;         entry:    Y position in H, X in L
                ;         exit:     nothing
                ;
0134 3E1B       XYOUT:    MVI  A,ESCAPE       ;First lead-in character
0136 CD2501               CALL CONOUT
0139 3E3D                 MVI  A,XY           ;Second lead-in character
013B CD2501               CALL CONOUT
013E 112020               LXI  D,OFFSET       ;Offset for cursor position
0141 19                   DAD  D              ;Added to HL
0142 7C                   MOV  A,H            ;Y out
0143 CD2501               CALL CONOUT
0146 7D                   MOV  A,L            ;X out
0147 CD2501               CALL CONOUT
014A C9                   RET
                ;
                ; CRLF:   display CR/LF pair on screen
                ;         entry:    nothing
                ;         exit:     nothing
                ;
014B F5         CRLF:     PUSH PSW
014C 3E0D                 MVI  A,CR
014E CD2501               CALL CONOUT
0151 3E0A                 MVI  A,LF
0153 CD2501               CALL CONOUT
0156 F1                   POP  PSW
0158 C9                   RET
                ;
                ; SPACE:  display a space on screen
                ;
                ; SPACE:  display a space on screen
                ;         entry:    nothing
                ;         exit:     nothing
                ;
0158 F5         SPACE:    PUSH PSW
0159 3E20                 MVI  A,BLANK
015B CD2501               CALL CONOUT
015E F1                   POP  PSW
015F C9                   RET
                ;
                ; CLEAR:  clear display
                ;         entry:    nothing
                ;         exit:     nothing
                ;
0160 F5         CLEAR:    PUSH PSW
0161 3E1A                 MVI  A,SCRCLR
0163 CD2501               CALL CONOUT
0166 F1                   POP  PSW
0167 C9                   RET
                ;
                ; PRINT: print string on display
                ;         entry:    DE = string address (terminated with $)
                ;         exit:     nothing
                ;
```

FIGURE 11-5. Assembled program using standard header files (*continued*)

```
0168 C5         PRINT:    PUSH B
0169 D5                   PUSH D
016A E5                   PUSH H
016B 0E09                 MVI  C,STRING
016D CD0500               CALL BDOS
0170 E1                   POP  H
0171 D1                   POP  D
0172 C1                   POP  B
0173 C9                   RET
                ;
                ;==================================
                ; PROGRAM STARTS HERE
                ;
0174 CD6001     GO:  CALL CLEAR               ;Clear the screen
0177 118301          LXI  D,MESSAGE           ;Point to message
017A CD6801          CALL PRINT               ;Print it
017D CD0F01          CALL CONIN               ;Get a keyboard response
0180 C30C01          JMP  STOP                ;End of program
                ;
0183 5468697320MESSAGE:  DB   'This is a sample message$'
                ;
019C                 END
```

FIGURE 11-5. Assembled program using standard header files (*continued*)

SUMMARY

This chapter has attempted to put a few of the pieces you learned about earlier (BDOS functions, assembly language programming, and CP/M memory locations) to work. Obviously, we could expand our simple example a great deal. Again, if you are interested in learning more about assembly language programming in CP/M, you should consider acquiring *The Programmer's CP/M Handbook*, which details at great length the things only briefly touched on in this book.

CHAPTER

12 MP/M, CP/NET, And CP/M Derivatives

The immense popularity of CP/M has spawned a number of similar operating systems. Like Cromemco's CDOS, some are direct descendants of CP/M but are not totally CP/M-compatible. Other "workalikes," I/OS and TP/M, for example, retain CP/M-compatibility and claim to improve on CP/M features. Digital Research expanded CP/M capabilities with MP/M and CP/NET and have extended the versions of CP/M available for 16-bit processors with CP/M-86 (for the Intel 8088 and 8086 CPUs) and CP/M-68K (for the Motorola 68000 CPU).

CP/M sales exceed those of all other microcomputer operating systems, including the Microsoft (IBM) DOS, Apple DOS, and Radio Shack TRSDOS. CP/M is available for both the Apple and Radio Shack computers, and 16-bit versions are now available with various add-on processor boards for many computers.

The popularity of CP/M has generated a growing library of CP/M-compatible software. Compared to application programs for other operating systems, CP/M-compatible software has developed largely for business applications.

You may have consciously chosen CP/M, you may not have had a choice, or you may simply have bought another operating system because you felt it offered additional features. In any case, it is important to learn the relationship between your operating system and CP/M to determine if your computer will run CP/M-compatible software. We discussed other operating systems in Chapter 2, where CP/M's history was presented, but we will go into more detail here, with particular emphasis on the differences you may discover.

The degree of compatibility between CP/M and other operating systems varies. Cromemco's CP/M-workalike, CDOS, cannot be used on an 8080-based system since it includes some Z80 instructions. CDOS also has several extensions, but the programs that utilize them cannot be run on a CP/M system. Other operating systems, like the I/OS and TurboDOS, claim to correct several CP/M "faults," but otherwise retain compatibility. Some, like MSDOS (originally 86-DOS), are not really compatible, since they have a different file format than what 8- and 16-bit CP/M utilize. Nevertheless, the MSDOS appears to a user to be very similiar to CP/M-86.

Erroneous assumptions about the compatibility of operating systems and application programs cause problems for everyone. To help avoid these pitfalls, we will clarify the compatibility of selected operating systems and discuss the features of MP/M and CP/NET, two Digital Research extensions of the CP/M family.

MULTI-USER AND MULTI-TASKING SYSTEMS

Until now we have described computer systems that perform one task for one user at a time. *Multi-tasking* computer systems perform a number of chores concurrently. Other names that refer to this computer setup are multi-user, time-sharing, time-slicing, multi-programming, and multi-terminal. Unfortunately, the microcomputer industry has changed some definitions that had previously referred to minicomputer and mainframe computer systems. In this text, multi-tasking refers to a microcomputer system performing two or more jobs simultaneously.

How does a multi-tasking computer system work? In a normal computer, a sequence of events occurs for each task. For example, when you press a key on the keyboard, the following (simplified) sequence occurs:

1. You press the key.
2. The keyboard sends the character to the computer.
3. The I/O device within the computer captures the character.
4. The CPU gets the character from the I/O device.
5. The CPU processes the character according to a set of instructions already in memory.

Although steps 1 through 3 take place at one keyboard, the CPU can perform step 5 (processing a character) for a second keyboard. When the CPU is waiting for the character from the first keyboard, it is idle.

Multi-tasking, in its simplest form, requires the CPU to perform a second job while it waits to continue processing the first job. The computer appears to perform two things simultaneously, since the tasks are measured in thousandths or millionths of a second.

Were everything as simple as our description, all computer systems would be multi-tasking devices. We must address one problem to describe fully the concept of multiple jobs on a single computer. Quite simply put, how do you know the two tasks will not interfere with each other? How does the CPU know when to work on which task?

The answer to both is, computer designers cheat. In a multi-tasking system the designers make some assumptions and take one of two conventional approaches:

1. Each user is given a time slice. If the slice of CPU time is of a fixed length, a user is not aware of another user's presence on the computer. Nor do the users notice

any appreciable slowing of the system since the computer normally wastes time in waiting for a user to do something. Multi-tasking thus provides certain advantages. For example, in I/O-bound systems where time is spent waiting for input to and output from various devices, such as in a word-processing system, the computer waits for keys to be pressed. This is clearly a good candidate for the time-slice system.

2. The CPU can also switch jobs each time it must wait for another device. A related method processes one job until another job demands CPU attention (this is called an *interrupt-driven system*). The differences between these two methods are more subtle than they first appear.

These may or may not be satisfactory methods for dividing CPU time. If the CPU rarely waits for I/O in one job, the second job may not be activated for quite some time. On the other hand, if one device constantly demands attention, the other devices are ignored. The result is the same: one task gets an advantage over the others.

These methods have been inaccurately described as polling systems. *Polling* is checking to see if a device is ready. A time-slice system may include polling. It is possible to implement a multi-tasking system without polling, however.

Microcomputer multi-tasking systems often combine these two methods. Each user has a time slice, but if the CPU must wait during that time slice or another device demands attention, the CPU alternates to another job before the time slice ends. This solves any problems resulting from unequal demands on the CPU from either the devices or the operator.

One way jobs demand attention from the CPU involves *interrupts*. When you press a key, a character needs to be processed; your input must reach the CPU before you release the key. In response, a special line monitored by the CPU is triggered, and the CPU immediately switches to the routine that fulfills that process. When this routine is done (the interrupt task), the CPU returns to the interrupted task.

A method of pseudo-multi-tasking involving multiple connected computers that share devices is known as *networking*. This concept involves two primary considerations:

1. The computers must be linked by a physical means (like a telephone connection or a simple cable) and a software means. The software means is called the *protocol*.
2. The way computers are linked depends on the interfacing capabilities of each computer in the network. In some instances all computers can use all devices on all other computers, while in others a hierarchy operates; one machine acts as a host to several others, or only certain linkages are allowed.

Yet another method now used to make a single computer perform multiple tasks is called *concurrent* processing by Digital Research. Currently available only for 16-bit versions, Concurrent CP/M allows the computer to be split into multiple task-oriented machines. You could have a word-processing program, a database program, and a number-processing program resident, each with a fraction of the computer's memory resources dedicated to it. In Concurrent CP/M, processing multiple tasks does not necessarily run simultaneously; normally you choose one of the tasks and function within it and then press a special key, which suspends the task you are on and takes you to another. If you are doing a lot of jumping around from task to task, Concurrent CP/M saves you the time (and extra typing) needed to load each new application.

With this introduction to multi-tasking, we can now turn our discussion to the features of CP/M's close relatives, MP/M and CP/NET.

MP/M

In general, this discussion pertains to what is known as MP/M version II, although most of the information is useful for the earlier MP/M version.

The letters MP/M stand for Multi-Processing Program Monitor. MP/M is an operating system for 8080 and Z80 computers that can control more than one console terminal and more than one program at each terminal. Thus, several users can "simultaneously" run several programs on one computer.

Differences Between MP/M and CP/M

You will notice three general differences between the operation of MP/M and CP/M: the prompt is different, there are new control characters, and there are new commands. Let us examine these differences between MP/M and CP/M:

The prompt. Like CP/M, MP/M displays the drive identifier of the currently logged drive (A, B, C, and so on) followed by a >. But MP/M also includes the currently logged user number (0-15, inclusive) before the drive identifier:

CP/M prompt	A>	drive A is the default
	B>	drive B is the default
	C>	drive C is the default.
MP/M prompt	0A>	user 0 on drive A
	4F>	user 4 on drive F
	3D>	user 3 on drive D.

Each user number is associated with a group of files on disk. Enter the USER command to switch to another user area on the disk.

Extra control characters. MP/M recognizes several control characters that CP/M does not. These are

Control Character	Description
^D	Detach console from current job
^Q	Restart console after ^S is pressed
^Z	End input from console.

A CONTROL-D lets you detach the console from a job. This is useful when a job requires little or no input from the console or when you wish to suspend one job to start another. You may reattach a job by typing ATTACH <cr> in response to the MP/M prompt.

A CONTROL-S stops the console display, just as it does in CP/M. However, unlike CP/M, only a ^Q will restart the console after a CONTROL-S is used.

A CONTROL-Z ends the input from the console device. You will rarely need CONTROL-Z. When the console functions like a disk device, CONTROL-Z sends an end-of-file marker.

Additional commands and utilities. MP/M has several new commands; note that several of them are basically the same as CP/M-PLUS extensions to the CP/M command set:

Command	Description
CONSOLE	Displays the console number.
DSKRESET	Enables the user to change diskettes.
GENHEX	Creates a hex file from a COM file (not the same as CP/M-PLUS).
PRLCOM	Creates a COM file from a special PRL file.
GENMOD	Creates a PRL file from a special HEX file.
SPOOL	Sends printer output to the spooling device.
STOPSPLR	Stops spooler output.
TOD	Sets or displays the time and date (similar to CP/M-PLUS DATE command).
SCHED	Schedules a task to be run automatically.
ABORT	Aborts a task, even if it is detached from the console.
ATTACH	Reattaches a detached job.
MPMSTAT	Displays MP/M status.
PRINTER	Selects the printer to be used.
SHOW	Displays disk status (similar to CP/M-PLUS).
SET	Sets the disk and file status, passwords, and time stamping (similar to CP/M-PLUS).

Different file types. Where CP/M uses the file type of COM for command (transient program) files, MP/M cannot use it. The reason is that all COM-type files are automatically loaded by CP/M at a fixed memory address, 0100 hex. Since MP/M supports multiple users, there can be no guarantee that a file starts at 0100 hex (one may already be there). MP/M gets around this by allowing something called *page relocatable* files, or PRL-type files. Any file with a type of PRL acts the same under MP/M as a transient program file (COM) does under CP/M.

MP/M will allow use of some COM-type files, but the system has to place those at the fixed memory location indicated earlier, which may not result in the most efficient use of memory space and may restrict other users from using a COM-type file as well.

More detailed descriptions of these new commands follow in the next section.

MP/M Commands

When you purchase MP/M you receive a number of programs unique to MP/M. All MP/M commands, except for the control characters, are transient commands or programs.

CONSOLE

There can be as many as 16 independent console devices in MP/M. These terminals are numbered console device 1, 2, and so on.

The console number is distinct from the user number, and the distinction is important. One fixed console number is assigned to each terminal. The user number, on the other hand, is associated with a group of files on disk.

To see which console you are using, type

CONSOLE<cr>

and MP/M replies

Console = x

where x is your console number.

DSKRESET

Unfortunately, several users may have to share one or two disk drives. What if one user must change the disk in the drive to access a different disk or to load another program? Remember, you must perform a warm start after changing disks in CP/M. With MP/M you want to perform that warm start for your job only, not for everyone else's.

DSKRESET selectively changes disks. Type the command with no other parameters to reset all disk drives on the system. Follow the command with a list of valid drive identifiers (A:, B:, and so forth), each separated by a comma, to reset only the drives you specify:

DSKRESET E:,N:,D:<cr>   Resets drives E,N,D

MP/M does not allow you to reset a drive if some task is using files on that drive. When that happens, you see

Disk reset denied, Drive x: Console y Program z

This message tells you which console and program still have open files on that disk. If your console is specified, complete your use of the program (at least finish using the files it is addressing) and then retry DSKRESET. If your console is not listed, you must either wait until the other user finishes before you can reset that disk drive, or check for another available drive.

You must use DSKRESET before removing a disk from the system, or else you may cause another user to have unrecoverable errors.

GENHEX

This program is the opposite of LOAD; it reads a COM-type file and creates a HEX-type file to be used either by LOAD or by GENMOD. Most users will not need this program.

PRLCOM

Files destined for MP/M with the PRL file type may be changed to files usable on CP/M-based systems (COM-type files) by using PRLCOM. The format of this command is

PRLCOM prltype.fil comtype.COM<cr>

This command line violates the common NEW=OLD convention of most commands.

GENMOD

With CP/M, LOAD changes the HEX file created by the assembler to a COM-type file that is loaded and executed by typing its name. MP/M locates an individual user program at the beginning of the memory dedicated to that user, but COM files always load beginning at 0100 hex. GENMOD converts a HEX-type file into a PRL-type file that can be loaded at some other memory address.

GENMOD reads a file consisting of two assembled versions of a program (each assembly with a different beginning location) and creates a file with the PRL file type. Two assemblies are required at different beginning locations because GENMOD compares the two resulting sets of object code to ascertain where specific addresses appear in the program. Since MP/M does not assume any one beginning location for a program, it identifies portions of the program that use specific locations so they can be changed to reflect the memory area where the program is loaded.

SPOOL

Several users on a system may share a single printer. Instead of sending your information directly to the printer, with MP/M you normally send your output to a disk file and then use SPOOL to print the file.

SPOOL maintains a queue of files to be printed. If user 1 asks SPOOL to print file, and user 2 asks for some printed report moments later, SPOOL will finish printing user 1's report first and then print the information for user 2. When you invoke SPOOL, it summarizes the queue and returns the MP/M prompt to your console. You are free for other jobs; the printer automatically prints your document according to the queue.

The format for this command is

SPOOL filename.typ, filename.typ, etc.<cr>

You may specify any number of files to add to the queue, each separated by a comma, up to the limitation of the command line length.

STOPSPLR

To stop the SPOOL function, type STOPSPLR followed by your console number. If you have any files waiting to be printed, they will all be removed from the queue. This is a drastic action and may result in a partially printed report; be sure you want to stop the printing of your files.

TOD

MP/M maintains a clock to track both date and time. Do not assume complete accuracy. First, if the computer shuts down for any time period, even a fraction of a second, MP/M just restarts the clock. Second, the clock's accuracy depends on how your MP/M system was implemented. If you are using a Digital Microsystems computer or an Intel MDS-based system, the clock functions exactly as Digital Research intended. Other implementations may or may not function properly.

To set the clock, use

TOD mm/dd/yy hh:mm:ss<cr>

Type in the month, day, year, hours, minutes, and seconds in exactly that order and format. Here is a valid entry:

TOD 01/16/80 10:00:00<cr>

This tells the computer it is 10 A.M. on the 16th day of January, 1980. When you type this command, MP/M will respond

Strike key to set time
THU 10/16/80 10:00:00

Press any key to begin the clock and return to MP/M. Any time you type TOD<cr>, you will see the current date and time as MP/M maintains it. Typing TOD P<cr> continuously displays the date and time until you press another key.

SCHED

The clock in your system allows you to schedule tasks automatically. The computer will perform these tasks when no one is using the system. This is especially useful for long reports that may slow the computer's response time. To schedule a task, use

SCHED mm/dd/yy hh:mm task<cr>

where task is a valid MP/M command line and mm/dd/yy hh:mm:ss is the exact date and time you wish the task to begin. You cannot specify the execution of tasks in increments shorter than one minute.

ABORT

To cancel any task, type ABORT TASK<cr>. If the task was invoked from a different console, you must add the console number from which you scheduled the task:

ABORT task #<cr>

MP/M's Internal Structure

MP/M is very similar in structure to CP/M. MP/M equipment requirements are

1. An 8080, 8085, or Z80 CPU
2. At least 32K of memory
3. At least one disk drive
4. A keyboard for input of characters
5. A printer or CRT for output of characters
6. A clock timer interrupt.

Consider how CP/M loads into memory (see Chapter 10). MP/M may be loaded with a cold start loader just like CP/M, or a special MP/M loader, a CP/M transient program, can be used to load and execute MP/M.

The internal structure of MP/M is similar to that of CP/M. Whereas CP/M had a Transient Program Area (TPA), Console Command Processor (CCP), Basic Disk Operating System (BDOS), and Basic Input/Output System (BIOS), MP/M has the following parts:

Command	Description
TPA	Transient Program Area.
MEMSEG	Between 1 and 8 memory segments, one for each user.
XDOS	Extended Disk Operating System.
BDOS	CP/M's Basic Disk Operating System with a bank-switching utility added.
XIOS	Extended Input/Output System.

For the most part, Chapters 10 and 11 apply to both MP/M and CP/M. Although MP/M adds to the CP/M structure, it does not significantly alter CP/M. Remember, MP/M has been expanded to include

16 user terminals
16 printers
16 drives, each up to 512 megabytes each.

MP/M does not support PUNCH and READER devices, as does CP/M. Where the CP/M BIOS describes one user terminal, reader, punch, and printer, the MP/M XIOS describes terminals and printers for each user. In other words, the concept has not been changed, but the operating system has been expanded to include information about all users. This is one reason MP/M requires more memory space than CP/M, even for only a single user.

Although their structures are similar, MP/M functions slightly differently from CP/M. CP/M always loads a utility program beginning at 0100 hex and stores it in a COM-type file. As already mentioned, MP/M retains this feature, but adds the ability to use PRL-type (page relocatable) files and to place or execute them beginning at any interval of 0100 hex (0100, 0200, 0300, and so forth).

Suppose two users have 48K of memory each, and each of their jobs requires only 20K of memory. If both jobs must start at location 0100 hex there is a major problem: each user will try to use 20K of memory beginning at 0100 hex, and the top 28K will not be used.

Some programs you buy from vendors other than Digital Research come only as COM-type files. They must be loaded and executed beginning at 0100 hex. Can two users use that program concurrently? No. But fortunately there is a solution. Most MP/M computers utilize a feature called *bank-selectable memory.* The 8080, 8085, and Z80 microprocessors can directly address only 64K of RAM. The key word is *directly.* Imagine you can tell a memory section to ignore all processes until it receives a special coded signal from the CPU. Another memory section pays attention to all processes until it receives that special coded signal, and then it ignores the proceedings. Your imagined system is a bank-selectable memory system.

With MP/M, each user usually gets one bank of memory. If you have two banks of 48K of RAM in your system, the first user has 48K from the first bank, the second user has 48K in the second bank, and MP/M reserves 16K of common memory area in the first bank. Look at the sample memory map shown in Table 12-1 and notice the addresses in the middle column. Both user 1 and user 2 have the same addresses for their programs, but they do not interfere with each other because MP/M uses only the currently active memory bank. You do not need to tell the system when to change memory banks; MP/M does this automatically.

If your memory address begins at an address other than 0100 hex, you must use PRL-type files rather than COM-type files to store programs. Digital Research provides its programs as PRL-type files. In addition, the Digital Research MAC assembler can create PRL files from assembly language programs. You can do this

TABLE 12-1: An MP/M Memory Map

Bank 1	Memory Address	Bank 2
	0000 hex	
Reserved for user 1 MP/M use		Reserved for user 2 MP/M use
	0100 hex	
User 1 program (TPA)		User 2 program (TPA)
	C000 hex	
MP/M (XDOS, BDOS, XIOS)		← not available (uses bank 1)
	FFFF hex	

with ASM, but with greater difficulty. Digital Research also includes RMAC (a relocatable assembler), LINK, and a library of common routines with MP/M so that you can create PRL-type files.

CP/NET

CP/NET is the Digital Research networking addition to the CP/M family of operating systems. CP/M is designed for a single user on a single computer system; MP/M, for multiple users on a single computer system; CP/NET, for multiple users on multiple computer systems.

The concept of computer networks differs slightly from multi-tasking. Multi-tasking tends to be hierarchical:

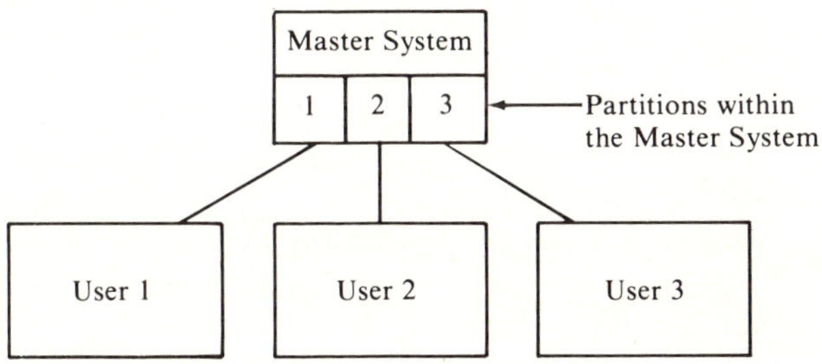

Each user is a separate entity; multi-tasking allows little or no interaction between users.

CP/NET operates on a different concept:

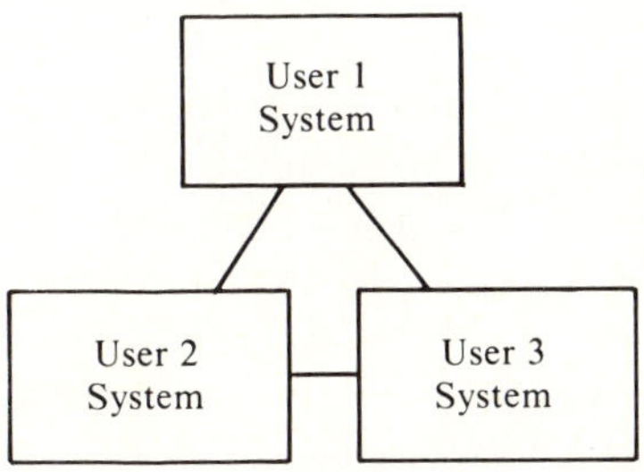

In CP/NET, each of the three users are represented as systems, not merely users. The logical linking between each user is more direct; there is no master system.

CP/NET requires at least one node in the network to act as a master. One user manages the network. The master node must have MP/M and disk drives. Other nodes may consist only of an 8080, 8085, or Z80 CPU and a minimum of 16K of memory. While these nodes need no other components, a terminal, more memory, and disk drives increase a node's functions. Considering these requirements for a CP/NET system, we will modify our diagram as follows:

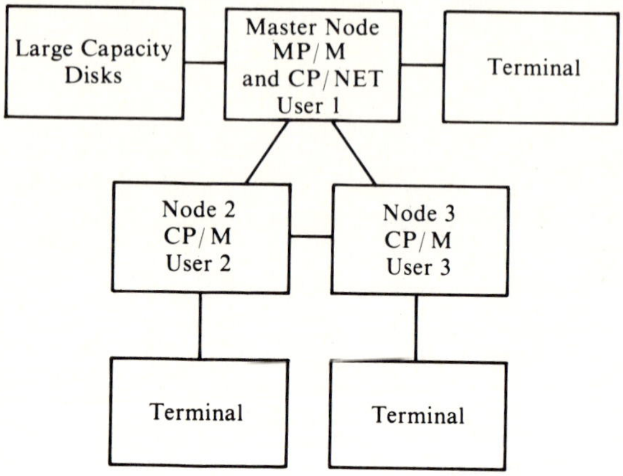

There are two primary advantages to a network system of computers: sharing of resources and speed of execution.

The primary shared resource of a microcomputer network is high-capacity disk drives. Because hard disk drives are expensive, it may be unreasonable to buy hard disk drives for each computer system. In addition, large database applications (storage, maintenance, and use of large bodies of data) may require all users to share one common file or group of files.

Another shared resource is usually a printer. There may be a typewriter-quality printer at one node, while another may have a faster but less-readable dot matrix printer. Since typewriter-quality printers are both expensive and slow, the faster dot matrix printer is more useful for rough drafts. But since each user in the network may send output to either printer, they can produce final copies with the typewriter-quality printer.

Each node on a CP/NET system can function independently and may be a separate computer. Nodes are connected to the network only to share a resource. A business might use CP/NET to consolidate several different machines into one system.

CP/NET nodes can use all MP/M and CP/M commands and programs; the exceptions are minimal. In addition, CP/NET includes some new commands:

Command	**Description**
LOGIN	Logs the user into the master node.
LOGOFF	Signs the user off the network.
SNDMAIL	Sends mail (text message) to another user.
RCVMAIL	Receives mail from another user.
BROADCST	Sends mail from the master node to all users.
MRCVMAIL	Receives mail at the master node from all users.

Command	Description *(Continued)*
NETWORK	Enables one node to use network devices.
LOCAL	Reassigns local devices in place of network ones.
ENDLIST	Sends CONTROL-Z to the list device.

CP/NET has not attracted a large number of users since its introduction. This is primarily because many computer manufacturers replace the BIOS in CP/M with a special "networking" BIOS that fools CP/M into thinking that it has the network's resources as its own. A number of microcomputer networks also work this way, and there is no particular disadvantage to this method over Digital Research's except that the creator of the networking system must provide a few extra programs to resolve contentions over network resources and to provide the mail functions CP/NET offers.

OPERATING SYSTEMS SIMILAR TO CP/M

Many software creators have tried to improve CP/M's control over the computing process. Most of these attempts have been based on CP/M version 1.4.

A number of other manufacturers provide CP/M-compatible operating systems. Some, like ADDS (Applied Digital Data Systems), have written operating systems that function like CP/M. Others have simply licensed CP/M from Digital Research and added a few features that reflect specific abilities of their equipment.

Figure 12-1 summarizes how the major operating systems similar to CP/M developed. Several other operating systems might fit into this outline; subtle changes in an

CP/M 1.3	lead to the development of	IMDOS (IMSAI DOS) CDOS CP/M 1.4
CP/M 1.4	lead to the development of	SDOS I/OS TP/M TurboDOS MSDOS CP/M 2.2 MP/M
CP/M 2.2	lead to the development of	CP/M-PLUS

FIGURE 12-1: The evolution of CP/M lookalike operating systems

operating system (CP/M 1.41 versus 1.42, for instance) are not reflected in this illustration; only major changes are shown. We will look briefly at each of the major CP/M relatives in the rest of this section.

Cromemco CDOS

Cromemco was one of the first microcomputer manufacturers. Its first products were not microcomputers but components used with IMSAI and Altair microcomputers. Rapid growth and careful attention to the order of new product development allowed Cromemco to introduce a complete system.

Cromemco's first disk-based system was the Z-2 computer. This system was housed in a rugged industrial-grade cabinet and included two built-in disk drives. Later, Cromemco designed the System 3, a computer for the business environment. Both computer systems were introduced with an operating system developed from CP/M by InfoSoft (then named TSA); the operating system was named Cromemco Disk Operating System (CDOS).

Originally, CDOS was little more than a rewrite of CP/M that took advantage of the Z80 microprocessor's enhanced capabilities. CDOS, however, evolved continuously, with more subtle refinements than CP/M. Cromemco has been able to update CDOS because it has full control over the design of the computer systems that utilize it. CDOS functions only with the Cromemco disk controller and a Z80 CPU. Digital Research has no control over the microcomputers that utilize CP/M, thus necessitating fewer changes.

CDOS Compatibility With CP/M

With each copy of CDOS, Cromemco includes this notice regarding its compatibility with CP/M:

> The Cromemco Disk Operating System (CDOS) is an original product designed and written in Z80 machine code by Cromemco, Inc. for its own line of microcomputers. However, due to the large number of programs currently available to run under the CP/M operating system, CDOS was designed to be upwards CP/M-compatible. Cromemco is licensed by Digital Research, the originator of CP/M, for use of the CP/M data structures and user interface. This means that most programs written for CP/M (versions up to and including 1.33) will run without modification under CDOS. This also means that programs written for CDOS will not generally run under CP/M.*

CDOS evolved from the first commercially available version of CP/M, version 1.3; it does not include features that Digital Research added to later versions. This is only a minor inconvenience if you use CDOS and try to run programs written for CP/M version 1.4; the differences between CP/M 1.3 and 1.4 are not so extreme as those between 1.4 and 2.2.

---

*From *Cromemco Users Bulletin,* Issue #1, December 1978.

A program using features of CP/M 2.2 (actually, any version after 2.0) most likely will not run on a CDOS-equipped computer. However, most programs written for CP/M version 2.2 do not necessarily use the added features. A program developed to run with EBASIC works equally well with CP/M version 1.4 or 2.2 and retains compatibility with CDOS. Versions of Microsoft BASIC and CBASIC2, especially the new compilers for these languages, may not work properly on your CDOS-equipped computer.

Do not believe that a program written for CP/M will run correctly on your CDOS system just because you can load and execute it. To guarantee that everything works correctly, you may need to test the programs thoroughly or buy a version of CP/M for your Cromemco computer.

The preferred choice is the second one. Remember Cromemco's advice on CDOS-CP/M compatibility: the CDOS file structure is the same, but some of the system functions are not. Use a CP/M operating system on your Cromemco machine to execute a CP/M program. This is more reliable and economical than modifying CP/M programs to fit CDOS.

CDOS Commands and Utilities

CDOS commands look like CP/M commands:

Command	Description
BYE	Returns to the Cromemco System Monitor.
DIR	Displays a disk file directory.
ERA	Erases a file or files from a disk.
REN	Renames a file.
SAVE	Saves a portion of memory in a disk file.
TYPE	Displays an ASCII file on the console device.

Cromemco includes these utility programs (transient commands):

Program	Description
BATCH	Submits a list of commands for execution.
DUMP	Displays hexadecimal representations of a disk file's contents.
EDIT	A simple character-oriented editor.
INIT	Initializes (formats and prepares) a disk.
WRTSYS	Copies CDOS from one disk to another.
XFER	Transfers files from a disk or device to another disk or device.
STAT	Displays statistics regarding the disk and devices.

These are the minimum commands and utilities supplied. New versions of CDOS (such as 1.07, 2.17, and later) include other utilities and enhance other commands and utilities. Early versions of the STAT program, for example, display the amount of disk space left, the number of directory entries, the names of any null files, and an error message for disk problems. The latest versions of CDOS include STAT programs that display all of these plus specific information on disk status, usage, and device assignments. This is just a brief example; to detail the differences between each version of CDOS and CP/M and explain how all CDOS commands work would require another book.

Some versions of CDOS include several other utility programs:

Programs	Description
CDOSGEN	Creates a different-sized operating system.
DEBUG	A debugging tool similar to DDT.
LINK	A linker program that takes compiled program code from Cromemco's languages and creates an executable file.
SCREEN	A sophisticated editor that works only with Cromemco terminals and may be used for system development or word-processing tasks.
MEMTEST	Tests Cromemco RAM and reports errors.

CP/M's Other Relatives

A number of CP/M workalike operating systems are now in existence, and each has advantages and disadvantages when compared to the standard CP/M operating system. The most popular of these workalikes are briefly described here.

I/OS

Formerly known as TSA/OS, I/OS was written by the same people who wrote CDOS. I/OS maintains compatibility with CDOS and CP/M, and this is its most obvious advantage. Recently, a multi-user version of I/OS, MULTI/OS, has evolved, users of MP/M may be interested in investigating the features of this system.

TP/M

TP/M is essentially a Z80 version of CP/M; it will not run on 8080- or 8085-based computers. TP/M's often-cited advantage over CP/M is that its use of Z80 instructions noticeably improves the overall speed of the operating system. Such claims, of course, are equipment specific, and you may or may not detect any noticeable differences in speed.

SDOS

SD Systems made some minor and cosmetic changes to CP/M in creating SDOS. However, SDOS's current version is a derivative of CP/M version 1.4 and therefore does not feature some of the improvements Digital Research made to CP/M when it introduced version 2.2.

TurboDOS

A relative newcomer to the CP/M workalike sweepstakes, TurboDOS introduces a number of state-of-the-art software concepts to the CP/M environment. The end result is a substantially faster operating system when disk-oriented tasks are performed. TurboDOS actually attempts to anticipate the sections of the disk the user will reference and to make sure that they are available when the user calls for them. In addition, some of the more aggravating aspects of CP/M, most notably the inability to exchange disks without telling CP/M, are eradicated by TurboDOS. A multi-user version of TurboDOS is also available.

CP/M for Zenith/Heath, Polymorphic, and Radio Shack Computers

Owners of early Zenith/Heath, Radio Shack Model I or III, or any Polymorphic computers need to be careful when purchasing CP/M for their systems. While CP/M may operate in the same manner as described in this book, its memory locations have been moved to reflect design differences in these computers. The relocation of CP/M and its reference points in memory require modifications to normally interchangeable CP/M programs. Make sure a program version is suitable for your machine if you have any of the following computers and use CP/M:

Poly 88
Polymorphic 8813
Radio Shack TRS-80 Model I
Radio Shack TRS-80 Model III
Heathkit H8
Heathkit H89
Zenith Z89

Each of these computers can be modified to run a standard CP/M operating system, but this should be done by a computer repairer.

Digital Equipment Corporation's CP/M-85/86

Digital Equipment Corporation (DEC) introduced a special version of CP/M for its Rainbow microcomputer that effectively combines 8- and 16-bit versions of CP/M. Since the Rainbow has both 8085 and 8088 processors, it can execute instructions destined for either version of CP/M. The manner in which DEC combined the two CP/Ms results in program files that may not be directly compatible with other machines, since a special "header" with the information on which processor to use and where to put the program in memory is used for some program files.

MP/M-816

Users of Godbout (or CompuPro) systems have available to them the "ultimate" mixture of CP/Ms as an operating system. Dubbed MP/M-816, it basically combines 8- and 16-bit versions of MP/M, allowing multiple users access to either 8- or 16-bit versions of CP/M programs.

CP/M-86 AND ALTERNATIVES

With the introduction of the IBM Personal Computer (PC) in 1981 the CP/M workalike competition extended itself to CP/M-86.

The initial operating system IBM provided with the PC was onc called, alternatively, IBM DOS or Microsoft DOS (generally shortened to MSDOS). In fact, this operating system turns out to be one introduced earlier as the 86-DOS, a product of Seattle Computer Products.

The 86-DOS was written before CP/M-86 was available, and possibly because of this, it incorporates an interesting cross of the features in 8- and 16-bit versions of CP/M. Microsoft purchased the rights and adapted 86-DOS to the IBM PC. The documentation provided with the resulting operating system is excellent; the user should be able to quickly learn to operate IBM DOS (or Microsoft DOS). IBM DOS's roots in 8-bit CP/M are clearly evident in the choice of file name size and file-naming conventions, the use of control characters to edit the command line, the prompt displayed on the screen, and many other "visible" aspects of the 86-DOS.

Where IBM DOS differs, however, is in the inner reaches of the operating system. Its BDOS calls are different than those for either 8- or 16-bit versions of CP/M, although they are clearly intended to be similar. Especially important, the layout of information on the disk is radically different in IBM DOS and CP/M versions. The arrangement of the directory and system tracks are different, and IBM DOS keeps different (and more detailed) information about the files on the disk.

The generic version of IBM DOS, called MSDOS, is an alternative to CP/M-86. Microsoft and Digital Research, once close partners in software development, have taken on an adversarial relationship over which of the two operating systems deserves to be the "standard" for 8086-based systems. Unfortunately, it looks like neither may win, as Microsoft has already introduced a non-compatible second version of the MSDOS (MSDOS 2.0) and announced their intention of creating yet another superset of the basic operating system, this time much like Xenix, their UNIX-derivative operating system.

Digital Research has introduced, for use on 8088/8086-based computers, CP/M-86, MP/M-86, and Concurrent CP/M-86, a single-user, multiple-task version of CP/M-86. Only Digital Research's 16-bit operating systems are directly compatible with the format of 8-bit disks. For users moving from Z80 to 8086-based systems, this may prove to be an important factor either because a data disk must be converted for use with MSDOS, or because an extra program that translates the disk format must first be loaded into the computer.

APPENDIX

A ASCII Character Codes

The American Standard Code for Information Interchange (ASCII) consists of a set of 96 displayed characters and 32 non-displayed characters. Most CP/M systems use at least a subset of the ASCII character set. When CP/M stores characters on a diskette as text, the ASCII definitions are used.

Several CP/M utility programs use the ASCII Character Code. Text created using ED is stored as ASCII characters on disk. DDT, when displaying a "dump" of the contents of memory, displays both the hexademical and the ASCII representation of memory's contents.

ASCII does not use an entire byte of information (i.e., 8 bits) to represent a character. ASCII is a 7-bit code, and the eighth bit is often used for *parity*. Parity is an error-checking method that assures that the character received is the one transmitted. Many microcomputers and microcomputer devices ignore the *parity bit*, while others require one of the following two forms of parity:

Even Parity
: The number of binary 1's in a byte is always an even number. If there is an odd number of 1's in the character, the parity bit will be a 1; if an even number of 1's is in the character, the parity bit is made a 0.

Odd Parity
: The total number of 1 bits in the character, including the parity bit, is always odd.

Alternative ways of *storing* the information by the computer include the 8-bit EBCDIC (Extended Binary Coded Decimal Interchange Code) used by IBM on their mainframe computers and a number of packed binary schemes primarily used to represent numerical information.

TABLE A-1. ASCII Character Codes

				b7→	0	0	0	0	1	1	1	1
				b6→	0	0	1	1	0	0	1	1
				b5→	0	1	0	1	0	1	0	1
b4	**b3**	**b2**	**b1**	**Row Col.**	**0**	**1**	**2**	**3**	**4**	**5**	**6**	**7**
0	0	0	0	0	NUL	DLE	SP	0	@	P	'	p
0	0	0	1	1	SOH	DC1	!	1	A	Q	a	q
0	0	1	0	2	STX	DC2	"	2	B	R	b	r
0	0	1	1	3	ETX	DC3	#	3	C	S	c	s
0	1	0	0	4	EOT	DC4	$	4	D	T	d	t
0	1	0	1	5	ENQ	NAK	%	5	E	U	e	u
0	1	1	0	6	ACK	SYN	&	6	F	V	f	v
0	1	1	1	7	BEL	ETB	'	7	G	W	g	w
1	0	0	0	8	BS	CAN	(	8	H	X	h	x
1	0	0	1	9	HT	EM	)	9	I	Y	i	y
1	0	1	0	10	LF	SUB	*	:	J	Z	j	z
1	0	1	1	11	VT	ESC	+	;	K	[	k	{
1	1	0	0	12	FF	FS	,	<	L	\	l	|
1	1	0	1	13	CR	GS	—	=	M	]	m	}
1	1	1	0	14	SO	RS	.	>	N	^	n	~
1	1	1	1	15	SI	US	/	?	O	_	o	DEL

NUL	Null	DC1	Device control 1
SOH	Start of heading	DC2	Device control 2
STX	Start of text	DC3	Device control 3
ETX	End of text	DC4	Device control 4
EOT	End of transmission	NAK	Negative acknowledge
ENQ	Enquiry	SYN	Synchronous idle
ACK	Acknowledge	ETB	End of transmission block
BEL	Bell, or alarm	CAN	Cancel
BS	Backspace	EM	End of medium
HT	Horizontal tabulation	SUB	Substitute
LF	Line feed	ESC	Escape
VT	Vertical tabulation	FS	File separator
FF	Form feed	GS	Group separator
CR	Carriage return	RS	Record separator
SO	Shift out	US	Unit separator
SI	Shift in	SP	Space
DLE	Data link escape	DEL	Delete

TABLE A-2. ASCII Character Codes in Ascending Order

Hexadecimal	Binary	ASCII	Hexadecimal	Binary	ASCII
00	000 0000	NUL	31	011 0001	1
01	000 0001	SOH	32	011 0010	2
02	000 0010	STX	33	011 0011	3
03	000 0011	ETX	34	011 0100	4
04	000 0100	EOT	35	011 0101	5
05	000 0101	ENQ	36	011 0110	6
06	000 0110	ACK	37	011 0111	7
07	000 0111	BEL	38	011 1000	8
08	000 1000	BS	39	011 1001	9
09	000 1001	HT	3A	011 1010	:
0A	000 1010	LF	3B	011 1011	;
0B	000 1011	VT	3C	011 1100	<
0C	000 1100	FF	3D	011 1101	=
0D	000 1101	CR	3E	011 1110	>
0E	000 1110	SO	3F	011 1111	?
0F	000 1111	SI	40	100 0000	@
10	001 0000	DLE	41	100 0001	A
11	001 0001	DC1	42	100 0010	B
12	001 0010	DC2	43	100 0011	C
13	001 0011	DC3	44	100 0100	D
14	001 0100	DC4	45	100 0101	E
15	001 0101	NAK	46	100 0110	F
16	001 0110	SYN	47	100 0111	G
17	001 0111	ETB	48	100 1000	H
18	001 1000	CAN	49	100 1001	I
19	001 1001	EM	4A	100 1010	J
1A	001 1010	SUB	4B	100 1011	K
1B	001 1011	ESC	4C	100 1100	L
1C	001 1100	FS	4D	100 1101	M
1D	001 1101	GS	4E	100 1110	N
1E	001 1110	RS	4F	100 1111	O
1F	001 1111	US	50	101 0000	P
20	010 0000	SP	51	101 0001	Q
21	010 0001	!	52	101 0010	R
22	010 0010	"	53	101 0011	S
23	010 0011	#	54	101 0100	T
24	010 0100	$	55	101 0101	U
25	010 0101	%	56	101 0110	V
26	010 0110	&	57	101 0111	W
27	010 0111	'	58	101 1000	X
28	010 1000	(	59	101 1001	Y
29	010 1001	)	5A	101 1010	Z
2A	010 1010	*	5B	101 1011	[
2B	010 1011	+	5C	101 1100	\
2C	010 1100	,	5D	101 1101	]
2D	010 1101	-	5E	101 1110	^
2E	010 1110	.	5F	101 1111	_
2F	010 1111	/	60	110 0000	`
30	011 0000	0	61	110 0001	a

TABLE A-2. ASCII Character Codes in Ascending Order (*continued*)

Hexadecimal	Binary	ASCII	Hexadecimal	Binary	ASCII
62	110 0010	b	71	111 0001	q
63	110 0011	c	72	111 0010	r
64	110 0100	d	73	111 0011	s
65	110 0101	e	74	111 0100	t
66	110 0110	f	75	111 0101	u
67	110 0111	g	76	111 0110	v
68	110 1000	h	77	111 0111	w
69	110 1001	i	78	111 1000	x
6A	110 1010	j	79	111 1001	y
6B	110 1011	k	7A	111 1010	z
6C	110 1100	l	7B	111 1011	{
6D	110 1101	m	7C	111 1100	|
6E	110 1110	n	7D	111 1101	}
6F	110 1111	o	7E	111 1110	~
70	111 0000	p	7F	111 1111	DEL

APPENDIX

B Disk Selections

The disks in each of the following categories may be single-density or double-density. Be sure to choose the proper density for your system. Double-density systems can usually be operated in single-density mode, so you may be using both varieties if you have such a system.

Systems Using 8-Inch Soft-Sectored Disks

Alspa
Altos
Cromemco FDC Controller
Cromemco System 3
Delta
Digital Microsystems
Discus
Dynabyte DB8/4
Hewlett-Packard 150
iCOM 3712, 3812
IMS 8000
IMSAI FDC2
IMSAI VDP-80
Intecolor (ISC) 8063, 8360, 8963
Intel MDS
Micromation
Morrow Discus
Mostek
Ohio Scientific C3
Pertec PCC 2000
Processor Technology Helios

Radio Shack TRS-80 Model II
Radio Shack TRS-80 Model I/Micromation
Radio Shack TRS-80 Model I/Omikron
Radio Shack TRS-80 Model I/Shuffleboard
Research Machines
SD Systems
Spacebyte
Tarbell
TEI
Thinker Toys
TRS-80. *See* Radio Shack
Vector Graphic System 2800

Systems Using 8-Inch Hard-Sectored Disks

MITS 3200, 3202
Processor Technology Helios II

Systems Using 5 1/4-Inch Soft-Sectored Disks

Actrix
Apple/SoftCard
AVL Eagle
BASF System 7100
Basis 101
Cromemco Z2D
DEC VT180
Digi-Log Microterm II
Durango F-85
Franklin Ace (with softcard)
Gnat
IBM Personal Computer
Hewlett-Packard HP-80 Series
Heath/Zenith double-density
iCOM 2411 Micro Floppy
IMS 5000
IMSAI VDP-40, -42, -44
Intertec SuperBrain
Kaypro 2, 4, 10
Kontron PSI-80
LNW
MSD
Osborne 1
Osborne Executive

Pied Piper
Polymorphic 8813
Quay 500, 520
Radio Shack TRS-80 Model I
Radio Shack TRS-80 Model I/FEC Freedom
Radio Shack TRS-80 Model I/Omikron
Radio Shack TRS-80 Model 4
RAIR
Research Machines
Sanco 7000
SD Systems
SuperBrain. *See* Intertec
TEI
Quay
Vector Graphic (current systems)
Xerox 820

Systems Using 5 1/4-Inch Hard-Sectored 10-Sector Disks

Heath H8 and H17, H27
Heath H89
Horizon
Meca
North Star Horizon
Vista V80
Vista V200
Zenith Z89

Systems Using 5 1/4-Inch Hard-Sectored 16-Sector Disks

Blackhawk (40 TPI)
CDS Versatile 3B (40 TPI)
CDS Versatile 4 (100 TPI)
COMPAL-80 (100 TPI)
Dynabyte (some models)
Exidy Sorcerer (100 TPI)
Micropolis Mod I (40 TPI)
Micropolis Mod II (100 TPI)
Nylac (40 TPI, 100 TPI)
REX (40 TPI)
Sorcerer. *See* Exidy
Vector Graphic (100 TPI)
Vector MZ (100 TPI)
Versatile. *See* CDS

APPENDIX

C Differences in CP/M Versions

The following tables (C-1 through C-4) describe the differences between versions of CP/M. Particular attention is paid to commands, line editing commands, BDOS functions, and disk specifications.

TABLE C-1. Commands Summary

Command	CP/M 1.3	CP/M 1.4	CP/M 2.2	CP/M-PLUS
Assembly Language	ASM DDT LOAD	ASM DDT LOAD	ASM DDT LOAD	MAC,RMAC SID HEXCOM XREF LIB LINK
Batch Utilities	SUBMIT	SUBMIT	SUBMIT XSUB	SUBMIT GET PUT
Change User Area			USER	USER
Copy Files	PIP	PIP[OPT]*	PIP[OPT]* +GRW	PIP[OPT]* +C,AXO,AXI
Directory	DIR* (one across display)	DIR* (one across display)	DIR* (four across display)	DIR* DIRS* DIR [OPTIONS]* (four across display)
* indicates wildcard (* and ?) file names allowed				

Table C-1. Commands Summary (*continued*)

Command	CP/M 1.3	CP/M 1.4	CP/M 2.2	CP/M-PLUS
Display File in Hex	DUMP (HEX only)	DUMP (HEX only)	DUMP (HEX only)	DUMP (ASCII and HEX)
Edit File	ED	ED (+/-V,0X 0V,X)	ED (+V default)	ED (separate input and output files)
Erase File	ERA*	ERA* (asks ALL? after *.* specification)	ERA* (asks ALL? after *.* specification)	ERA* ERASE* ERA [OPTIONS]* (asks ALL? after *.* specification)
Miscellaneous Utilities				DATE HELP INITDIR PATCH SETDEF
Rename File	REN	REN	REN	REN* RENAME*
Save Memory	SAVE	SAVE	SAVE (does not alter TPA)	SAVE (new version)
Statistics Device Assignment	STAT (space only)	STAT* (files assign. R/O attr)	STAT* (VAL, DSK, USR, $att)	SHOW (space only) DEVICE SET
System Generation	SYSGEN MOVCPM	SYSGEN MOVCPM	SYSGEN MOVCPM	COPYSYS GENCPM
Type File	TYPE	TYPE	TYPE	TYPE TYPE [OPTIONS]

* indicates wildcard (* and ?) file names allowed

TABLE C-2. Line-Editing Commands Summary

Command	CP/M 1.3	CP/M 1.4	CP/M 2.2	CP/M-PLUS Nonbanked	CP/M-PLUS Banked
A					x
B					x
C	x	x	x	x	x
E		x	x	x	x
F					x
G					x
H (BACKSPACE)			x	x	x
I (TAB)			x	x	x
J (LINEFEED)			x	x	x
K					x
M (RETURN)	x	x	x	x	x
P	x	x	x	x	x
R		x	x	x	x
S	x	x	x	x	x
U	x	x	x	x	x
W					x
X		x	x	x	x
DEL, RUBOUT	x	x	x	x	x

TABLE C-3. BDOS Functions Summary

Function	CP/M 1.3	CP/M 1.4	CP/M 2.2	CP/M-PLUS
0-5	x	x	x	x
6			x	x
7-9	x	x	x	x
10	x	x	Improved	Improved
11	x	x	x	x
12	Lift head	Lift head	Return version number	Return version number
13-14	x	x	x	x
15	x	x	Improved	Improved
16	x	x	x	x
17-19	x	x	Improved	Improved
20-21	x	x	x	x
22-24	x	x	Improved	Improved
25-27	x	x	x	x
28-36			x	x
37-152				x (Some undefined)

TABLE C-4. Disk Specifications Summary

Item	CP/M 1.3	CP/M 1.4	CP/M 2.2	CP/M-PLUS
Maximum number of drives	2	4	16	16
Maximum storage per drive	1M	1M	16M	512M
Maximum file size	128K	128K	8M	32M
Maximum number of files	64	64	Expandable	Expandable
Access method	Sequential		Sequential or random	
Location of disk characteristics	BDOS	Disk parameter block	BIOS disk parameter block	BIOS disk parameter block

APPENDIX

D File Types Commonly Used in CP/M

This appendix lists and describes each CP/M file type (extension).

TABLE D-1. CP/M File Types

File Type	Meaning	File Type	Meaning
.ASC	File containing ASCII text	.NDX	Index file (MicroPro, Ashton Tate)
.ASM	Assembly language source program file	.OBJ	Machine code (object code) file
.BAK	Backup file	.OVL	Program overlay file
.BAS	BASIC source program file	.OVR	Overlay file (MicroPro, Sorcim)
.BRS	Banked-resident system process (MP/M)	.PAS	Pascal source program file
.C	C source program file	.PCO	Pascal run-time program file (Sorcim Pascal/M)
.CAL	SuperCalc data file	.PLI	PL/I source program file
.CMD	Directly executable transient program (CP/M-86)	.PRL	Page-relocatable file (MP/M)
.COB	COBOL source program file	.PRN	Assembly language print listing file
.COM	Directly executable transient program	.REL	Relocatable machine code (object code) file
.CRF	Program cross-reference file	.RSP	Resident-system process file (MP/M)
.DAT	Data file	.SPR	System process file (MP/M)
.DOC	Document/text file	.SRC	CP/M Users' Group source file
.ERL	Pascal/MT+ relocatable file	.SUB	Command file for SUBMIT program
.FOR	FORTRAN source program file	.TEX	Document file (TEX)
.H	C program header file	.TOK	Pascal/MT+ intermediate language file
.HEX	Intel HEX-format object code file	.TXT	Document/text file
.HLP	Help information file	.XRF	Cross-reference file
.INT	CBASIC intermediate code program file	.$$$	Temporary file, or improperly saved, unusable file
.IRL	Indexed library file		
.LIB	Library file		
.MAC	Macro assembly language source program file		

APPENDIX

E CP/M Prompts

This appendix lists the prompts CP/M will put on your computer display. A description of each prompt is also provided.

TABLE E-1. CP/M Prompts

Prompt	Definition
X>	CP/M waiting for command; drive X: is currently logged drive.
#X>	MP/M or CP/M-PLUS waiting for command; drive X: is currently logged drive; current user or console number is #.
*	PIP or Microsoft's BASIC compiler, FORTRAN compiler, COBOL compiler, Pascal compiler, or EDIT waiting for command.
:*	ED waiting for command.
#:*	ED waiting for command; character pointer is on line number #.
-	DDT waiting for command.
#	SID waiting for command.
#>	SuperCalc waiting for command (where # is the number of characters in command so far).
	dBASE II waiting for command.
HELP>	HELP waiting for command.

APPENDIX

F Error Messages

This appendix* lists the error messages that emanate from standard CP/M and its utility programs. It does not include any error messages from the BIOS; these messages, if any, are the product of the programmers who wrote the various versions of the BIOS for specific computers.

The error messages are listed in alphabetical order, followed (in parentheses) by the name of the program or CP/M component outputting the message. All messages are shown here in uppercase, but the actual messages may contain lowercase letters. Additional characters that are displayed to "pretty up" the message have been omitted. For example, the message ** ABORTED ** is listed as ABORTED.

In general, the system prints an error message because CP/M cannot continue a task until you correct the error. Most CP/M error messages are short but clear enough to convey a general idea of the problem encountered. However, some programs from firms other than Digital Research occasionally use numbers to represent error messages, as in "Error #1." This is done to save internal computer-memory space, but it forces you to look up the error in the manual to find out what happened.

If you encounter an error message you do not understand, first try to eliminate or narrow the possibilities. If you're still stumped as to what to do next, consult the vendor who sold you the computer. If all else fails, write to the vendor who created the software, explaining exactly what you did and what the computer reported back to you.

? (CCP)

The CCP displays this message if you enter a command name and there is no

*Adapted from *The Programmer's CP/M Handbook* by Andy Johnson-Laird. Copyright © 1983. Used by permission of Osborne/McGraw-Hill, Inc. All rights reserved.

corresponding COMMAND.COM file on the disk.

It is also displayed if you omit the number of pages required as a parameter in the SAVE command.

? (DDT, SID)

DDT and SID output this cryptic error message under several circumstances. You must use context (and some guesswork) to determine what has gone wrong. Here are some specific causes of problems:

- DDT or SID cannot find the file that you have asked it to load into memory. Exit and investigate using DIR or STAT (the file may be set to system status and therefore not be visible with DIR).
- There is a problem with the data in the HEX file that you have asked DDT or SID to load. This could be a bad checksum on a given line or an invalid field somewhere in the record. Try TYPEing the HEX file out on a console or use an editor to examine it. It is rare to have only one or two bad bits/bytes in a HEX file; it is more likely for large amounts of the file to have been corrupted. Therefore, you may be able to spot the trouble fairly readily in this way. If you have the source code for the program, reassemble it to produce another copy of the HEX file. If you do not have the source code, there is no reliable way around this problem unless you are prepared to create the HEX file by hand—a difficult and tedious task.
- DDT or SID fails to recognize the instruction you have entered when using the A (Assemble) command to convert a source code instruction into hexadecimal. DDT and SID do not like tabs in the line (although they appear to accept them), nor do they like hexadecimal numbers to be followed by the letter H. Check that the mnemonic and operands are valid as well.

??= (DDT)

This cryptic notation is used by DDT when you are using the L (list disassembled) command to display some part of memory in DDT's primitive assembly language form. DDT cannot translate all of the 256 possible values a byte can have. Some of them are not used in the 8080 instruction set. When DDT encounters an untranslatable value, it displays this message as the instruction code, followed by the actual value of the byte in hexadecimal.

You will see this if you try to disassemble code written for the Z80 central processor, which uses unassigned 8080 instructions. You will also see it if you try to disassemble bytes that contain ASCII text strings rather than 8080 instructions.

ABORTED (PIP)

This message is displayed if you press any keyboard character while PIP is copying a file to the LST: device.

ABORTED (STAT)

If you enter any keyboard character while STAT is working its way down the file directory setting files to $DIR (directory), $SYS (system), $R/W (read/write), or $R/O (read-only) status, then it will display this message, stop what it is doing, and execute a warm boot.

By contrast, if you used the STAT *.* form to display all of the files on a disk, there is no way that the process can be aborted.

ASSIGN A PASSWORD TO THIS FILE (SET)

Password protection has been selected for the file, but no password has been assigned.

AUXILIARY DEVICE REDIRECTION NOT IMPLEMENTED (GET, PUT)

Because of the manner in which the BIOS was implemented, neither AUXOUT nor AUXIN can be redirected for file use.

BAD CHARACTER, RE-ENTER (GENCPM)

A non-numeric character was encountered. You must supply input to GENCPM using valid numbers. Retype your entry.

BAD CLOSE (SAVE)

SAVE was not able to close the file correctly after writing to it. The problem is most likely that the file is write-protected. Try making the file read/write and SAVE again.

BAD DELIMITER (STAT)

If your BIOS uses the normal IOBYTE method of assigning physical devices to logical devices, you can use STAT to perform the assignment.

STAT displays this message if it cannot find the = in the correct place.

BAD LOAD (CCP)

This is probably the most obscure error message that emanates from CP/M. You will get this message if you attempt to load a COM file that is larger than the transient program area. Your only recourse is to build a CP/M system that has a larger TPA.

BAD LOGICAL DEVICE ASSIGNMENT (DEVICE)

You typed the name of an invalid device. Use only CONIN:, CONOUT:, AUXIN:, AUXOUT:, or LST:.

BAD PARAMETER (PIP)

PIP accepts certain parameters in square brackets at the end of the command line. This message is displayed if you enter an invalid parameter or an illegal numeric value following a parameter letter.

BAD PASSWORD (RENAME)

You supplied the incorrect password. Try again with the correct password.

BANK ONE NOT ALLOWED (GENCPM)

Bank 1 of memory is not available during system generation.

BAUD RATE CANNOT BE SET FOR THIS DEVICE (DEVICE)

Only physical devices that can have their baud rate set may use the command you typed. Check the attributes of the device you specified to see if it allows baud rate specification, or type the name of a valid device when you reenter the command.

BDOS ERROR ON d: BAD SECTOR (BDOS)

BDOS displays this message if the READ and WRITE functions in your BIOS ever return indicating an error. The only safe response to this message is to type a CONTROL-C. CP/M will then execute a warm boot. If you type CARRIAGE RETURN, the error will be ignored—with unpredictable results.

A well-implemented BIOS should include disk error recovery and control so that the error will never be communicated to BDOS. If the BIOS gives you the option of ignoring an error, do so only when you are reasonably sure of the outcome or have adequate backup copies so you can recreate your files.

BDOS ERROR ON d: FILE R/O (BDOS)

You will see this message if you attempt to erase (ERA) a file that has been set to read-only status. Typing any character on the keyboard causes BDOS to perform a warm boot operation. Note that BDOS does not tell you *which* file is creating the problem. This can be difficult to determine when you use ambiguous file names in the ERA command. Use the STAT command to display all the files on the disk; it will tell you which files are read-only.

This message is also displayed if a program tries to delete a read-only file. Again, it can be difficult to determine which file is causing the problem. Your only recourse is to use STAT and try to infer which of the read-only files is the culprit.

BDOS ERROR ON d: R/O (BDOS)

This looks much like the previous message, but it refers to an entire logical disk instead of a read-only file. However, it is rarely output because you have declared a disk to be read-only. The more usual circumstance when you would see this error is if you change disks without typing a CONTROL-C; CP/M will detect the new disk and, without any external indication, will set the disk to read-only status.

If you or a program then attempts to write any data to the disk, the attempt will be trapped by BDOS and this message displayed. Type any character on the keyboard to cause a warm boot and then proceed.

BDOS ERROR ON d: SELECT (BDOS)

BDOS displays this message if you or a program attempts to select a logical disk for which the BIOS lacks the necessary tables. BDOS uses the value returned by SELDSK to determine whether a logical disk "exists" or not.

If you were trying to change the default disk to a nonexistent one, you will have to press the RESET button. There is no way out of this error.

However, if you were trying to execute a command that accessed the nonexistent disk, then you can type a CONTROL-C and CP/M will perform a warm boot.

BREAK x AT y (ED)

This is another one of those cryptic messages that you cannot possibly second-guess. The table below explains the possible values of x. The value y refers to the command ED was executing when the error occurred.

x	Meaning
#	Search failure. ED did not find the string you asked it to search for.
?	Unrecognized command.
0	File not found.
>	Buffer full. ED's internal buffer is now full.
E	Command aborted.
F	Disk or directory full. You will have to determine which is causing the problem.

CANNOT CLOSE DESTINATION FILE (PIP, GENCOM, HEXCOM, LIB-80, LINK-80)

The programs listed display this message if the destination disk is physically write-protected. If it is write-protected, remove the protection and repeat the operation.

If the disk is not protected, you have a hardware problem. The directory data written to the disk either is being written to the wrong place, even to the wrong disk, or is not being recorded on the medium.

CANNOT CLOSE FILES (ASM, MAC, RMAC)

The assemblers display this message if they cannot close their output files because the disk is physically write-protected, or if there is a hardware problem that prevents data from being written to the disk. See the previous paragraph.

CANNOT CLOSE, READ-ONLY? (SUBMIT)

SUBMIT displays this message if the disk on which it is trying to write its output file, $$$SUB, is physically write-protected. Do not confuse this with the disk being *logically* write-protected.

The standard version of SUBMIT writes the output file onto the current default disk; so if your current default disk is other than drive A:, you may be able to avoid this problem by switching the default to A: and then entering a SUBMIT command with the drive on which the SUB file is located.

CANNOT DELETE FILE (GENCOM)

CP/M-PLUS must be able to write a new file to the disk; either the file it is trying to write is read-only, or it is password-protected. Remove the protection from the file and try again.

CANNOT HAVE BOTH CREATE AND ACCESS TIME STAMPS (SET)

Both create and access time stamps cannot be used. Select one or the other and try again.

CANNOT LABEL A DRIVE WITH A FILE REFERENCED (SET)
You cannot mix files and drives when labeling a disk.

CANNOT OPEN SOURCE FILE (HEXCOM)
The HEX file you specified was not found.

CANNOT READ (PIP)
PIP displays this message if you attempt to read information from a logical device that can only output, such as the LST: device.

PIP will also display this message if you confuse it sufficiently, for instance, by entering PIP FILE1=FILE2;FILE3.

CANNOT REDIRECT FROM BIOS (GET, PUT)
Your system has an invalid BIOS. Contact the manufacturer of your system.

CANNOT SET BOTH RO AND RW (SET)
You can set a file to read-only or read/write, but not to both. Select one and try again.

CANNOT SET BOTH SYS AND DIR (SET)
You can set a file to directory or system, but not to both. Select one and try again.

CANNOT WRITE (PIP)
Similarly, PIP displays this message if you attempt to output information to a logical device that can only be used for input, such as the RDR: device.

CAN'T DELETE TEMP FILE (PIP)
A temporary file exists that is read-only. Change its attributes to read/write and try again.

CHECKSUM ERROR (LOAD, HEXCOM)
LOAD and HEXCOM display this message if they encounter a line in the input HEX file that does not have the correct checksum for the data on the line.

LOAD also displays helpful information to pinpoint the problem. Unfortunately, the checksum value is not displayed. You need to use TYPE or an editor to inspect the HEX file in order to see exactly what has gone wrong.

CHECKSUM ERROR (PIP)
If you ask PIP to copy a file of type HEX, it will check each line in the file, making sure that the line's checksum is valid. If it is not, PIP will display this message. Unfortunately, PIP does not tell you which line is in error—you must do this by inspection or recreate the HEX file and try again.

CLOSE ERROR (XREF)
XREF could not write the XRF file. Check to see if the disk is protected or that a disk is in the drive.

CLOSE OPERATION FAILED (COPYSYS)
COPYSYS could not write the CPM3.SYS file. Check to see if the disk is protected, that enough space exists on the disk, or that a disk is in the drive.

CLOSING FILE HELP.xxx (HELP)

An error was encountered in processing the file. Use DUMP to examine the file and ascertain the problem.

COM FILE FOUND AND NULL OPTION (GENCOM)

GENCOM was looking for RSX files, not COM files. Either do not use the NULL option, or make sure the appropriate files are present on the disk.

COM FILE REQUIRED (DIR, ERASE, RENAME, TYPE)

CP/M-PLUS requires a COM file for each of the above commands when some of the extended options are specified. Make sure the appropriate files are present on the default drive.

COMMAND BUFFER OVERFLOW (SUBMIT)

SUBMIT displays this message if the SUB file you specified is too large to be processed. SUBMIT's internal buffer is only 2048 bytes. You must reduce the size of the SUB file, remove any comment lines, or split the file in two, with the last line of the first file submitting the second to give a nested SUBMIT file.

COMMAND TOO LONG (SUBMIT)

The longest command line that SUBMIT can process is 125 characters. There is no way around this error other than to reduce the length of the offending line. You will have to find this line by inspection; SUBMIT does not identify the line.

You can remove a few characters from a command line by renaming the COM file you are invoking with a shorter name, or by using abbreviated names for parameters if the program will accept these.

COMMON ERROR (LINK-80)

An undefined common block was selected. Make sure that you specified the correct name or file.

CORRECT ERROR, TYPE RETURN OR CTL-Z (PIP)

This message is a carryover from the days when PIP read hexadecimal data from a high-speed paper tape reader. If PIP detected the end of a roll of paper tape, it would display this message. The user could then check to see if the paper tape had torn or had reached the end. If there was more tape to be read, the user could enter a CARRIAGE RETURN to resume reading tape, or enter a CONTROL-Z to serve as the end-of-file character.

Needless to say, it is unlikely that you will see this message if you do not have a paper tape reader.

CPMLDR ERROR: FAILED TO OPEN CPM3.SYS

CPM3.SYS is not present on the disk.

CPMLDR ERROR: FAILED TO READ CPM3.SYS

CPM3.SYS contains errors.

CP/M ERROR ON d: DISK I/O BDOS FUNCTION = xx FILE = filename.typ

CP/M ERROR ON d: INVALID DRIVE BDOS FUNCTION = xx FILE = filename.typ

CP/M ERROR ON d: READ/ONLY DISK BDOS FUNCTION = xx FILE = filename.typ

CP/M ERROR ON d: READ/ONLY FILE BDOS FUNCTION = xx FILE = filename.typ

This is CP/M-PLUS's BDOS error message. First the type of error is specified; then you are told what function and file CP/M-PLUS was trying to use when the error was encountered.

DATE AND TIME STAMPING INACTIVE (DIR)

You asked for the DATE option, but the disk directory has not been initialized for date and time stamping.

DESTINATION IS R/O, DELETE (Y/N)? (PIP)

PIP displays this message if you try to overwrite a disk file that has been set to read-only status. If you type an upper- or lowercase Y, PIP will overwrite the destination file. It leaves the destination file in read/write status with its directory/system status unchanged. Typing any character other than Y makes PIP abandon the copy.

You can avoid this message altogether if you specify the "w" option on PIP's command line. PIP will then overwrite read-only files without question.

DEVICE REASSIGNMENT NOT SUPPORTED

ENTER NEW ASSIGNMENT OR HIT RETURN (DEVICE)

The device assignment you specified does not exist. Enter a valid device assignment, or press RETURN to cancel the DEVICE command.

DIRECTORY ALREADY RE-FORMATTED (INITDIR)

You asked for date and time stamping to be initialized on a disk where it is already present.

DIRECTORY FULL (SUBMIT)

This message is displayed if the BDOS returns an error when SUBMIT tries to create its output file, $$$SUB. As a rough and ready approximation, use STAT *.* to see how many files and extents you have on the disk and erase any unwanted ones. Then use STAT DSK: to find out the maximum number of directory entries possible for the disk.

You may also see this message if the file directory has become corrupted, or if the disk formatting routine leaves the disk with the file directory full of some pattern other than E5H.

You can assess whether the directory has been corrupted by using STAT USR:. STAT then displays the user numbers containing files. If the directory is corrupt, you will normally see user numbers *greater* than 15.

It is not easy to repair a corrupted directory. ERA*.* erases only the files for the current user number, so you will have to enter the command 16 times, once for each user number from 0 to 15. Alternatively, you will have to reformat the disk.

DIRECTORY NEEDS TO BE REFORMATTED FOR DATE/TIME STAMPS (SET)

You must use INITDIR on a disk before specifying the DATE option in SET.

DIRECTORY OR DISK FULL (ED, LIB-80, LINK-80, GENCPM, HEXCOM)

Self-explanatory.

DISK READ ERROR (PIP, GENCPM, HEXCOM, LIB-80, LINK-80)

DISK WRITE ERROR (SUBMIT)

DISK WRITE ERROR (PIP)

These messages will normally be preceded by a BIOS error message. They will be displayed only if the BIOS returns indicate an error. As was described earlier, this is unlikely if the BIOS has any kind of error recovery logic.

DO YOU WANT ANOTHER FILE? (Y/N) (PUT)

Press Y to redirect output to an additional file; otherwise press N.

DRIVE DEFINED TWICE IN SEARCH PATH (SETDEF)

You can specify a drive only once in a SETDEF order.

DRIVE READ ONLY (ERASE, RENAME)

You must make the drive read/write before erasing or renaming a file.

DRIVE SPECIFIED HAS NOT BEEN DEFINED (GENCPM)

Buffers have not been allocated for the drive you specified.

DUPLICATE INPUT RSX. (GENCOM)

Two or more RSX files with the same name were specified. GENCOM uses only the first of the RSX files.

DUPLICATE RSX IN HEADER. REPLACING OLD BY NEW.

THIS FILE WAS NOT USED. (GENCOM)

The specified RSX file is already attached to the COM file. The old file is replaced by the new one.

END OF FILE, CTL-Z? (PIP)

PIP displays this message if, during the copy of a HEX file, it encounters a CONTROL-Z (end-of-file). Again, the underlying idea is based on the concept of paper tape: seeing this message, you can look at the tape in the reader, and if it really is at the end of the roll, enter a CONTROL-Z on the keyboard to terminate the file. If there is any other character, PIP will read the next piece of tape.

END OF LINE EXPECTED (DEVICE, GET, PUT, SETDEF)

A character other than a valid parameter or end of line was found; any remaining characters on the line will be ignored.

EQUALS (=) DELIMITER MISSING AT LINE NN (GENCPM)

The equal sign is missing in the line specified.

ERROR AT END OF LINE (DEVICE, GET, PUT, SETDEF)

An error was detected at the end of the input line.

ERROR : CANNOT CLOSE FILES (LOAD)

LOAD displays this message if you have physically write-protected the disk on which it is trying to write the output COM file.

ERROR : CANNOT OPEN SOURCE (LOAD)

LOAD displays this message if it cannot open the HEX file that you specified in the command tail.

ERROR : DISK READ (LOAD)

ERROR : DISK WRITE (LOAD)

These two messages would normally be preceded by a BIOS error message. If your BIOS includes disk error recovery, you would not normally see these messages; the error would have been handled by the BIOS.

ERROR : INVERTED LOAD ADDRESS (LOAD)

LOAD displays this message if it detects a load address less than 0100H in the input HEX file. It also displays the actual address input from the file, so you can examine the HEX file looking for this address in order to determine the likely cause of the problem.

Note that DDT, when asked to load the same HEX file, will do so without any error — but it will probably damage the contents of the base page as well.

ERROR : NO MORE DIRECTORY SPACE (LOAD)

Self-explanatory.

ERROR ON LINE N (SUBMIT)

SUBMIT displays this message if it encounters a line in the SUB file that it does not know how to process. Most likely you have a file that has type SUB but does not contain ASCII text.

The first line of the SUB file is number 001.

FILE ALREADY EXISTS; DELETE IT? (Y/N) (PUT, RENAME)

Press Y to delete an existing file of the name you specified and replace it with the new one, or press N to cancel your command.

FILE CANNOT FIT INTO GENCPM BUFFER: filename.SPR (GENCPM)

There is not enough memory to generate the system you specified.

FILE ERROR (ED)

The disk or directory is full, and ED cannot write any more information to disk.

FILE EXISTS (CCP)

The CCP displays this message if you attempt to use the REN command to rename an existing file with a name already given to another file.

Use STAT *.* to display all of the files on the disk. DIR will only show those files that have directory status, and you may not be able to see the file causing the problem.

FILE EXISTS, ERASE IT (ED)

The destination file you specified already exists. Try another name, or erase the old file of the same name.

FILE IS READ/ONLY (ED, PUT)
ED displays this message if you attempt to edit a file that has been set to read-only status.

FILE NAME ERROR (LIB-80)
The source file name is invalid.

FILE NOT FOUND (STAT, DUMP, ED, GENCOM, GET, SET)

FILENAME NOT FOUND (PIP)
These programs display their respective messages if you specify a nonexistent file. This applies to both specific and ambiguous file names.

FIRST COMMON NOT LARGEST (LINK-80)
You must link files and keep the library in the proper order, with the largest common declaration first.

FIRST SUBMITTED FILE MUST BE A COM FILE (GENCOM)
A COM file must be the first file in the list at the end of the command. Either specify the NULL option or redo the file list.

HELP.DAT NOT ON CURRENT DRIVE (HELP)
For HELP to function, the file HELP.DAT must be on the default drive or in the chain of drives searched.

ILLEGAL COMMAND TAIL (DIR)
The command line has an invalid format or option list.

ILLEGAL DATE/TIME SPECIFICATION (DATE)
You used the incorrect date or time format.

ILLEGAL FILENAME (SAVE)
You did not type a valid file name and type.

ILLEGAL FORMAT VALUE (DIR)
Only SIZE and FULL options can be used for display formats.

ILLEGAL GLOBAL/LOCAL DRIVE SPEC MIXING (DIR)
You cannot mix DRIVE options with a file name specification that also uses a drive specifier.

ILLEGAL OPTION OR MODIFIER (DIR)
An invalid option or abbreviation was used in the command.

INCORRECT FILE SPECIFICATION (RENAME)
You did not specify a valid file name and type.

INDEX ERROR (LINK-80)
The index in an IRL file contains invalid information.

INSUFFICIENT MEMORY (GET, LINK-80, PUT, SUBMIT)
Your system does not have enough memory to allocate the appropriate buffers. You may have too many nested SUBMIT commands.

INVALID ASSIGNMENT (STAT)
STAT can be used to assign physical devices to logical devices by means of the IOBYTE system described earlier. It will display this message if you enter an

illogical assignment. Use the STAT VAL: command to display the valid assignments.

INVALID CHARACTER AT LINE NN (GENCPM)

A non-numeric character was encountered.

INVALID COMMAND (GET, PUT)

Self-explanatory.

INVALID CONTROL CHARACTER (SUBMIT)

SUBMIT is supposed to be able to handle a control character in the SUB file—the notation being ^x, where x is the control letter. In fact, the standard release version of SUBMIT cannot handle this notation at all. A patch is available from Digital Research to correct this problem.

Given that this patch has been installed, SUBMIT will display this message if a character other than A to Z is specified after the circumflex (^) character.

INVALID DELIMITER (DEVICE, GET, PUT, SETDEF)

You used the wrong delimiter; for example, a [was used where a = was expected.

INVALID DESTINATION (PIP)

You specified an invalid device or drive.

INVALID DIGIT (PIP)

PIP displays this message if it encounters non-numeric data where it expects to have a numeric value.

INVALID DISK ASSIGNMENT (STAT)

STAT displays this message if you try to set a logical disk to read-only status and you specify a parameter other than R/O. Note that there is no leading $ in this case (as there is when you want to set a *file* to read-only).

INVALID DRIVE IGNORED AT LINE NN (GENCPM)

Drives must be A-P only.

INVALID DRIVE NAME (USE A,B,C, OR D) (SYSGEN, SETDEF, GENCPM, TYPE, COPYSYS)

This message is displayed if you attempt to load the CP/M system from, or write the system to, a disk drive other than A, B, C, or D.

INVALID FILE

INVALID FILENAME

INVALID FILE SPECIFICATION (ED, ERASE, GENCOM, GET, PIP, SET, SUBMIT, PUT, TYPE)

The file name typed does not conform to the file-naming conventions used by CP/M.

INVALID FILE INDICATOR (STAT)

STAT outputs this message if you specify an erroneous file attribute. File attributes can only be $DIR, $SYS, $R/O, or $R/W.

INVALID FORMAT (PIP)

PIP displays this message if you enter a badly formatted command, for example, a + character instead of a =, which on some terminals are on the same key.

INVALID HEX DIGIT (LOAD, HEXCOM)
LOAD and HEXCOM display this message if they encounter a nonhexadecimal digit in the input HEX file, where only a hex digit can appear. LOAD and HEXCOM then display additional information to tell you where in the file the problem occurred.

INVALID MEMORY SIZE (MOVCPM)
MOVCPM displays this message if you enter an invalid memory size for the CP/M system size you want to construct.

INVALID NUMBER (DEVICE)
A number in the range 0-255 was expected but not found.

INVALID OPTION (DEVICE, GET, SETDEF)

INVALID OPTION OR MODIFIER (DIR, GET, PUT)

INVALID PARAMETER (MAC, RMAC)

INVALID PARAMETER AT LINE NN (GENCPM)
Self-explanatory.

INVALID PASSWORD (ED, PIP)
Self-explanatory.

INVALID PHYSICAL DEVICE (DEVICE)
Self-explanatory.

INVALID REL FILE (LINK-80)
The file indicated is not a valid REL or IRL type file.

INVALID RSX TYPE (GENCOM)
The file type must be of type RSX.

INVALID SCB OFFSET (GENCOM)
You must specify an SCB offset of 00H-64H only.

INVALID SEPARATOR (PIP)
PIP displays this message if you try to concatenate files and use something other than a comma between file names.

INVALID SOURCE (PIP)
You specified a device or drive that is not valid.

INVALID SYM FILE FORMAT (XREF)
The symbol table XREF found has invalid information.

INVALID TYPE FOR ORDER OPTION (SETDEF)
The ORDER option must be of type SUB or COM to be valid.

INVALID USER NUMBER (PIP)
PIP displays this message if you enter a user number outside the range 0-15 with the [Gn] option (where n is the user number).

INVALID WILDCARD (RENAME)
You inappropriately used *, ?, or another character that RENAME did not

recognize as a wildcard character.

INVALID WILD CARD IN THE FCB NAME OR TYPE FIELD (GENCOM)
You cannot use wildcard characters in a GENCOM file name.

LOAD ADDRESS LESS THAN 100 (HEXCOM)
The program origin is less than 100H.

MAIN MODULE ERROR (LINK-80)
More than one main module was encountered by LINK.

MAKE ERROR (XREF)
The directory is full on the specified drive.

MEMORY CONFLICT —CANNOT TRIM SEGMENT (GENCPM)
The defined memory segment overlaps another segment. GENCPM could do nothing about the problem.

MEMORY CONFLICT —SEGMENT TRIMMED (GENCPM)
The defined memory segment overlaps another segment. GENCPM trimmed one of the segments to fit.

MEMORY OVERFLOW (LINK-80)
There is not enough memory to complete LINK.

MINIMUM NUMBER OF BUFFERS IS 1 (GENCPM)
The first drive must have at least one buffer defined.

MISSING DELIMITER OR UNRECOGNIZED OPTION (ERASE)
The ERASE command line format is invalid.

MISSING PARAMETER VARIABLE AT LINE NN (GENCPM)
The line is missing a variable name.

MISSING LEFT PARENTHESIS (GENCOM)

MISSING RIGHT PARENTHESIS

MISSING SCB VALUE
The SCB option is expected to be enclosed by parentheses.

MORE THAN FOUR DRIVES SPECIFIED (SETDEF)
You may only have four drives in a SETDEF search command.

MULTIPLE DEFINITION (LINK-80)
The same symbol was specified for more than one of the modules being linked.

NO DIRECTORY LABEL EXISTS (SHOW)
The disk has no directory label.

NO DIRECTORY SPACE (ASM, COPYSYS, GENCOM, MAC, PIP, RMAC, SAVE)
Self-explanatory.

NO DISK SPACE (SAVE)
Self-explanatory.

NO FILE (CCP, DIR, ERASE, LIB-80, LINK-80, PATCH, RENAME, TYPE)

The CCP displays this message if you use the REN (rename) command, and it cannot find the file you wish to rename.

The programs listed display this message if they cannot find the file you specified.

NO HELP.HLP FILE ON THE DEFAULT DRIVE (HELP)

Self-explanatory.

NO INPUT FILE PRESENT ON DISK (DUMP)

The file you requested does not exist.

NO MEMORY (ED, CCP)

ED displays this message if it ever runs out of memory for storing the text you are editing.

NO MODIFIER FOR THIS OPTION (GENCOM)

A modifier was specified but it was not expected by GENCOM; therefore, it was ignored.

NO MODULE (LIB-80)

The requested module cannot be found by LIB.

NO MORE SPACE IN THE HEADER FOR RSXS OR SCB INITIALIZATION (GENCOM)

The header has room for only 15 entries, and you have exceeded that maximum.

NON-SYSTEM FILE(S) EXIST (DIRS)

Self-explanatory.

NO OPTIONS SPECIFIED (SET)

An option must be present.

NO PRN FILE (XREF)

The PRN file was not found.

NO RECORDS EXIST (DUMP)

Only a directory entry exists for the file you specified; the file does not yet contain information.

NO SOURCE FILE ON DISK (SYSGEN, COPYSYS)

This error message is misleading. SYSGEN does not read source code files. The message should read "INPUT FILE NOT FOUND."

NO SOURCE FILE PRESENT (ASM, MAC, RMAC)

In this case, the assemblers really do mean that the source code file cannot be found. Remember that the assemblers use a strange form of specifying their parameters. The assemblers use the file name that you enter and then search for a file of that name, but with the file type ASM. The three characters of the file type that you specify are used to represent the logical disks on which the source, hex, and list files, respectively, are to be placed.

NO SPACE (CCP, SAVE)

The CCP displays this message if you use the SAVE command, and there is insufficient room on the disk to accommodate the file.

NO 'SUB' FILE FOUND (SUBMIT)

NO 'SUB' FILE PRESENT

SUBMIT displays this message if it cannot find a file with the file name you specified and with a type of SUB.

NO SUCH FILE TO RENAME (RENAME)

The file you wanted to rename was not found.

NO SYM FILE (XREF)

The SYM file was not found.

NOT A CHARACTER SOURCE (PIP)

PIP displays this message if you attempt to copy characters from a character output device, such as the auxiliary output device (known as PUN: by PIP).

NOT ENOUGH AVAILABLE MEMORY

NOT ENOUGH MEMORY

NOT ENOUGH MEMORY FOR SORT (DIR, INITDIR)

There is not enough memory to sort or store the directory information.

NOT ENOUGH ROOM IN DIRECTORY (INITDIR)

There is not enough directory space for date and time stamping.

NOT RENAMED, FILE READ ONLY (RENAME)

Files must be read/write to be renamed.

OPEN FILE NONRECOVERABLE (PIP)

A bad disk sector or format was encountered.

OPTION ONLY FOR DRIVES (SET)

The specified option is not valid when it is used with a file name.

OPTION REQUIRES A FILE REFERENCE (SET)

You must supply a file name to use the requested option.

OPTIONS NOT GROUPED TOGETHER (DIR)

You can use only one set of brackets when specifying options.

OUT OF DATA SPACE (COPYSYS)

There is not enough space to save the CPM3.SYS file.

OUTPUT FILE READ ERROR (MAC, RMAC)

The output file was not written properly; most likely the disk is full.

OUTPUT FILE WRITE ERROR (ASM)

ASM will display this message if the BDOS returns an error from a disk write operation. If your BIOS has disk error recovery logic, you should never see this message.

OVERLAPPING SEGMENTS (LINK-80)

LINK needed memory used by another segment when it attempted to write the current segment to memory.

PAGE AND NOPAGE OPTION SELECTED

NO PAGE IN EFFECT (SET)

You specified both the PAGE and NOPAGE options. NOPAGE was used.

PARAMETER ERROR (SUBMIT)

SUBMIT uses the $ to mark points where parameter values are to be substituted. If you have a single $ followed by an alphabetic character, SUBMIT will display this message. Use $$ to represent a real $.

PASSWORD ERROR (DUMP, ERASE, GENCOM, TYPE)

You typed an incorrect password.

PERMANENT ERROR, TYPE RETURN TO IGNORE (SYSGEN)

SYSGEN displays this message if the BIOS returns an error from a disk read or write operation. If your BIOS has disk error recovery logic, you should never see this message.

PHYSICAL DEVICE DOES NOT EXIST (DEVICE)

You specified an invalid or undefined physical device.

POSSIBLE INCOMPATIBLE DISK FORMAT (COPYSYS)

The system disk and output disk have different formats.

PUT> (PUT)

You specified PUT FILE [NO ECHO] and the program requires user input. Either restart the session using the ECHO option or type the appropriate response.

PUT ERROR: FILE ERASED (PUT)

The PUT file could not be closed; therefore, it was erased.

QUIT NOT FOUND (PIP)

PIP displays this message when it cannot find the string specified in the [Qcharacter string^Z] option, meaning "Quit copying when you encounter this string."

RANDOM READ (SUBMIT)

An error occurred when a temporary file was read.

READ ERROR (CCP, TYPE)

The CCP displays this message if the BIOS returns an error from a disk read or write operation. If your BIOS includes disk error recovery logic, you should not see this error message.

READING FILE (GENCPM, HELP)

An error occurred during an attempt to read the file specified.

READ ONLY (GENCOM, SET)

The drive or file specified is read-only or write-protected.

RECORD TOO LONG (PIP)
A HEX record exceeds 80 characters in length.

REQUIRES CP/M 2.0 OR NEWER FOR OPERATION (PIP)

REQUIRES CP/M VERSION 2.0 OR LATER (XSUB)
Self-explanatory.

REQUIRES CP/M 3.0 OR HIGHER (DATE, DEVICE, DIR, ERASE, GENCOM, HELP, INITDIR, PIP, SET, SETDEF, SHOW, RENAME, TYPE)
You cannot use these programs without CP/M-PLUS.

R/O DISK (PIP)
The disk specified is read-only.

R/O FILE (PIP)
The file specified is read-only.

SORT STACK OVERFLOW (DIR)
There is not enough memory to sort file names in memory.

SOURCE FILE INCOMPLETE (SYSGEN, GENCPM)
SYSGEN or GENCPM displays this message if the file you have asked it to read is too short. Use STAT to check the length of the file.

SOURCE FILE NAME ERROR (ASM, MAC, RMAC)
The assemblers display this message if you specify an ambiguous file name, that is, one that contains either * or ?.

SOURCE FILE READ ERROR (ASM, MAC, RMAC)
The assemblers display this message if they encounter problems in reading the input source code file. Check the input file using the TYPE command or an editor.

START NOT FOUND (PIP)
PIP displays this message when it cannot find the string specified in the [Scharacter string^Z] option, meaning "Start copying when you encounter this string."

SYMBOL TABLE OVERFLOW (ASM, XREF)
ASM and XREF display this message when you have too many symbols in the source code file. Your only recourse is to split the source file into several pieces and arrange for ORG (origin) statements to position the generated object code so that the pieces fit together.

SYMBOL TABLE REFERENCE OVERFLOW (XREF)
The symbol table is too large.

SYNCRONIZATION ERROR (MOVCPM)
Apart from the spelling error, this message is designed to be cryptic. MOVCPM displays it when the Digital Research serial number embedded in

MOVCPM does not match the serial number in the version of CP/M that you are currently running.

SYNTAX ERROR (LIB)
The LIB command is invalid.

SYSTEM FILE NOT ACCESSIBLE (ED)
ED displays this message if you attempt to edit a file that has been set to system status. Use STAT to set the file to directory status.

TOO MANY ENTRIES IN INDEX TABLE (HELP)
There is not enough memory available to hold the topic table while creating HELP.HLP.

TOO MANY FILES (STAT)
STAT displays this message if there is insufficient memory available to sort and display all of the files on the specified disk. You should try limiting the number of files it has to sort by judicious use of ambiguous file names.

TOPIC: NOT FOUND (HELP)
The topic you requested does not exist.

TOTAL FILE SIZE EXCEEDS 64K (GENCOM)
A COM file cannot exceed 64K in length.

TRY 'PAGE' OR 'NO PAGE' (TYPE)
You specified an invalid option for TYPE.

UNABLE TO ALLOCATE DATA DEBLOCKING BUFFER SPACE (GENCPM)

UNABLE TO ALLOCATE DIR DEBLOCKING BUFFER SPACE

UNABLE TO ALLOCATE SPACE FOR HASH TABLE
There is not enough space to allocate the specified function in the generated system.

UNABLE TO CLOSE HELP.xxx (HELP)

UNABLE TO MAKE HELP.xxx
HELP.HLP or HELP.DAT could not be saved because there was not enough disk or directory space.

UNABLE TO FIND FILE HELP.HLP (HELP)
Self-explanatory.

UNABLE TO OPEN .SPR (GENCPM)
The file specified could not be found by GENCPM.

UNBALANCED MACRO LIBRARY (MAC, RMAC)
A MACRO definition was started, but a matching ENDM was not found.

UNDEFINED START SYMBOL (LINK-80)

UNDEFINED SYMBOLS
The symbol specified is not defined in any of the modules LINK encountered.

UNEXPECTED END OF HEX FILE (PIP)
An end-of-file was found before the termination hex record.

UNRECOGNIZED DESTINATION (PIP)
PIP displays this message if you specify a destination device that is illegal.

UNRECOGNIZED DRIVE (SHOW)
Self-explanatory.

UNRECOGNIZED INPUT (SHOW)
Self-explanatory.

UNRECOGNIZED ITEM (LINK-80)
Self-explanatory.

UNRECOGNIZED OPTION (GENCOM, SHOW)
Self-explanatory.

USER ABORTED (PIP)
You stopped a PIP option by pressing CONTROL-C.

VERIFY ERROR (PIP)
If you use the [V] (verify) option of PIP when copying to a disk file, PIP will write a sector to disk, read it back, and compare the data. PIP displays this message if the data does not match.

If there is a problem with your disk system, you should have seen some form of disk error message preceding this one. If there is no preceding message, then you have a problem with the main memory on your system.

WARNING: PROGRAM INPUT IGNORED (SUBMIT)
The line includes a <, but the program does not require the additional input; therefore, it was ignored.

WRITE ERROR (XREF)
No disk or directory space was available to write the XRF file.

WRITE PROTECTED? (COPYSYS)
The drive that the system is to be copied to is read-only.

WRITING FILE (GENCPM, HELP)
The file could not be written because of insufficient disk or directory space.

WRONG CP/M VERSION (REQUIRES 2.0) (STAT)
Self-explanatory.

WRONG PASSWORD (SET)
The specified password is incorrect.

(XSUB ACTIVE) (XSUB)
This is not really an error message, but you may mistake it for one. XSUB is the eXtended SUBMIT program. Without it, SUBMIT can only feed command lines to the CCP. XSUB allows character-by-character input into any program that uses the BDOS to read console input.

XSUB is initiated by being the first command in a SUB file. Once initiated it stays in memory until the end of the SUB file has been reached. Until that happens, XSUB will output this message every time a warm boot occurs as a reminder that it is still in memory.

XSUB ALREADY PRESENT (XSUB)

XSUB will display this message if it is already active and you attempt to load it again.

ZERO LENGTH SEGMENT NOT ALLOWED (GENCPM)

A valid segment cannot have a length of 0.

0FFFFH IS AN INVALID VALUE IN THE DPH DIRECTORY BCB ADDRESS FIELD (GENCPM)

The directory BCB field must be at 0FFFE or lower to be valid.

APPENDIX

G Sources of Information

The previous edition of this book listed a large number of magazine articles that related to CP/M. In the three years since that bibliography appeared, the number of possible entries has climbed to such a level that a complete listing would fill a book. For the sake of brevity, we have included in this appendix a listing of the most useful books and magazines providing information on CP/M.

Books

Barbier, Ken. *CP/M Assembly Language Programming*. Englewood Cliffs, N.J.: Prentice-Hall, 1983.

A beginner's guide to CP/M assembly language programming. Not as thorough as Waite and Lafore's *Soul of CPM,* but easy to read and understand.

Brigham, Bruce, ed. *CP/M Summary Guide*. Glastonbury, Conn.: Rainbow Associates, 1980.

A useful computer-side reference that reprints and summarizes the commands available with CP/M, DESPOOL, MAC, TEX, CBASIC, and BASIC-80.

Cortesi, David. *A Programmer's Notebook: Utilities for CP/M-80*. Reston, Va.: Reston Publishing Co., 1983.

A book full of assembly language utilities and subroutines. A disk is available for those who do not want to type the listings into their computers. A very valuable book for programmers.

_____ _____ .*Inside CP/M: A Guide for Users and Programmers*. New York: Holt Rinehart & Winston, 1982.

A useful book, especially for assembly language programmers; includes valuable material for using the MAC assembler and useful, well-organized appendixes.

Dennon, Jack. *CP/M Revealed.* Rochelle Park, N.J.: Hayden Book Co., 1983.

A curious collection of miscellany about assembly language programming under CP/M. This book does not begin to cover everything needed to program well under CP/M, but what it does provide is useful and well presented.

Fernandez, Judi, and Ruth Ashley. *Using CP/M*. New York: John Wiley & Sons, 1980.

A primer of CP/M commands and syntax, this self-teaching book conveys technical information in a question-and-answer format. Another version of this book addresses CP/M-86 for the IBM PC.

Johnson-Laird, Andy. *The Programmer's CP/M Handbook.* Berkeley: Osborne/McGraw-Hill, 1983.

The follow-up book to *CP/M User Guide.* Deals primarily with assembly language programming, but also includes examples of programming with C under CP/M.

Miller, Alan. *Mastering CP/M.* Berkeley: Sybex, 1983.

A book that aims for an audience somewhere between readers of *CP/M User Guide* and experienced CP/M programmers. Much of the book centers on the disk I/O operations that are at the heart of CP/M.

Murta, Stephen, and Mitchell Waite. *CP/M Primer.* Indianapolis: Howard W. Sams & Co., 1980.

A good book for novice CP/M users.

Townsend, Carl. *How to Get Started With CP/M.* Beaverton, Oreg.: dilithium Press, 1981.

A simple overview of the CP/M operating system.

Waite, Mitchell, and Robert Lafore. *Soul of CP/M.* Indianapolis: Howard W. Sams & Co., 1983.

A solid and well-written beginner's guide to assembly language programming under CP/M-80.

Weber, Jeffrey. *CP/M Simplified.* Cleveland: Weber Systems, 1982.

An introduction to CP/M. Not particularly well organized, but a great deal of useful information is presented.

Zaks, Rodnay. *The CP/M Handbook With MP/M.* Berkeley: Sybex, 1980.

Discusses CP/M and MP/M commands, programs, and facilities.

Other books of interest to CP/M users include those on BASIC (Microsoft BASIC-80, CBASIC), C, SuperCalc, WordStar, and 8080/8085/Z80 assembly language programming.

Magazines

Several magazines regularly address the CP/M world, with articles of interest to CP/M users in almost every issue. Check your local computer or software store or a well-stocked magazine rack for these titles:

CP/M Review
: Mainly of interest to new or potential purchasers of CP/M systems.

Datacast
: Published irregularly, this magazine does a good job of explaining what the CP/M and application program manuals were trying to tell you. Look for back issues at your computer store. Most of the staff went to *User Guide*.

Dr. Dobbs Journal
: A great source of information for CP/M assembly language, FORTH, and C programmers. The back issues have been published in book form by Hayden and include complete source code for the C, BASIC, and FORTH languages.

InfoWorld
: The only weekly news magazine for microcomputer users. Features news and software reviews of interest to CP/M users.

Lifelines
: A hard-to-find but often useful magazine dedicated to CP/M software.

Microsystems
: Hard-core users and hobbyists like this magazine's articles, which center around programming in assembly language and C and discuss exotic and high-performance hardware.

Personal Software
: A new magazine that periodically covers CP/M software.

User Guide
: Very much like *Datacast*; attempts to explain commonly used software for CP/M systems in terms computer novices can understand. An invaluable aid.

Glossary

ASCII. American Standard Code for Information Interchange refers to the computer's internal recognition of the letters, numbers, and symbols of English or another language. Appendix A provides a complete listing of these representations.

Assembly Language. Assembly language consists of mnemonics that represent machine instructions the computer will perform. For example, instead of "11001001" (the machine instruction), the mnemonic RET instructs the computer to return to a location stored by the computer.

BASIC. Beginners All-purpose Symbolic Instruction Code is an intermediate language; each instruction in BASIC will generate a number of equivalent assembly language instructions executed as they are encountered. (*See also* Interpreter.)

Batch Processing. Batch processing refers to any process that collects instructions and data (by terminals, keypunches, optical card readers, and so forth) and delays processing until a large batch accumulates.

Booting/Bootstrap. Booting, or bootstrap, initializes a computer system by copying an operating system into the internal memory of a computer from a disk or tape.

Buffer. A buffer is an area within the computer's memory that temporarily stores input from or output to any peripheral computer device (like a disk drive). It allows the central processing unit to process information more quickly than it would from a slower mechanical device such as a printer, disk drive, punch, or keyboard.

Byte. The storage capacity of a microcomputer's memory, or its disks, is always described as some number of bytes. A byte, consisting of 8 *bits,* is a memory unit capable of storing a single ASCII character. For example, the letter A or the number 1 could be stored in one byte of memory. A number without a decimal point is usually stored in two bytes of memory, while a number with a decimal point may require five or more bytes of memory. Memory size is usually expressed not as thousands of bytes, but rather as some number of K (Kilo-) bytes. In reality, however, 1K equals 1024 because all computers are binary machines that count in twos. You will get the number 1024 if you double 2 to give 4, then double 4 to give 8, and keep on doubling in this fashion ten times.

Call. A call instructs the computer to transfer control to another section of memory where the required routine is located. Calls are used often in computing, since many processes divide into subroutines; instead of duplicating the same routine in several memory locations, the routine is stored in one location and called as necessary. When the call is completed, the computer returns control to the instruction immediately following the one that originally made the call.

Central Processing Unit. The CPU is the brain of a computer; all information passes through it.

Close. To close a file is to finish (at least temporarily) any processing associated with it. CP/M does not completely update a file until it is closed.

COBOL. COmmon Business Oriented Language instructs the computer in English-like sentences such as ADD SALES-AMT TO TOTAL-AREA. COBOL programs are easy to read, but require a lot of space. COBOL is a standardized language; it is the same no matter what computer uses it. It is used primarily by large businesses and the government.

Compiler. A compiler translates high-level language programs into executable machine language programs. You generate the original program with an editor or word processor and then compile the program. The compiler first checks your program for errors, then translates it into an executable program. (*See also* Interpreter.)

Configuration. Configuration applies either to programs or to the operating system. To configure a program means to change its operating parameters. To configure the operating system means to let it know what input/output devices are to be used during standard operation. In CP/M, BIOS (Basic Input Output System) must be configured to your individual equipment. This operation is usually done by computer professionals.

Console Device. On most CP/M systems the console device is a standard terminal with both a keyboard and CRT display; on some the keyboard and display may be separate units. Some older systems use a typewriter-like computer printer (one that has a keyboard for input) as the primary console device, but this practice has diminished with the advent of low-cost video displays.

Data. Data refers to any information the computer processes or stores. An important distinction must be made between instructions to the computer and data the computer processes. A computer distinguishes between data and instructions entirely by context. One missing piece of information can cause strange results.

Directory. The directory provides a table of contents of the disk. It stores the name of each file and other information that CP/M uses to find the file as well as its current use.

DMA. Normally, information must pass through the CPU when traveling from disk to computer memory and vice versa. Direct Memory Access bypasses the CPU, and information goes directly to and from memory. While the disk drives perform a DMA transfer, the CPU simply waits for the process to be completed. DMA transfers are generally faster than if the CPU werc involved.

Documentation. Documentation is all the information about a piece of computer equipment or software. Your computer system manuals are documentation.

Driver. A driver is a set of software instructions that is used to control the operation of a unit of hardware. For example, to run your disk system you must have drivers that correctly apply to your equipment. CP/M's drivers are in BIOS (Basic Input Output System).

8080/8085. The 8080 and 8085 microprocessors were designed by Intel. The 8080 is a second-generation CPU chip and the first to have widespread appeal. The 8080 has eight internal registers: A and Flag, B and C, D and E, H and L. Its instruction set (the instructions that it can directly interpret) is somewhat limited compared to later CPU designs. For example, the 8085 added more hardware interrupts, serial line, and two software instructions that were not available in the 8080. Other than these features, the 8085 works identically to the 8080.

Execute. To execute a program means the computer performs all the instructions that make up that program.

File. A file is a set of data or instructions stored on a disk or tape. One complete program might be stored in a file named PROGRAM.BAS, for instance. A data file is commonly used to hold information used by a program, such as names and addresses, recipes, or household finances.

File Name/File Type. The file name in CP/M has two sections: a name of up to eight characters followed by a period and, after the period, a unique type identifier called a file type. CP/M locates the file by the file name and file type.

Floppy Disk. A floppy disk is a flexible storage medium that records information read or written by the computer.

Formatting. Formatting puts dummy (nonsense) information onto a disk prior to use. It also verifies whether the disk can be read from and written to.

Hard Disk. Hard disks are made up of polished metal surfaces, or platters. The platters are coated with magnetic oxide. In a fixed disk drive the platters are permanently fixed (and sealed) within the drive; you cannot remove the medium without ruining the drive. In hard disk drives that are not fixed, the media are encased in removable plastic cartridges.

Hex. Hex, short for hexadecimal, refers to math base 16, a numbering system that counts 0 1 2 3 4 5 6 7 8 9 A B C D E F. The smallest computer unit of meaning (a byte—eight 1's or 0's) consists of two hex digits. Thus 11110000 becomes F0 hex.

Interpreter. An interpreter is used by a language such as BASIC to interpret and execute program statements in real time. Because of this translation process, interpreted programs are almost always slower in execution than are programs in machine language format. *See also* Compiler.

Interrupt. An interrupt is a hardware signal or a software instruction to the CPU to stop after processing the current instruction and execute a special set of instructions.

Library File. A library file contains a set of standard routines you can add to new programs. You can write a complete program from various library files.

Machine Code/Machine Language/Machine Instructions. These all refer to the lowest level of instructions; they are directly understood and executed by the computer.

Machine Dependent. If a program or device is machine dependent, it will operate only with a particular set of equipment.

Macro. Macros are commonly used in assembly language programs to generate either repeated code or conditional code (if/then statements).

Media. Media is the material on which information is stored. Floppy disks and cassette tapes are media.

Memory Location. Computer memory locations are defined by addresses. A specific memory location can store one byte of information.

Minifloppy. Minifloppy, a trademark of Shugart Associates, refers to their 5 1/4-inch floppy disks. Other manufacturers also produce 5 1/4-inch floppy disks.

Modem. A modem (MOdulator/DEModulator) is a device that converts computer data and/or instructions into frequencies at the sending end and converts frequencies back to the original information at the receiving end. A modem is needed at both the sending and receiving stations for proper operation. Telephone lines are commonly used to carry the modulated signals. Generally modems are extremely slow devices.

Operating System. The operating system coordinates all the activities performed by the computer but usually (as in the case of CP/M) does not perform complicated procedures (programs do that).

Packed Binary Code. The major use for this coding scheme is to produce binary-coded decimal (BCD) numbers. In this system each decimal digit of a number is represented by a combination of four binary digits (bits). It thus allows two decimal numbers to be stored in one byte.

Punch. A punch device punches holes in a card or paper tape. Before the advent of floppy disks, data or programs were stored on punch cards or paper tape.

RAM. Random Access Memory is the primary storage area of a computer. The information stored in RAM is lost when power is disconnected.

Random Access. Disk systems use two storage methods: random access and sequential access. Random access implies that you may read pieces of information at random. Random access files are accessed by a record number (location within a group of records). In order to find a record quickly and accurately, random files use records of the same length and indexes for locating individual records.

Read. To read is to obtain information from a file or a memory location. To read a file is get the information from the file and transfer it to memory (or another device).

Reader. A paper tape reader reads the holes punched by the paper punch device and interprets them according to a predetermined code.

Register. A register is an internal temporary storage area within a CPU. Only assembly and machine language programmers are interested in register contents. (*See* 8080 and Z80.)

Reset. Reset instructs the computer to restart from an initialization state. It is accomplished by either turning the system off and then on again or pressing the RESET button.

ROM. Read Only Memory can only be read from; you cannot change the information stored in it. Routines that don't change like the system bootstrap or a system monitor (which controls the computer at a higher level than does CP/M) are often put into ROM.

Routine. A routine is a set of modules (related instructions) that performs specific tasks. Routines make up programs but are not programs in themselves. For example, a routine might input one character, see if a key was pressed, display one character, or turn on the disk drive motor.

Run-Time. Sometimes modules are referred to as run-time routines or run-time code. Another name for this is executable code.

Sectors and Tracks. When information is stored on a cassette tape, it is stored as a single track of data along the length of the tape. When information is stored on a disk, the surface of the disk is divided into a number of concentric tracks. Each track is divided into a number of sectors so that CP/M, given a sector and track number, can access any point on the disk surface.

Sequential Access. Elements of a sequential access file are accessed in order. If you want to read element number ten, you must first read the preceding nine elements. Sequential storage methods are used when the amount of data to be stored cannot be anticipated. Sequential files have an end-of-record marker, and you may have elements of varying length (called variable-length records).

Skewing. Skewing relates to how information is physically stored on a disk. Information is assigned to non-adjacent locations (the first part of the information is put in sector 1, the second in sector 18, the third in sector 25, and so forth). This weaving of information is handled completely by CP/M.

Source. Source code refers to a program in its original state. Since programs are sometimes compiled, or translated into machine language, the distinction between source and run-time is important. In addition, *source* describes any original data or program, and *backup* refers to a copy of the source.

Statement. A statement is one complete instruction (or combination of instructions) to a computer. The complexity of a statement (think of it as a computer sentence) depends entirely on the language used and the programmer's style.

Status. Computer devices are either ready or not ready. When the computer is to use a device (for example, a printer), it checks its status; it checks to see if the device is ready. Unfortunately, status schemata are not standardized. A positive voltage emitted from a device can mean either that it is ready or not ready, depending on the manufacturer's design. CP/M performs status checks automatically, assuming that a proper BIOS has been created.

Tape. Computer tape is like audio tape. It usually consists of 1/2-inch or 1-inch tape wound onto reels. Computers store a higher density of information on a tape than do home tape recorders, and the information is stored differently via digital pulses rather than analog representations. Tape is an easy-to-handle and inexpensive medium for storing data or programs. Unfortunately, tape has two problems relating to home computer systems:

1. Unlike tape drives used with minicomputers or mainframe computers, tape drives used with small computers are extremely slow.
2. Tape is not suited for random access. The longer the tape, the longer the wait for record location.

Utility Program. A utility program is typically used for system operation (STAT, PIP, and so on). In contrast, an application program is ordinarily used to perform high-level tasks such as spreadsheets, data bases, accounting, and word processing.

Wildcard. A wildcard is a global parameter that remains constant throughout a process and accepts any specification. For example, in the CP/M command STAT B:*.ASM, * is a global parameter since anything can fill that position in the command line.

Write. To write is to place information into a file or memory location. To write to a file is to transfer the information from memory or another device into the file.

Write-Protect. You cannot add information to a write-protected disk; it can only be read. An 8-inch disk's write-protect notch appears on the bottom of the disk; a minifloppy disk's write-protect notch appears on the right side of the disk. The STAT command also write-protects disks and files.

Z80. The Z80 chip is a complete redesign of the 8080. While it retains full compatibility (it can execute all of the 8080 instructions exactly as the 8080 does), it introduces a number of other features. In addition to the 8080 register set, the Z80 contains a duplicate set, referred to as the A' and Flag', B' and C', D' and E', H' and L'. Indexing, a special type of computer instruction, is allowed, and the use of advanced RAM chips is simplified.

Index

Other Osborne/McGraw-Hill Publications

An Introduction to Microcomputers: Volume 0—The Beginner's Book, 3rd Edition
An Introduction to Microcomputers: Volume 1—Basic Concepts, 2nd Edition
Osborne 4 & 8-Bit Microprocessor Handbook
Osborne 16-Bit Microprocessor Handbook
8080A/8085 Assembly Language Programming
6800 Assembly Language Programming
Z80® Assembly Language Programming
6502 Assembly Language Programming
Z8000® Assembly Language Programming
6809 Assembly Language Programming
68000 Assembly Language Programming
Running Wild—The Next Industrial Revolution
The 8086 Book
PET® Personal Computer Guide
CBM™ Professional Computer Guide
Osborne CP/M® User Guide, 2nd Edition
Apple II® User's Guide, 2nd Edition
Some Common BASIC Programs
Some Common Pascal Programs
Practical BASIC Programs
Practical Pascal Programs
Science and Engineering Programs—Apple II® Edition
A User Guide to the UNIX™ System
PET® Fun and Games
Commodore 64® Fun and Games
Assembly Language Programming for the Apple II®
VisiCalc®: Home and Office Companion
Discover FORTH
Your ATARI™ Computer
Wordstar® Made Easy, 2nd Edition
Armchair BASIC
Data Base Management Systems
The HHC™ User Guide
VIC 20™ User Guide
6502 Assembly Language Subroutines
Z80® Assembly Language Subroutines
8080/8085 Assembly Language Subroutines
The VisiCalc® Program Made Easy
Your IBM® PC: A Guide to the IBM® Personal Computers
Your Commodore 64™
The Programmer's CP/M® Handbook
The Home Computer Software Guide
Your IBM® PC Made Easy
Graphics Primer for the IBM® PC
The MBASIC® Handbook
Advanced Pascal Programming Techniques
54 VisiCalc® Programs
54 SuperCalc® Programs
Using dBASE II®